C

ON BEING HUMAN
Essays from the Fifth Shi'i Muslim Mennonite Christian Dialogue

Harry J. Huebner
Hajj Muhammad Legenhausen
Editors

CMU Press
Winnipeg, Manitoba
2013

CMU Press
500 Shaftesbury Blvd.
Winnipeg, Manitoba, R3P 2N2

All rights reserved. No part of this publication may be reproduced in any form or by any means, electronic or mechanical, including photocopying, recording, or any information storage and retrieval systems, without permission in writing from the publisher.

Cover photo and design: Annalee Giesbrecht
Back cover photo credit: CMU Communications and Marketing
Layout: Harry Huebner

Printed in Canada by Friesens Corporation, Altona Manitoba

MIX
Paper from responsible sources
FSC® C016245

Library and Archives Canada Cataloguing in Publication

Shii Muslim Mennonite Christian Dialogue (Conference) (5th : 2011 : Winnipeg, Man.)
    On being human : essays from the fifth Shi'i Muslim Mennonite Christian dialogue / Harry J. Huebner, Hajj Muhammad Legenhausen, editors.

This volume includes papers from the fifth round of interfaith dialogue exchanges between a group of Mennonite Christian and Shi'i Muslim scholars and clerics, held June 1-4, 2011, at Canadian Mennonite University, Winnipeg, Manitoba, Canada.
ISBN 978-0-920718-94-0 (pbk.)

    1. Theological anthropology—Islam—Congresses. 2. Theological anthropology—Christianity—Congresses. 3. Christianity—Relations--Islam—Congresses. 4. Islam—Relations—Christianity—Congresses. I. Huebner, Harry, 1943- II. Legenhausen, M.
III. Title.

BP172.S55 2011   297.2'83
C2013-904029-3

Copyright © 2013
CMU Press

In the Name of God!

Surely, man has lost, except for those who believe, and perform good deeds, and commend the truth, and commend patience.
   (The Qur'an—Surah al-`Asr: 103:1-4)

... what are human beings that you are mindful of them, mortals that you care for them? Yet you have made them a little lower than God, and crowned them with glory and honor
   (The Bible—Psalm 8:5-6).

Contents

In Memoriam	9
Welcome Presentation – Gerald Gerbrandt	11
Introduction	16

Part I: Sacred Texts

Mohammad Ali Shomali – Man in the Qur'an — 29

Gordon Zerbe – Human Nature and Destiny in Biblical Perspective — 39

Mohammad Fanaei Eshkevari – The Perfect Man in Islamic Mysticism — 60

Part II: Perfection

Jo-Ann A. Brant – The Way of Perfection in the Christian Tradition — 77

Aboulhassan Haghani – Perfection According to the Qur'an — 94

Part III: Culture

Harry J. Huebner – Sin and Grace in Christian Perspective — 109

Ali Mesbah – Religion, Culture, and Social Well-Being from an Islamic Perspective — 129

David W. Shenk – Culture and Faith in a Mennonite-Christian Perspective — 141

Part IV: Human Rights

Abolfazl Sajedi – Islam and Human Rights: Equality and Justice   159

Peter Dula – Who is My Neighbour? Human Rights and Acknowledgement   168

Part V: Gender

Abbas Ali Shameli – Islamic Womanology: Toward the Development of Engendered Islamic Culture and Values   185

W. Derek Suderman – Created as Male and Female: 'ADAM, Gender, and the Legacy of Disobedience   211

Part VI: The Self

Mohammad Motahari Farimani – The Role of Turning to the Self: Introspection in Qur'anic Discourse   233

Jeremy M. Bergen – Conscience, Dissent, and Church: Theological Anthropology in Mennonite Perspective   244

Contributors   265

In the Name of Allah, the Beneficent, the Merciful

In Memoriam
Professor A. James Reimer

Verily, we belong to God, and, verily, unto Him do we return. (2:156)

Dear friends, Peace be unto you. *Al-salamu ʿalaykum.*

As we meet here in Winnipeg to discuss the religious anthropologies of our scriptures, we notice with heavy hearts the empty place of Jim Reimer. In Persian, when we miss someone, we say, "*Jāyesh khālī ast*" (His place is empty); and Prof. Reimer's place is very empty today, all the more so, as we remember the last time we gathered at the Imam Khomeini Education and Research Institute in Qom, when Prof. Reimer proposed the topic of religious anthropology for the symposium in which we are participating here. We extend our condolences to his colleagues, students, friends and family, as we mourn the loss of our dear colleague, teacher, friend and brother, Professor A. James Reimer. Professor Reimer shared himself with us in honest and open dialogue. Indeed, his participation provides an exemplar that we hope will continue to guide us in our continued sharing and dialogue. Religious dialogue with Prof. Reimer was true collaboration in a common project of service to God and searching for truth. In this project we learned how a great intellect struggles toward understanding, and how to join with him in that struggle. But our dialogue has been at least as much a matter of profound friendship as it has been about any intellectual quest, a friendship which manifested the care and consideration and ready willingness to give of himself characteristic of genuine authentic fraternity, and it is in the spirit of that fraternity that we remember him today.

We pray that God will bestow His divine grace on our work together, and grant us the blessings of collegiality, intellectual learning, friendship and fraternity, as we cherish the memory of Prof. Reimer in our continued common attempts to pursue the truth and attain nearness to the one God whom we worship.

Peace!

Written by Professor Hajj Muhammad Legenhausen
on behalf of the administration and faculty of
The Imam Khomeini Education and Research Institute
Qom, Iran. This statement was read on June 1, 2011 at
the opening ceremonies of Dialogue V in Winnipeg.
It was then passed on to Jim's widow Margaret Loewen Reimer.

Welcome to Muslim-Mennonite Dialogue

Gerald Gerbrandt

Presented at the opening of the dialogue on June 1, 2011

It is a privilege to welcome all the participants for this, the fifth in this series of Muslim-Mennonite dialogues. I am pleased to welcome the Mennonite dialogue members, as well as guests from CMU and the larger Mennonite community. But I am especially pleased to welcome our Muslim guests from Iran. You have come a long way for this event, with at times uncertainty about visas. So we are glad you made it safely and are here with us.

Some years ago CMU adopted a vision statement which included four commitments, the third of which reads: "Generous Hospitality . . . Radical Dialogue." When drafting that statement we were not thinking specifically about this dialogue, but the Mennonite-Muslim dialogue reflects that commitment in a wonderful way.

Dialogue is a term we use often, frequently with inadequate attention to what it means. It is not discussion about matters that are unimportant. It also is not discussion among people who agree with each other on everything. Productive dialogue requires partners committed to sharing honestly and frankly, about themselves and their understandings of God and life. It requires commitment to listening carefully to the other, with openness and full intention of learning from the conversation. The goal in genuine dialogue is not consensus or full agreement, but genuine understanding and learning.

It is my impression that through the earlier rounds of dialogue an important relationship has developed between our two communities, and the dialogue participants. I have not had the privilege of being a participant in any of the previous dialogues, but I hear that these were significant events. I understand they are occasions when scholars who are dedicated representatives of their faith tradition and committed to their sacred texts share their understandings of those texts with the goal of learning from each other. Through these conversations people have come to know each other better, they have come to trust each other more, and they have become genuine friends.

With that comment I am reminded of someone who is not present here tonight, but who has played a significant role in these dialogues—Dr. A. James Reimer, someone who was also a very good friend of mine. He shared with me more than once that originally he had been drafted into these conversations, as sometimes happens, but once in them, he could not leave them. He could not leave because through these conversations he came to understand God and his Christian faith better, and because through them he developed profound friendships with his Muslim dialogue partners.

Tonight I extend a warm welcome to our guests who have come from Iran to carry on conversation with fellow believers and searchers. You are valued partners. I am confident that the next few days will once again produce insightful and stimulating conversation, greater understanding of our own faith tradition as well as that of the dialogue partner, and deepened relationships. I also trust that our CMU campus will serve you well, a place where your needs are met, and you are comfortable for conversation and encounter.

The topic of the last dialogue was Peace and Justice in the two traditions. I am pleased that the proceedings of that event now are available with the publication to be launched later this week. For this the fifth in the series of dialogues the topic is on Anthropology, or more specifically, "Human Nature and Destiny: Explorations into Theological Anthropology."

Questions around who we are as human beings are critical for how we live and act and think and speak. The way we answer these questions impacts everything else. The conversation over the next few days thus is extremely important, and appropriate for dialogue between Christians and Muslims.

I might quibble gently about the use of the adjective "theological" in the title. It may not be inaccurate, but it is redundant. In both of our traditions a non-theological understanding of the human being, of our nature and destiny is impossible. In both traditions God is the creator—we have been created by God, and understand ourselves in relationship to God. And yet the term reminds us of that, especially when we look outside of our faith traditions into the larger dominant secular culture. At least here in North America, the tendency is often to think of humans apart from their nature as creatures created by God.

As someone who loves what we call the Old Testament, I naturally turn to the opening chapters of Genesis when I think about the topic of anthropology. I think of these opening chapters as a kind of prolegomena to our Scripture, chapters which provide the basic or foundational framework for the rest of scripture and its account of God and God's actions in relationship to the world God created. It thus is not surprising that these chapters provide a rich resource for the question of who we are as human beings.

Given that there will be a dozen or so scholars speaking to various aspects of the theme over the next few days, it may be foolish for me to say anything, but since experience makes it clear to me that foolishness is part of our human nature, I will be bold enough to share a few brief observations.

The opening chapters of Genesis touch on the nature of the human from many perspectives, even including how male and female are related to each other, but at its most foundational level, I see these chapters as making two foundational statements. On the one hand, they highlight the very high view of the human held by Scripture. On the other hand, they note the distorted, or as Christian theology has traditionally put it, the fallen nature of humanity. These two themes are not the ends of a continuum, where our task is to determine where on the continuum the truth is, but are held simultaneously, with the truth not some point between the extremes, but rather, in an affirmation of both simultaneously.

The high view of humanity is reflected in the statement that God created us in their own image. I am not using the pronoun "their" because I want to be inclusive and avoid the masculine pronoun for God, but because that is what the text says:

> Then God said, "Let *us* make humankind in *our* image, according to *our* likeness; and let them have dominion over the fish of the

sea, and over the birds of the air, and over the cattle, and over all the wild animals of the earth, and over every creeping thing that creeps upon the earth. So God created humankind in his own image, in the image of God he created them; male and female he created them. (Gen. 1:26-27, emphasis mine)

I expect there may be further reflection over the next few days over what exactly this means, so I will leave that entirely, but the high view of the human is clear. We have been created in the image of God, with a mandate from God to have dominion over the rest of the earth. This high view is not only present in this verse, but resurfaces repeatedly elsewhere. For example, when Genesis chapter one speaks of the different days of creation, after each creative act Genesis recounts that God looked at his creation, and it was good, but after the creation of the human we read, "God saw everything that he had made, and indeed, it was very good" (Gen. 1:31). Later passages in scripture then build on this affirmation.

One of the clearest examples of this is found in Psalm 8, that wonderful psalm which praises God the creator:

> ... what are human beings that you are mindful of them, mortals that you care for them? Yet you have made them a little lower than God, and crowned them with glory and honor. (Ps. 8:5-6)

God has wonderfully made us, made us in God's own image, and given us dominion and stature in the world,

But then there is the other theme. The stories of Genesis 3 and 4 and 6 and 11 all make this point. In Genesis 3 Adam and Eve disobey God and eat from the forbidden fruit, leading to their being exiled from the Garden of Eden. In Genesis 4 Cain murders his brother Abel. In Genesis 6 we read of God looking down on the wickedness of humankind, and sending a flood to purge his creation. But even the righteous Noah gets drunk after surviving the flood. This theme reaches a climax in Genesis 11 where we see human hubris in the effort to build a tower which is to reach into the heavens.

And so the opening chapters of Genesis present humans as both the crowning achievement of God's creation acts, and yet at the same time, as imperfect or distorted mortals who have an inevitable tendency to imagine themselves to be God, or those in absolute control, with full knowledge. Just like these are not ends of a continuum, I also do not take them as having a chronological order. It is not that humans were made perfect, and became imperfect. Rather, even as humans were created only a little lower than God, at the same time, they, or perhaps I should say "we," are flawed or defective, tempted to think we are omniscient, but actually, limited in perspective. This is integral to our humanity.

I have focused on the opening chapters of Genesis. It is my reading of scripture that these themes continue throughout. But I will not go there tonight. I give you the opportunity and encouragement to pursue these further, expand and refine them, and perhaps correct them in your further conversation.

I do welcome all of you, and pray that God will give sharp minds, attentive ears, and humble hearts as you speak with each other.

In His Name, Exalted

INTRODUCTION

The papers collected in this volume were delivered at the fifth Mennonite-Shi'ite dialogue, which took place in Winnipeg, Canada, at the Canadian Mennonite University, on June 1-4, 2011. The dialogue series began as a result of an initiative by the Mennonite Central Committee (MCC), after having provided relief assistance following the earthquake in Rudbar, Gilan, Iran, in 1990. Building on the cooperation between the Iranian Red Crescent and MCC, eventually a statement of understanding was signed by Ayatullah Misbah and Ron Mathies, in 1997, on the basis of which cooperation was begun between the Imam Khomeini Education and Research Institute in Qom and the MCC that included a student exchange program and other efforts to promote greater mutual understanding. One of the outcomes of this cooperation has been a series of theological conferences with alternating venues in Canada and Iran since 2002. Most of the papers delivered at these dialogues have been published subsequent to the conferences.[1] Thus, this volume is witness to a much

---

[1] "The Challenge of Modernity: Shi'ah Muslim-Mennonite Christian Dialogue," *Conrad Grebel Review*, Fall, 2003, available at: https://uwaterloo.ca/grebel/sites/ca.grebel/files/uploads/files/CGR-Fall-2003.pdf; "Revelation and Authority: Shi'ah Muslim-Mennonite Christian Dialogue II," *Conrad Grebel Review*, Winter, 2006, https://uwaterloo.ca/grebel/sites/ca.grebel/files/uploads/files/CGR-Winter-2006.pdf; M. Darrol Bryant, Susan Kennel Harrison, and A. James Reimer, eds., *On Spirituality: Essays from the Third Shi'i Muslim Mennonite Christian Dialogue* (Kitchener: Pandora Press, 2010); Harry J. Huebner and Hajj Muhammad Legenhausen, eds., *Peace and Justice: Essays from the Fourth Shi'i Muslim Mennonite Christian Dialogue* (Winnipeg: CMU Press, 2011). For a review of these dialogues, see A. James Reimer, "Preface:

broader and continuing discussion between (mostly) North American Mennonites and Iranian Shi'ah, and the continuing exchange of ideas is a manifestation of the friendships that have grown ever deeper as we have come to better understand one another.

In addition to serving as a historical record, the collection and publication of these essays serve several purposes: they show how Mennonite and Shi'ite scholars seek to make themselves understood to those of other traditions without assuming any expertise in the histories and theologies of those addressed. Because the essays are addressed to an audience that includes others, namely, those outside our own tradition, each of the essays may be seen as an introduction to the topic discussed. Because the essays are addressed to a mixed audience that includes scholars from the author's own tradition, they seek to explain elements of their traditions in ways that will be at least tolerable for their colleagues. So, these are not the usual sorts of academic articles to be found in scholarly journals. The journal literature seeks to carry a specific academic tradition forward in accordance with the developing standards internal to that tradition, often by defending a controversial view within the tradition. Our essays are reflections on what the authors believe, and what they believe to be fairly well attested within their communities—this is not by any means to say that the views are those held by all scholars of the community. Each thinker offers a unique approach to the issues, one with which others in their community might take issue; but the point of the essays is not to promote new theories. The point is to promote mutual understanding. The essays thus reflect the authors' ideas of how best to convey what they hold to be not only their personal beliefs, but the beliefs of their communities, to an audience that is not expected to share these beliefs. Surprises abound as discussions reveal astonishing similarities across denominational lines and differences in basic concepts where similarities were assumed. The authors do not attempt to prove that their views are correct or that those of their dialogue partners are wrong. Indeed, what is most lacking in this collection is the give and take of the questions and answers after the delivery of each paper and

---

Ten Years of Shi'ah Muslim Mennonite Christian Dialogue," in *Peace and Justice*, 15-20.

the informal discussions that took place. So the essays may also be read as an invitation to explore the issues in dialogue with Mennonites and Shi'ah and to observe the similarities and differences displayed in the thinking of Mennonites and Shi'ah, both in contrast to one another and within each group.

Mennonites and Shi'ah both have a history of dissent within their broader societies. Both Mennonites and Shi'ah claim that their deepest convictions were violated by the religious institutions that came to dominate the majority. Both formed communities of dissent whose members have been subject to the violence of those whom they criticized. Both have a legacy of martyrdom. When the Mennonites were first introduced to the Shi'i religious scholars in Qom, and *The Martyrs' Mirror* was described for them, there was an immediate sympathetic reaction.

The topic of discussion for the dialogue sessions reflected in these pages was theological anthropology. The topic was suggested by the late A. James Reimer at the close of the previous session on peace and justice in Qom. Prof. Reimer thought that in order to better understand the similarities and differences on the topics that had already been discussed, we would have to review our beliefs about what it means to be human. There was general agreement.

Dissent gives a particular edge to the concept of being human. Anabaptists and the early Shi'ah appealed to scripture in order to show that the majority communities had gone astray and that believers were bound by the general covenant between God and humanity to reform themselves. Of course, the precise nature of the covenant is understood differently in Christianity and Islam; but the structural parallels are striking. The experience of dissent is one in which appeals to conscience are made. The ability of each individual to freely choose between the path of the dissenters or the path of perdition is essential to the dissenting view of being human. The proper free choice which accords with scripture and conscience is the choice indicated by divine guides. The divine guides are understood differently by Christians and Muslims. For Christians, divine guidance comes in the life and teachings of Christ, while for the Shi'ah, this guidance is dispensed by the prophets (among whom Christ is included) and the twelve Imams. The divine guide not only offers teachings, but exhibits the proper way of living in his own life. As such, those sent by God establish an ideal of human perfection toward which believers are to strive. In traditions of dissent, the ideal of human perfection is held up as a target with the observation that the larger community is widely missing the mark, or is not even aiming in the right direction. The alternative posed by the dissenting community is not only an individual choice guided by scripture, conscience, and divine paradigms, but requires the establishment of communities of believers. Humans are social creatures and our religious pursuits, successes and failures take place in the various contexts of human cultures. For Mennonites, the social development of faith has focused on the building of communities of believers intentionally committed to the discipline of the church. For the Shi'ah, the focus has been on the establishment of a virtuous society, including the various aspects of culture and its institutions, from education to government. Both on the individual and social levels, there can be no success through human efforts alone; and believers turn to God for grace and mercy. The question of the relation between individual effort, sin, and grace has been especially prominent in Christian thought, especially since the Reformation, and has no close counterpart in Islamic thought, although Muslims generally affirm the need for good works and faith, which can only be achieved with divine aid. Social dimensions of being human that demand special attention and which have been posed as challenges to religious views include questions of human rights and the changing roles of women in religious societies. Both Mennonites and Shi'ah struggle with these issues in complex ways. Finally, both our communities struggle with tensions between individual conscience and commitment to the structures that shape religious social life. For Muslims, ideas about how to fulfill the duty to establish a just Islamic society have been especially divisive; but there has also been a tremendous emphasis on the personal spiritual journey, inwardness, and knowledge of one's true self, and questions continue to be raised about how to reconcile these demands. For the Anabaptist tradition, the issue of church discipline has been divisive while the need to respect individual conscience has been maintained. Perhaps a part of what it means to be human in both traditions is to live toward ideals of perfection with cognizance of human flaws and limitations, conflicts and discrepancies, through which we can only find direction by divine aid. For dissenting communities, these challenges to the radical discipleship of Mennonites and to the submission to Allah of Muslims are properly understood in contrast to that against which religious dissent is articulated; and in understanding these challenges we learn what our faith traditions teach about being human.

In order to help the reader steer through the essays, a very brief overview of the papers follows. Our collection is divided into six parts. *Part I: Sacred Texts* begins with the contribution of Mohammad Ali Shomali, "Man in the Qur'an," in which there is a review of the good and bad qualities by which we are described in the Qur'an. Emphasis is given to the choice given to the individual to cultivate good qualities or sink into depravity. Success in choosing the path of self-improvement depends, according to the Qur'an, on having faith and performing good works. This essay is followed by Gordon Zerbe's "Human Nature and Destiny in Biblical Perspective," in which human nature is shown to be described in the Bible through salvation history: creation, fall, and restoration. While Shomali's paper finds the scriptural description of man to focus on the essential moral choice, Zerbe's finds it in the course of development from creation and fall to the restoration of humanity's relationship with God. A developmental account of human nature is also suggested by Mohammad Fanaei Eshkevari, in "The Perfect Man in Islamic Mysticism." This paper may be considered a transition to the discussion of perfection. It treats the notion of the human perfection in the Qur'an and in Islamic mysticism. The development is not from fall to restoration, but from a state of being lost to a gradual approach to human perfection through spiritual discipline. Both the Bible and the Qur'an emphasize that human beings are two-sided--both human dignity and sinfulness. Christians understand being human through the doctrine of salvation in which history is prominent. In Islam there is less concern with historical narrative, and instead the focus is on stories with a moral. While the human sinfulness is not seen as being quite as radical as it is in Christianity, the divine intervention to guide us is through a divine model and guide. In Islam, we are not reconciled with God through anything but our own faith and good works by divine aid and mercy. Nothing plays a role comparable to that of Christ in Christianity; although both Christians and Muslims see humans as sinful and in need of divine aid.

Fanaei Eshkevari's introduction of the theme of the human perfection serves as a good introduction to *Part II: Perfection*, which begins with Jo-Ann Brant's "The Way of Perfection in the Christian Tradition," according to which there are three main roads available toward human perfection: (1) perfection through the imitation of divine generosity; (2) perfection through the endurance of suffering; and (3) perfection through sanctification or holy living as children of God. The concept of perfection in the New Testament is about neither the perfectibility of individual gifts, the cultivation of good qualities, nor the individual achievement of a moral perfection. Instead, it is the way by which we, as God's creatures, can participate in God's perfection at God's invitation within the context of an imperfect world by following Christ. Despite the differences between Muslim and Christian perspectives on moral improvement, Aboulhassen Haghani's "Perfection According to the Qur'an" displays a remarkable correspondence to many of the points in Brant's paper. Muslims are called to perfection, although the perfection of God is unattainable. Nevertheless, one can strive toward perfection through obedience to God and in hope for His mercy; and one can, for example, approach divine kindness by exhibiting kindness to others. Human nobility and greatness is especially manifest in traditions related to Imam Husayn who was able to display these features through suffering and martyrdom.

Part III: Culture, opens with Harry J. Huebner's theological essay, "Sin and Grace in Christian Perspective." The concepts of sin and grace have a contested history in the Christian theological tradition, while Islamic theology has not been divided over the nature of the corresponding concepts of sin (*isiyan*) and grace (*lutf*). Huebner guides us through some of the tangles over these topics in the Christian tradition, and in so doing dispels some common misgivings that Muslims often have about what Bonhoeffer called "cheap grace." Muslims will agree with the main points with which Huebner concludes. An account of human sinfulness is needed to understand the human, and divine grace is needed to lead us from sin and to a life in which we show kindness toward others as we hope in God's kindness toward us. Sin is a distortion of human nature, but does not destroy human perfectibility. We need divine aid to escape the grasp of sin. The

Christian is called to faithfulness after repentance and finds the ability to resist the power of evil through Christ, while for the Shi'ah the calling is through the Prophet and Imams and the power to resist is sought by direct recourse to God. The Christian finds that we can see our own nature best by looking to Christ; the Muslim looks to the Perfect Man as a way to find inner direction to our true selves. Huebner writes: "Grace is rooted in God's covenant faithfulness toward sinful human beings. That is, God does not deal with us according to our actions but according to God's mercy and righteousness." For the Muslim, God does deal with us according to our actions as prescribed in our covenant relation to Him. However, there is hope in divine mercy if we repent for what has been done contrary to the covenant, and even the unrepentant sinner deserving eternal damnation might be forgiven because of divine mercy that has no limits. Resistance to the seductions of sin is manifest in an exemplary way by the divine guides. The call to true Christianity is not an appeal to cheap grace, but to work for peace and justice even when this entails personal sacrifice. As God forgives us, we also are enjoined to forgive others and in so doing to restore our communities. Prayer and submission are required as we seek God's grace, forgiveness, and reconciliation with Him and as we seek to manifest these in our relations with others. These are all points on which Muslims and Christians can find common cause. In Ali Mesbah's "Religion, Culture, and Social Well-Being from an Islamic Perspective," we find an outline based on the teachings of the Qur'an of the kind of society that Muslims are called upon to build. First, people in the ideal society are to comply with divine commands in order to achieve felicity. Second, people seek to live in a responsible manner, aware of their abilities and of how God wants us to use them. Third, people are to recognize their responsibility to the environment as divine stewards. Fourth, they are to help one another and all other human beings. Fifth, they are to establish social relations based on justice and benevolence through such social institutions as the family, economy, state, law, and education. Cultural variety is one of the major themes of David Shenk's "Culture and Faith in a Mennonite-Christian Perspective." This paper is filled with fascinating vignettes of Christian missionary work and reflections on the diversity of cultural expressions that Mennonite churches can manifest in different parts of the world that serve as evidence against the claim that the Mennonite churches reject all elements of culture outside those associated with the original movement. Although mission activity has often been a source of tensions between Muslim and Christian communities, who have tended to see one another as rivals, there may yet be hope for some cooperation on the mission front, as well.

The discussion of religion and culture naturally leads to discussion of the political and social aspects of culture, among the most prominent of which are taken up in *Part IV: Human Rights* and *Part V: Gender*. In his "Islam and Human Rights: Equality and Justice," Aboulfazl Sajedi defines a human right as a privilege one has in virtue of being human. Focus is on justice and equality as human rights in Islam. Islam emphasizes brotherhood and equality, and supports justice and the removal of any kind of oppression and unfair discrimination. One result of the right to equality and justice is to accept the equal value of men and women and to reject any discrimination between them in this regard. A more critical view of the concept of human rights is found in Peter Dula's "Who is My Neighbour? Human Rights and Acknowledgement." In this paper, Dula dissents from the absolutism about human rights that characterizes much contemporary liberal political writing. He engages Wolterstorff's defense of human rights, and finds it less than fully convincing. The primary concern of the Bible is the claims that others have upon us. The language of human rights can help to bring this to attention, but it can also obscure it. In the end, the language of human rights is supported as a minimalist framework, while emphasis is placed on the more demanding account of the good based on the teachings of Jesus.

In Abbas Ali Shameli's "Islamic Womanology: Toward the Development of Engendered Islamic Culture and Values," the study of women is proposed as a subfield of anthropology. In accordance with the general project for Islamic social sciences, an Islamic study of woman based on Islamic sources, as well as the study of culture and values is recommended. The author argues that women's activism in social and political affairs is consonant with Islamic teachings, despite the differences in responsibilities recognized by Islam. In "Created as Male and Female: 'ADAM, Gender, and the Legacy of Disobedience," Derek Suderman considers the story of the fall in Genesis and its implications for gender relations. It is argued that the word "Adam" is used in two senses: first as a general term for the human being that includes both males and females; and second, as a proper name for the first male human. Ambiguities in the text of Genesis yield a responsibility for the Christian to interpret the text in accordance with Christian principles, so that the text should not be misused to justify male domination.

Our collection ends with a return to the self in *Part VI: The Self*. Mohammad Motahari Farimani, in his "The Role of Turning to the Self': Introspection in Qur'anic Discourse," demonstrates that through the Qur'an and certain questions that it raises, God directs us to look within, or turn to the self. This is no simple matter of immediate introspection, however, for the real self is to be distinguished from a false or imaginary self. Service to God is found to be identical to service to the true or real self. In the final article, "Conscience, Dissent, and the Church: Theological Anthropology in Mennonite Perspective," Jeremy Bergen points out various tensions between the ideal of being true to one's conscience and commitment to community, both of which have been prominent in Anabaptist and Mennonite history; and these tensions are further complicated by the modern notion of moral autonomy as action governed by conscience. Bergen supplements his paper with a report of some of the discussion at the conference with Muslims about these issues, and finds places where Mennonite and Shi'i positions seem to support one another, especially in the distinction between real and imaginary selves presented by Farimani.

None of the conference participants argues for the superiority of their own positions where they conflict with those of other traditions. Instead, all seek to elucidate their own positions in a way that can be understood by others. None seeks to impose their presumptions about the other, but demonstrate a willingness to recognize both points where we differ and points on which we seem to converge. One reason for the convergence is the heritage of dissent. Although the papers and conference are aimed at promoting understanding between Mennonites and Shi'ah on the topic of being human, understanding comes in degrees from superficial to profound. Depth of understanding occurs when the views of those whom we seek to understand resonate with our own views, even when there are contradictory positions that must not be overlooked. The cognitive and emotional legacies of our histories of dissent may help us to understand how Mennonites and Shi'ah are able to resonate with one another despite their differences; but the friendships that continue among us can only be fully appreciated as the grace of God, or *lutf Allah*, for which we give thanks.

Hajj Muhammad Legenhausen
Harry J. Huebner

PART I

SACRED TEXTS

In the Name of Allah, the Beneficent, the Merciful

Man in the Qur'an

Mohammad Ali Shomali

God and man are the two most important topics of the Qur'an and one may even suggest that the relation between God and man is the central topic of the Qur'an. There are many verses in the Qur'an about man in general. Of course, this is in addition to many cases in which specific human beings are mentioned. Among those verses that characterize man in general, there are some that refer to virtues and gifts of man and there are others that refer to negative qualities of man. To be able to have a complete picture of man in the Qur'an we need to study all these verses and examine carefully the qualities they ascribe to man. In what follows, I will first refer to positive aspects, i.e., good qualities and virtues of man, and then refer to bad qualities and vices attributed to man. Finally, I will try to present an overall picture of man in the Qur'an.

Good Qualities
Man is the only creature of God capable of becoming the vicegerent of God on earth. Man is created for a purpose and not by chance. According to the Qur'an, God the Wise has created man to become His vicegerent. The Qur'an says:

> When your Lord said to the angels, "Indeed I am going to set a viceroy on the earth," they said, "Will You set in it someone who will cause corruption in it, and shed blood, while we celebrate Your praise and proclaim Your sanctity?" He said, "Indeed I know what you do not know." (2:30)

O David! Indeed We have made you a vicegerent on the earth. So judge between people with justice, and do not follow desire, or it will lead you astray from the way of God. Indeed those who stray from the way of God—there is a severe punishment for them because of their forgetting the Day of Reckoning. (38:26)

It can be understood from the Qur'an that it is only humans who bear the divine trust and fulfil the goal of creation:

We offered the trust to the heavens and the earth and the mountains, but they refused to carry it and were afraid of it, and man carried it. Surely he is very unjust, very ignorant. (33:72)

Man has the greatest capacity for knowledge. When God wanted to demonstrate Adam's qualifications for becoming His vicegerent, instead of giving this position to the angels, He stressed Adam's capacity for learning all the facts. The Qur'an says:

And He taught Adam all the names, then presented them to the angels; then He said: Tell me the names of those if you are right. (2:31)

"Names" here means "realities." When the angels thought that they were more qualified than Adam to be appointed as His vicegerent, God, the Most Glorious, wanted to prove that the angels were wrong. The Almighty taught Adam all the facts, and then asked the angels if they were true in their claim; then they would have to reveal those facts to Him. But they were not able to do so. Thus, we can understand from this verse that man is capable of attaining all knowledge. Of course, this implies that the angels did not have the capacity to learn more; otherwise they could have said that they too were able to learn all the facts.

Man can know his Creator through innate knowledge. Man has no need to use external ways for knowing God. If we go deep into our spirits, we can understand that we are created, that we have a Lord. To illustrate this point with an example, a person went to Imam Ja'far al-Sadiq ('a) and asked him to prove the existence of God, the Most Glorious. The Imam ('a) asked him whether he ever travelled on a ship. The man answered positively. Then the Imam ('a) asked him whether in his travels a situation ever arose when there was a danger that the ship would sink, so that people began to panic and were afraid that the ship would be wrecked and they would die as a result. The man again gave an affirmative answer. The Imam ('a) then asked: "Did you think of any power that could have saved you then?" When the man said, "Yes," the Imam ('a) concluded, "That is God, the Omnipotent."

This knowledge may not be active in everyone, but normally when we are in danger and we feel no one can help us, it is awakened and activated. Referring to man's natural inclination towards God, the Qur'an says:

> Then set your face upright for the religion in the right state—the nature made by God in which He has made men; there is no altering of God's creation; that is the right religion, but most people do not know. (30:30)

The term *fitrat* refers to the way man is created by God. In particular, we should refer to two dimensions of man's God-given nature: knowledge and desire. Therefore, we can say that every person is instinctively aware of God and has an affinity towards Him through his innate God-given knowledge and desire.

God has breathed from His spirit into man. Besides the corporeal body, there is a spiritual element in human beings which is so valuable that God attributes it to Himself. Of course, God has no spirit so that it can be given to man; it is to honour the human spirit that God told the angels:

> So when I have proportioned him and breathed into him of My spirit, then fall down in prostration before him. (15:29)

When we attribute spirit to God, it is something symbolic, just like the House of God. Although everything is created by God, certain things are more precious and respected than others, so God attributes them to Himself in a special way. In any case, the angels were commanded to prostrate before Adam ('a) only after God had instilled the divine spirit into Adam. This spirit is the origin and the source of all virtues of human beings.

Man is honoured by God.

> And surely We have honoured the children of Adam, and We have carried them in the land and the sea, and We have given them to excel by an appropriate excellence over most of those whom We have created. (17:70)

Man is free to choose his destiny. Man is the master of his own fate. Man has been guided, but not forced to follow this guidance; man is free to follow it or not. Of course, man will be accountable for his choice. The Qur'an says:

> Surely we have shown him the way; he may be grateful or ungrateful. (76:3)

Man is able to judge and decide what is right and what is wrong. To a large extent man understands what is good and what is bad and therefore the Prophets were not sent to teach moral values to mankind that were entirely unknown to them and start from scratch; rather they came to remind them of what they already knew and help them in the process of self-purification as well as teaching new ideas. This God-given power can be understood from the following verses:

> And the soul and Him who perfected it. Then He inspired it to understand what is right and wrong for it. (91:78)

> Know that the Apostle of God is among you. Should he obey you in many matters, you would surely suffer. But God has endeared faith to you and made it appealing in your hearts, and He has made hateful to you faithlessness, transgression and disobedience. It is such who are the right-minded—a grace and blessing from God, and God is all-knowing, all-wise. (49:7-8)

Man will never be satisfied by anything except by the remembrance of God and drawing near to Him.

> Those who believe and whose hearts are set at rest by the remembrance of God; now surely by God's remembrance are the hearts set at rest. (13:28)

Every human being tries to reach his Lord. A person who wishes to acquire infinite wealth also tries to reach God, but his mistake is that he misunderstands his Lord and goes after something insecure and transient. For man, the only way to be satisfied is to make one's soul aware of God. The Qur'an says:

> O man! Surely you strive (to attain) to your Lord, a hard striving until you meet Him. (84:6)

Although everyone will finally meet His Lord, it will not be the same experience for everyone. For some people, it will be the most joyful experience they will ever have and for some it will be very worrying and disturbing:

> Some faces will be fresh on that day, looking at their Lord, and some faces will be scowling on that day. (75:22-24)

> That day some faces will be bright, laughing and joyous. And some faces on that day will be covered with dust, overcast with gloom. (80:39-41)

Man should try to return to God in peace and tranquillity:

> O soul at peace! Return to your Lord, pleased, pleasing! Then enter among My servants! And enter My paradise! (89:27-28)

To obtain peace and tranquillity, human soul needs the remembrance of God:

> Those who have faith, and whose hearts find rest in the remembrance of God. Look! The hearts find rest in God's remembrance! (13:28)

God has made nature manageable for man. Human beings are enabled to utilize the land, the seas, space, plants, and animals to their own benefits and ends:

> And He has made subservient to you whatsoever is in the heavens and whatsoever is on the earth, all, from Himself; most surely there are signs in this for a people who reflect. (45:13)

> It is He who created for you all that is in the earth. (2:29)

Man is created to serve God the Glorious.

> And I have not created the jinn and the men except to serve Me. (51:56)

This verse shows that one of the goals of our creation is to serve God. The ultimate perfection of human beings cannot be achieved except through the worship of Almighty God.

Man cannot know himself unless he knows God. Failing to know or remember God leads to ignorance or forgetfulness about himself:

> And do not be like those who forgot God, so He made them forget their own souls. It is they who are the transgressors. (59:19)

The Prophet Muhammad (s) is quoted as saying: "Whoever knows himself has known his Lord."

Bad Qualities

As said before, we can describe man in two different ways: in general or specifically with regard to certain individuals. If an individual is blamed in the Qur'an for having an undesirable quality this does not necessarily mean that all human beings are bound to be like that. Here we want to mention some undesirable attributes of human beings in general that are mentioned in the Glorious Qur'an:

Man is unjust and ignorant. These two qualities are expressed in the following verse:

> Surely he is very unjust, very ignorant. (33:72)

Thus, human beings suffer from ignorance and injustice. Of course, the unjust act is not restricted to others. It can be applied to the person himself.

> Every person who breaks Divine laws, has oppressed himself. (95:61)

If a person does not pray or fast then he has been unjust to himself. When a person beats someone or robs him of his money, he is initially doing a disservice to himself, then to the other person. Committing a sin is just like drinking poisoned water: if this person drinks poison, he is hurting himself. The same logic can be applied when he harms another being. The consequence of his ill acts is that he destroys the bases of his inherent God-given purity.

Man is ungrateful.

> And it is He who has brought you to life, then He will cause you to die, then bring you to life (again); most surely man is very ungrateful. (22:66)

Man rebels when he considers himself free from need.

> Indeed man becomes rebellious when he considers himself without need. (96:6-7)

Human beings feel self-sufficient when they enjoy the status of wealth, health, or position. When a man has no money or social position or is not from an important family, he is not inordinate. To illustrate, one of the companions of the Prophet (s) was quite poor. He asked the Prophet (s) for help and was given some money. That money was blessed and had good effects. Day by day his money increased. He used to pray behind the Prophet (s), but as his money increased, his worship decreased. The Prophet (s) began to feel concerned about him so one day he asked the man to pay the money back. When he paid it back, his money was no longer blessed. He became poor again and started to attend the mosque regularly and say his prayers behind the Prophet (s).

Man is impatient.

> And man prays for evil as he ought to pray for good and man is ever hasty. (17:11)

Man shows total reliance on God when he is in trouble and difficulty. Of course, as said before, when our difficulties disappear we think we have become self-sufficient and our reliance on God also diminishes. This fact is expressed in the following verse:

> And when affliction touches a man, he calls on Us, whether lying on his side or sitting or standing but when We remove his affliction from him, he passes on as though he had never called on Us on account of an affliction that touched him. (10:12)

Man is miserly.

> Say: if you controlled the treasures of the mercy of my Lord, then you would withhold (them) from fear of spending, and man is very miserly. (17:100)

Man is greedy.

> Surely man is created of a greedy temperament; being greatly grieved when evil afflicts him, and niggardly when good befalls him, except those who pray. (70:19)

Man is inquisitive. He is interested in disputing and arguing about everything more than is needed. The Scripture presents such an idea:

> And certainly We have explained in this Qur'an every kind of example; and man is most of all given to contention. (18:54)

Man is weak. The Qur'an says:

> And man is created weak. (4:28)

Conclusion

According to the Glorious Qur'an a human being is a responsible being and has the capability of either following the right path or going astray. A man is able to choose either of these qualities, cultivate them, nurture them, and strengthen them in his being.

The bad attributes or vices are not such that they can prevent a human being from reaching perfection, because the vices are of three kinds: First, some are necessary implications of human creation and one cannot prevent them. For example, as we saw above, man is weak and has many limitations in his existence and actions. These kinds of attributes will not be questioned or punished. God explains these imperfections to make us aware of our weakness and to prevent us from taking pride in ourselves.

Second, some are implications of human creation but are not necessary. This means that human nature inclines one toward vice, but it can be resisted. To explain this point philosophically, we should say that human nature is not a sufficient condition or a complete cause *(al-illah al-tāmmah)* of moral vice. It is just the incomplete or partial cause *(al-illah al-nāqisah)*. It is up to human beings to submit themselves to their nature or to resist. For example, growing up in a bad family tends to result in vice, but this is only an incomplete cause. Returning to our own discussion, the human being has a greedy temperament, but he can control and direct his temperament to any direction he wants. He can even use it to acquire infinite perfection.

Third, some vices are caused by the human being himself, i.e., by his free will and are not due to human or individual nature. For example, if a human being is a liar, this is because he himself has chosen to lie.

Thus, we understand that the vices cannot prevent us from perfection, and that God, the Most Merciful and Forgiving, will never punish us for those nature-given attributes. Man possesses capabilities and potentialities as well as freewill. It is up to him to decide what to do or obtain. In the Glorious Qur'an, God says:

> Most surely man is in loss, except those who believe and do good, and enjoin on each other truth, and enjoin on each other patience. (103:2-3)

According to the above verses, all human beings are in a state of loss because they are losing their lives and their bodily and mental powers. The only exceptions are those who believe, do good, and invite each other towards truth and patience. These people spend their lives or powers or properties to get divine pleasure and salvation. So, what they get or obtain is more than what they spend or lose. The Qur'an says:

> Certainty We created man in the best make. Then We tendered him the lowest of the low. Except those who believe and do good, so they shall have a reward never to be cut off. (95:4-6)

Again the same fact is seen. God has created man in the best way. Then it is up to him to be the lowest of the low or to be higher than other creatures, even angels.

Human Nature and Destiny in Biblical Perspective

Gordon Zerbe

My assigned subject matter is a broad one, and I hope to provide an adequate overview, while at the same time offering insights into a few particular debates among Christian theologians on this topic. And I will seek to draw attention to some distinctive perspectives found in the Mennonite tradition.

To highlight some images pertaining to the theological anthropology of the Bible, I begin with some excerpts from the Apostle Paul (dated ca. 50–56). Their significance will perhaps only become apparent by the end of this paper:

> Just as we have borne the image of the earthly human [Adam], we will also bear the image of the heavenly human [Christ]. (1 Corinthians 15:47)

> [The human being] is sown a psychic body (*sōma psychikon*), it is raised a pneumatic body (*sōma pneumatikon*). (1 Corinthians 15:44)

> For as all die in Adam, so all will be made alive in Christ. 1 (Corinthians 15:22)

> Just as through one man Error (Sin) came into the world, and Death came through Error, and so Death spread to all humanity because all have erred . . . so one man's righteous act leads to righteousness of life for all humanity . . . Where Error abounded, Grace abounded all the more, So that, just as Error exercised

> dominion in Death, so Grace might also exercise dominion through justice-righteousness unto the life of the age to come through our Lord Jesus Christ. (Romans 5:12, 18b, 21)

> For God has imprisoned all humanity in disobedience so that God may be merciful to all humanity. (Romans 11:32)

The Bible offers no overall theory of the human being, but offers hints as to the nature of humanity in the course of its general narrative. The Bible is much less interested in an exposition of the human *being* in an "essentialist" or "ontological" sense, than in expounding on the modalities, imperatives, and challenges of human *living* that are intrapersonal, God-ward (theological-spiritual), ethical (behavioural), and socio-political (having to do with allegiance, dominions, and identity). Some hints as to some assumptions about the basic constitution and character of humanity often appear only implicitly, and secondarily to these broader concerns of human living. Theologian Jürgen Moltmann puts the matter similarly: "The question 'What is man?' is always a question involving a comparison. It is never posed in the abstract, any more than man occurs in isolation."[1] For Moltmann, that comparison puts humanity in relationship to other creatures and the entire globe, in relation to the ethnic and historical variation among human beings and human groups (in personal, interpersonal, social and political realities), and ultimately in relation to God. And the Christian view of humanity competes with other prevailing images of the human being, for instance, from various biological, psychological, sociological, secular, industrial, or political perspectives.

---

[1] Jürgen Moltmann, *Man: Christian Anthropology in the Conflicts of the Present* (Philadelphia: Fortress Press, 1974), 4. For an exploration of theological anthropology in connection with the specifically crucified Jesus, embracing God's pathos for and solidarity with the human condition, see his *The Crucified God: The Cross of Christ as the Foundation and Criticism of Christian Theology* (New York: Harper & Row, 1974), 267–340; his major topics are: The Experience of Human Life in the Pathos of God; Ways towards the Psychological Liberation of Man; and Ways towards the Political Liberation of Man.

To summarize quite broadly, the Bible presents humanity in relational and functional terms, not essentialist terms. Moreover, the depiction is often multi-sided. For instance, the Bible presents humanity in terms of both proximity and distance to God. The human being is both a transient creature but also dignified with God's image;[2] humanity is characterized as dependent and accountable to God, and still as co-creator (e.g., of culture and history) and co-regent with God (in creation). Similarly in relation to animals and the rest of creation; the Bible posits both proximity (and solidarity) and distance. In relation to other human beings, the Bible presents people as both individual beings, with individual ontogeny and responsibility, but also as a collective, corporate being (living in a family, clan, society) that can be characterized as a singularity that has corporate responsibility, more than just an aggregate.[3] The human being is created male and female, and has both a physical aspect and a soulish-spiritual aspect (including volitional, rational, appetitive dimensions). The human being is pictured as having a remarkable capacity for evil and violence, but at the same time a notable potential for goodness and peace (especially in humanity's restored condition). In the diversity of human culture, there is both unimaginable variation but also amazing similarity. The human being is constituted with freedom and individual self-determination, but at the same time is bound by limits and constraints, and powers beyond oneself. In sum, humanity is a paradoxical creature, whose outcome cannot be determined ahead of time, in the abstract, in essence. In the history of Christian theology, however, emphases have swung like a pendulum on both sides of these various continua, as theologians have sometimes chosen to emphasize one aspect of the human condition to the neglect of another.

The Bible's view of humanity is best understood in light of its overall plan. Taken as a whole, despite its diversity and multiple subplots, the Christian Bible presents a grand narrative of redemption and restoration. The literary theorist Northrop Frye, for instance, claims

---

[2] E.g., E. Jacob, "The Nature and Destiny of Man," in *Theology of the Old Testament* (New York: Harper & Row, 1958), 151–53. A variety of texts are cited.

[3] Jacob, *Theology of the Old Testament*, 153–56.

that the coherent unity of the Bible is created and governed by its "U-shaped plot" characteristic of the genre of comedy.[4] (He doesn't mean comedy in the sense of being funny and light, but in the ironic sense that things are not always as they seem, having a plot line with a good measure of the paradoxical in contrast to that of simple romance, where the righteous good guys always win, or tragedy, where the hubristic hero always fails.) As pertaining to humanity, we can schematize this epic story in three topical movements, as exemplified in the texts from the Apostle Paul cited above: (1) Humanity as created and intended; (2) Humanity as subject to degradation (through Error [Sin] and Death); (3) Humanity in the process of re-creation, toward Justice-Righteousness and Life (through God's work in Jesus Christ).

This three-fold pattern also informs explicitly or implicitly the shape and content of confessions of faith in the Protestant Christian tradition. Confessions of faith in the Protestant tradition have been a way to summarize and systematize the core teachings of the Bible that pertain to "faith and life," or doctrine and ethics, for the purpose of teaching (catechetical) purposes, but also as a way to distinguish ways of understanding the Bible from other Christian traditions.[5] Meanwhile, confessions of faith have also come to serve as a guide to interpret the Bible as a whole, even though confessions of faith acknowledge that they are subject to the more primal authority of Scripture.[6] In this

---

[4] Northrop Frye, *The Great Code* (Toronto: Academic Press, 1982).

[5] E.g., John H. Leith, ed., *Creeds of the Churches: A Reader in Christian Doctrine from the Bible to the Present* (3d ed. Atlanta: John Knox Press, 1982).

[6] E.g., *Confession of Faith in a Mennonite Perspective* (Scottdale/Waterloo: Herald Press, 1995), 8; *Confession of Faith of the General Conference of Mennonite Brethren Churches* (Winnipeg/Hillsboro: Kindred Publications, 1999), 5: "The Bible is our written authority. As Anabaptists, we believe that authoritative interpretation of the Bible is the result of corporate reflection under the guidance of the Holy Spirit. This confession is the result of such a process and not only describes how the Mennonite Brethren Church in Canada and the United States interprets the Bible for our context but is also an authoritative guide for biblical interpretation, theological identity, and ethical practice."

Confessions of faith in the Anabaptist-Mennonite tradition have evolved over the past 500 years, and influences from various theological streams can be

paper, then, I will summarize core themes in two recent Mennonite confessions of faith (MC, 1995; MB, 1999)[7] that correlate with the Bible's three-stage drama, as a way to sketch the theological anthropology of Scripture.

Humanity as Created and Intended
Beginning, then, with the topic of humanity as created and intended, we can discern the following emphases in contemporary Mennonite confessions of faith: (1) the creation of humanity, as both male and female, in the image of God; (2) the resulting "special dignity" of humanity [MC] as the "crowning act" of creation [MB]; (3) the design of human beings (a) "to live in fellowship with God" [MB], or "for relationship with God" [MC], (b) to live "in mutually helpful relationships with each other" [MB], "to live in peace with each other" [MC], and (c) "to rule and care for creation as a sacred trust" [MB], "to care for creation out of reverence and honour for the Creator" [MC]; (4) the essential "goodness" of humanity [MC]; and (5) as given the freedom of choice, "to obey or to disobey God" [MB], "blessed with the abilities to respond faithfully to God" [MC, explained in the

---

discerned. But there are nevertheless some consistent emphases which distinguish them as expressions of Anabaptist-Mennonite faith and practice. See Howard John Loewen, *One Lord, One Church, One Hope and One God: Mennonite Confessions of Faith* (Elkhart, IN: Institute of Mennonite Studies, 1985); K. Koop, ed., *Confessions of Faith in the Anabaptist Tradition, 1527–1660* (Kitchener, ON: Pandora Press, 2006). As typical of other Protestant confessions of faith, contemporary Mennonite confessions of faith begin with articles on God, the Trinity, and Revelation, and proceed to a treatment of Humanity in the context of Creation more generally, moving into the topic of Sin and Evil (and thereby the "human condition") and then to Salvation (the transformation and redemption of humanity). Further articles then expand on crucial Christian practices (ethics) and the nature of the church (ecclesiology), and then culminate with an article on God's final triumph and the resurrection.

[7] See above, n. 6. The two confessions are available online at http://www.mennolink.org/doc/cof/intro. And http://www.mbconf.ca/home/-products_and_services/resources/theology/confession_of_faith. Accessed on April 20, 2013.

commentary as "the ability to choose the bond of a covenant with God or to choose bondage to sin"].[8]

Notably absent is any reference to different parts of the human being e.g., body or soul; the commentary to the MC confession clarifies that the term "image of God" "refers to human beings as a whole rather than to one particular aspect of the person" (29). In this way, contemporary Mennonite confessions of faith indirectly stress the human being as a holistic being, not as a dualistic being that is comprised of distinct parts (body and soul/spirit) that while now unified can somehow be separated. While this is consistent with the main emphasis of Scripture, this has not been the view of mainstream Christianity. Already by the middle of the second century CE Christian theologians adopted an anthropology influenced by Greek philosophy as a way to explain the biblical message, positing a dichotomous body-soul dualism along with a notion of the soul's immortal and conscious existence after death, and this became the assumption of almost all strands of Christianity.[9] Similarly, Lutheran, Reformed, and some earlier Mennonite confessions of faith specifically claim such a dualism, along with the notion of the soul's immortality.[10]

In connection with this dualistic assumption, the history of Christian theology has also seen variety of opinion (speculation) and considerable debate on the subject of the origin of the soul in the individual; that is, how and when was it infused with the body. Three main approaches to the question of the soul's origin and how it was infused in the body can be observed in the course of Christian theology. This topic is not addressed in Scripture, but many theologians sought to develop a view in the area that was consistent with Scripture. (1) Some early theologians considered the soul to be pre-existent, that is, created at the beginning of the world. Origen (185–254 CE), for instance, drew on Plato's doctrine of the pre-existence and transmigration of the soul, and combined this view with a notion of the pre-temporal "fall" of the

---

[8] A variety of Scriptural passages are cited as the basis for these convictions, and for other statements.

[9] E.g., J. N. D. Kelly, *Early Christian Doctrines*, rev. ed. (San Francisco: Harper & Row, 1978), 163–88; L. Berkhof, *Systematic Theology* (Grand Rapids: Eerdmans, 1939), 191–96.

[10] Augsburg (1530); Westminster (1646); Waterlander (1577), Articles 8, 9, 10; Thirty-three Articles (1617); Ris Confession (1766/1895), Articles 5, 32.

soul, reading Genesis 1–3 as a cosmic myth, such that "original sin" marked human souls before they were infused in a particular person. (2) Others, labeled "creationists," held that God creates a new soul at the birth of every individual (e.g., Jerome, ca. 347–420 CE). (3) In the West, the theory of "traducianism" (via a "channel") gained ground, adduced first by Tertullian (ca. 160–220 CE). In this view, the soul as well as the body originates by propagation from parental ancestry: human nature was created in its entirety by God and is ever-increasingly individualized as the human race multiplies. This view was usually wedded to a "realistic" theory of human nature and original sin (see below), such that all human beings were "in Adam" and thus literally sinned "in Adam" with a taint passed on through the semen (Tertullian). Augustine (354–430) eventually sought to combine both the creationist and traducianist positions, denying a thoroughgoing theory of corporeal translation of original sin (with the creationists against the traducianists), while admitting to a kind of spiritual translationism. Thomas Aquinas (1225–1274), though a creationist, solved the problem of original sin by positing that it was translated through the semen like a natural infection (*Summa* 1-2.81.1), but noted that this has nothing to do with the translation of the rational soul (traducianism, by contrast, correlated the translation of the soul with the transmission of original sin).[11]

But even these theories could not fully satisfy the question of when precisely the body and the "rational soul" were united in a new human being, that is, when did life become fully "human." Thomas Aquinas gave this problem attention more than some others. Aquinas believed that vegetables had a "vegetative soul," which in animals was absorbed in the "sensitive soul;" both of these in turn were absorbed by the "rational soul," which especially gave humans the gift of intelligence, and by ancient standards, "personhood." Following a biological paradigm, Aquinas believed that in the case of a human fetus, God introduces the rational soul only after the fetus has gradually acquired first a vegetative soul, and then a sensitive soul. Only at the point where a body is fully formed is the rational soul created (*Summa* 1.90; cf. *Summa contra gentiles* 1.76.2; 1.118.2); the embryo only has the "sensitive soul" (*Summa* 1.90). Accordingly, he is also of the belief that

---

[11] See L. Berkhof, *Systematic Theology*, 191–201.

embryos will not take part in the resurrection of the dead, before the rational soul has been infused in them (*Summa*, Supplement 80.4); they are not fully human beings.[12]

Parenthetically, one might also observe in this connection the rather tragic results of other debates regarding the "rational soul" in the late medieval and early colonial era of Europe, including the debates as to whether women and "savages" also shared fully in having "rational souls," that is, were as fully "human" as European men.

As noted above, Mennonites have avoided this matter in confessional statements and in theological discussions, especially because the Bible, in the main, does not offer any clear guidance in this area, and instead treats the human being in holistic terms, albeit with both bodily and soulish-mental "aspects" or dimensions. But with increasingly complex ethical questions pertaining to the beginning of life on the horizon, Mennonites along with other Christians will be facing mounting questions about the nature and beginning of human life and personhood. Indeed, recent developments in evolutionary biology and neuropsychology have caused considerable rethinking of the body-soul dynamic within the human being among Christian theologians.[13]

---

[12] See Umberto Eco, "On the Soul of the Embryo," in *Turning Back the Clock: Hot Wars and Media Populism* (Orlando: Harcourt, 2007), 277–80.

[13] E.g., Nancey Murphy, *Religion and Science: God, Evolution, and the Soul* (Scottdale: Herald Press, 2002); idem, *Bodies and Souls, or Spirited Bodies?* (Cambridge: Cambridge University Press, 2006); Warren S. Brown, Nancey Murphy, and H. Newton Malony, eds., *Whatever Happened to the Soul?* (Minneapolis: Fortress Press, 1998); Warren S. Brown and Malcolm A. Jeeves, "Portraits of Human Nature: Reconciling Neuroscience and Christian Anthropology," *Science and Christian Belief* 11 (1999): 139–50; Philip Heffner, *The Human Factor: Evolution, Culture, and Religion* (Minneapolis: Fortress Press, 1993); John R. Russell, N. Murphy, T. Merering, M. Arbib, eds., *Neuroscience and the Person* (Vatican City State: Vatican Observatory, 1999); J. P. Moreland and Scott B. Rae, *Body and Soul: Human Nature and the Crisis in Ethics* (Downers Grove: InterVarsity, 2000); William Hasker, *The Emergent Self* (Ithaca: Cornell University Press, 1999); Kevin Corcoran, ed., *Soul, Body, and Survival* (Ithaca: Cornell University Press, 2001); Joel B. Green, ed., *What About the Soul? Neuroscience and Christian Anthropology* (Nashville: Abingdon, 2004).

The Hebrew Bible (Old Testament) treats the human being as a unity, and there is no trace of Greek-style body-soul dualism. While there are indeed terms for the inner dimensions and essential life force of the human person, these do not come close to the sense that *psychē* (soul) had for Greek thinking, especially in the Platonic tradition. *Nephesh*, while usually translated as *psychē* in the Greek Old Testament (Septuagint, LXX) beginning in the second century BCE (Latin, *anima*), and often translated "soul" in English translations, designates the vitality or life principle of the human being, but extends to include the feelings, passions, will, or even the mentality of a person. The term *ruʻakh*, typically translated by *pneuma* in Greek and by "spirit" in English (from the Latin *spiritus*), is used for every kind of wind or breath, and can also be used to denote the whole range of emotional and volitional life, overlapping considerably in meaning with *nephesh* when used of humans. (Indeed, both terms also describe the essential life force of animals; see below.) But neither of these terms is used to refer to a distinct part of the person that is capable of surviving the death of the *basar* (Greek., *sarx*, English, flesh). As G. E. Ladd puts it: "both [terms] designate the human being as a whole viewed from different perspectives."[14]

In the intertestament period of Early Judaism (III BCE–I CE), however, both *pneuma* and *psychē* become conceived as entities capable of separate existence, persisting after death. And in some writings of Early Judaism, the body is perceived as a burden to the soul (a theme showing obvious dependence on Greek perspectives). Generally speaking, *pneuma* comes to represent the human being in its God-ward dimension, while *psychē* comes to represent the person in its human dimension.[15]

When we turn to the New Testament, we find that the anthropology of Paul's writings (ca. 50–56 CE) and the earliest stratum of the Gospels

---

[14] G. E. Ladd, *A Theology of the New Testament* rev. ed. (Grand Rapids: Eerdmans, 1993), 501. Along the same lines: H. W. Wolff, *Anthropology of the Old Testament* (Philadelphia: Fortress Press, 1974); Jacob, *Theology of the Old Testament*, 158–62. Even dualists concede this general conclusion, such as L. Berkhof, *Systematic Theology*, 193.

[15] For a sample of texts, see Ladd, *Theology*, 501–502.

(ca. 50s–60s CE) follows the perspective of the Old Testament (Hebrew Bible): terms such as *sōma* (body), *psychē*, or *pneuma* do not denote separate faculties or parts of the individual but different dimensions or ways of viewing the whole person.[16] (But it should be noted, however, that when Paul refers to the human "spirit," he does not refer to something intrinsic to humanity, but to the divine spirit that is apportioned to humanity.)[17] In general, Paul and the earliest translators of the Jesus tradition use Greek words but install Hebrew meanings (Jesus spoke Hebrew-Aramaic, but the New Testament is written in Greek). And even when Paul uses Greek terms with no exact equivalent in Hebrew (e.g., *syneidēsis*, "conscience, consciousness"), he does so in the framework of a basically Hebraic framework (for instance, absorbing *syneidēsis* within the Hebraic notion of "heart").[18] Paul thus characterizes a human being in the present order of time as a *sōma*

---

[16] For instance, in Romans 12:1–2 *sōma* ("body") is used to denote the whole person, whereas in Romans 13:1 *psychē* ("soul") is used to denote the whole person ["let every soul (person) be subordinate to the prevailing authority"]. Origen, however, whose father had been martyred for the faith, and who argued that the obedience to any human authority was never absolute, made much of the fact that Paul advised Christians to be subordinate only with their "souls," not with their entire being. See M. Reasoner, *Romans in Full Circle: A History of Interpretation* (Louisville: Westminster/John Knoz Press, 2005), 129–31.

[17] E.g., G. Fee, *God's Empowering Presence: The Holy Spirit in the Letters of Paul* (Peabody: Hendrickson, 1990), 24–26; Ladd, *Theology*, 512.

[18] See Gordon Zerbe, "Paul on the Human Being as a 'Psychic Body': Neither Dualist nor Monist," *Direction* 37/2 (2008): 168–184. Available at http://www.directionjournal.org/article/?1527. For arguments in favour of a dualistic structure of the human being in Paul, see e.g. R. Gundry, *SŌMA in Biblical Theology: With an Emphasis on Pauline Anthropology* (Cambridge: Cambridge University Press, 1976), 147–56; J. Knox Chamblin, "Psychology," in *Dictionary of Paul and His Letters*, ed. G. F. Hawthorne, R. P. Martin, D. G. Reid (Downers Grove: InterVarsity, 1993), 765–75; John W. Cooper, *Body, Soul, and Life Everlasting: Biblical Anthropology and the Monism-Dualism Debate*, 2d ed. (Grand Rapids: Eerdmans, 2000); idem, "Biblical Anthropology and the Body-Soul Problem," in *Soul, Body, and Survival*, ed. Kevin Corcoran (Ithaca: Cornell University Press, 2001), 218–28.

psychikon (roughly, "psychic body"; usually wrongly translated as "natural body"), but the person in the age to come as a *sōma pneumatikon* (pneumatic body).[19] (Note that Paul also follows the trend noted above, using *psychē* especially for the animation of the human body in the present age, but *pneuma* for the animation that is especially responsive to God and constitutive in the age to come.) Paul knows of no disembodied soulish-spiritual human entity: human beings always have bodies indissolubly connected with a life force that animates them.

In later writings of the New Testament, however, it is apparent that patterns of dualistic Greek anthropology and psychology have increasingly begun to shape conceptions of human beings and their destiny.[20] As noted above, by the middle of the second century CE, a Greek-style dualism becomes the unquestioned understanding of the constitution of the human being, and has been seriously challenged only in the past two centuries of Christian theology. On the other hand, the biblical witness would also not support a reductionist monism (materialism, physicalism), in which there is no room for human uniqueness and relating with God.[21]

The reason this issue is important is that dualistic conceptions of the person tend to have strong correlation with inadequate approaches to Christian soteriology and ethics. In Christian theology at least, strongly dualistic conceptions of the person have led to narrow views of the "atonement" and a preoccupation with matters of the "soul" (for instance, the stress on "saving souls") in contrast to the material, physical, social, or even earthly concerns that are also a crucial focus of the Bible's missional and ethical mandate. Indeed, in the history of Christianity, the stress on the hope for individual immortality and glorification of disembodied human souls after death (the ascent of the soul to heaven), has often clouded out the primary biblical hope for

---

[19] 1 Corinthians 15:44.

[20] E.g., Matthew 10:28; Luke 8:55; 16:19–31; Hebrews 12:9; Revelation 6:9–11; 20:4.

[21] See especially Nancey Murphy, *Bodies and Souls, or Spirited Bodies?*, 1–37. See also Joel B. Green, "'Bodies—That Is, Human Lives'," 149–73; idem, "Scripture and the Human Person: Further Reflections," *Science and Christian Belief* 11 (1999): 51–63.

corporate resurrection in the renewal of the whole of creation in the age to come.[22]

As noted above, humanity is given a dignified role in creation, as very close in relationship to God.[23] At the same time, however, the Bible's emphasis on the correlation of humans and animals as fellow creatures has become increasingly recognized in Christian theology in recent years. In the creation account of Genesis 1, first birds and fish are created, and then all animals. All are designated as "living creatures [*nephesh khayyah*]" (Gen. 1:20, 24, 30); then humans are created in the same pattern. In Genesis 2, humanity's proximity to the earth is stressed: "the Lord God formed the human [*'adam*] from the dust [*'aphar*] of the ground [*'adamah*], and breathed into his nostrils the breath [*nishmah*] of life [*khay*]; and the human became a living being [*nephesh khayyah*]." The same term is then used to describe all the animals (Gen. 2:19). And in Genesis 3, the divine voice asserts that life will last "until you return to the ground [*'adamah*], for out of it you were taken; you are dust [*'aphar*] and to dust you shall return" (Gen. 3:19). Later all humans and all animals are designated together as "all flesh that has the breath [*ru'akh*] of life" (Gen. 6:17; 7:15; cf. simply "all flesh," Gen. 6:12, 13; 7:16; 9:15; "the living of all flesh," Gen. 6:19; 8:17; 9:5, 6). Also indicating the sense of proximity to and regard for animals in the Hebrew Bible is the fact that both the first humans and the animals were directed to be vegetarian (Gen. 1:29–30). And later the text decries the "violence" of all living beings against each other (Gen. 6:11, 13), indicating the Hebraic sense that even the animal food chain

---

[22] The notion of an "intermediate state" before the general resurrection, in which righteous souls immediately enter a state of glory after leaving the dead body, was first propounded by Irenaeus (ca. 180 CE), and has become the prevailing view of mainstream Christianity, until the last two centuries.

[23] Besides the core text on being made in the divine image (Gen. 1:26–28) is the similar statement in Psalm 8: "When I look at your heavens, the work of your fingers, the moon and the stars that you have established; What are human beings [Heb., *'enosh*] that you are mindful of them, mortals [lit., son of Adam, *ben 'adam*] that you care for them? Yet you have made them a little lower than God [or, divine beings, *'elohim*] and crowned them with glory and honor. You have given them dominion over the works of your hands." (Ps. 8:3–6a)

represents something contrary to God's original design. The permission to eat animal meat is later given as a concession (Gen. 9:1-7). Accordingly, in Isaiah's prophetic vision of the age to come, all life will return to the primordial condition such that even all animal violence and violence between humans and animals will end in the peaceable kingdom (Isa. 11:6-9; 65:25). Similarly, just as God renewed a covenant with all living flesh after the flood (Gen. 9:11-17), so also a covenant with all flesh will be restored in Hosea's vision of the age to come (Hosea 2:18). As the Psalmist claims: "you save humans and animals alike, O Lord" (Ps. 36:6).

Humanity as Subject to Degradation, through Error (Sin) and Death
We turn, then, to the degradation of humanity (and all creation) through the entry of Error (Sin) into the world. This, too, is a core element of Mennonite confessions of faith, as with other Christian creeds and confessions, considered to be presuppositional to a doctrine of salvation (soteriology). The following themes are stressed: (1) The first humans yielded to sin, and Sin thereby entered the world. The sin of Adam and Eve "affects all" [MC][24] humans, but at the same time, all humans choose to sin, and so are responsible and accountable. (2) Sin is thus constitutive and universal in the human condition. (3) Sin is not just one thing: it includes both personal acts contrary to God's will, but it is also a power that enslaves humanity at multiple levels: "The enslaving nature of sin is apparent in the powers of evil, which work through both individuals and groups and in the entire created order. These powers, principalities, and elemental spirits of the universe often hold people captive and work through political, economic, social, and even religious systems to turn people away from justice and righteousness" [MC].[25] (4) The consequences of Sin in the world are multiple: (a) "human nature is distorted" [MB]; the image of God in humans is "marred" [MC]; (b) "people are alienated from God and creation," and from "each other and themselves" [MB], "unable to

---

[24] For references to MC and MB confessions of faith see n. 7 above.

[25] Similarly, MB Confession, Art. 4: "Sin opens individuals and groups to the bondage of demonic principalities and powers. These powers also work through political, economic, social and even religious systems to turn people away from holiness, justice, and righteousness."

worship God rightly" [MC]; (c) "all face eternal separation from God" [MB]; we become "separated from God" [MC Commentary: choosing "bondage to sin. . . . leads to final separation from God"]; (d) "spiritual and physical death" have entered the world, and "creation is under the bondage of decay" [MB]; "the powers of domination, division, destruction, and death have been unleashed in humanity and in all creation" [MC]. (5) Moreover, humans are unable to solve the problem on their own: "all humans are under the domination of sin and, on their own, are unable to overcome its power" [MB]; "because of sin and its consequences, the efforts of human beings on their own to do the good and to know the truth are constantly corrupted" [MC].

Significantly, the two major Mennonite confessions of faith do not use the classic term "Fall" to describe the degradation, culpability, or incapacity of humanity, even though they use the biblical terminology of "falling short" of the glory of God [MB] or of the Creator's intent [MC] (taking up the phrase from Rom. 3:23). In addition, they specifically avoid the terminology of "original sin" that developed in Christian theology (by contrast, "original sin" is specifically treated in Lutheran and Reformed confessions, for instance). Contemporary Mennonite confessions affirm the universality of sin and its consequences, but without positing the concept of "original sin." (Original sin in Christian theology, despite its varied understanding, can be defined as the sinful state and condition in which humans are born [as a result of Adam's sin, not original creation itself], and embraces the notions of "original guilt" [by virtue of Adam's sin imputed or transmitted to all his descendants], "original pollution" [or, "inherent corruption," or "total depravity," both the absence of original righteousness and the presence of positive evil], or "total inability" [or, the "bondage of the will"].) While not denying some sort of primal significance to the sin of the first human beings, Mennonite confessions have avoided seeking a precise theory as to its nature and consequences, and its transmission to all human beings. Instead, Mennonites have usually tilted to the side of emphasizing the actual sin of all human beings, their accountability before God, and the freedom of the will.[26]

---

[26] E.g., Balthasar Hubmaier, "Freedom of the Will, I & II [1527]," in *Balthasar Hubmaier: Theologian of Anabaptism* (Scottdale/Kitchener: Herald

And beyond stressing individual culpability, Mennonite confessions also stress the reality of bondage to powers beyond ourselves (whether cosmic or terrestrial) that keep us from the good. It should be observed, however, that even those Christians who argue for some strong sense of "original sin" or the moral "inability" of humanity apart from Christ, do not suppose that humans are completely unable to do good apart from their transformation in Christ. It is supposed that the "unredeemed" are able to perform some virtue in the social and civic sphere, but that at a fundamental level they are not able to perform God's will and respond to God on their own, in their "original" condition. Thus, for these Christians, the first step of faith or repentance can only come as a gift of grace.[27]

Christian confessions of faith, including Mennonite confessions, have drawn especially on the theology of the Apostle Paul for an articulation of the human condition (including the notion of "original sin" and the "bondage of the will"). In the articles pertaining to anthropology and soteriology, more texts are cited from Paul than the remainder of the biblical writers combined. This is partly because Paul offers the most explicit comment on these matters, even though not addressing them as such. Paul's theology, however, has been the subject of vigorous debate and varied explanations, not least because of its thoroughgoing apocalyptic (millenarian) texture that is hard to translate into modern conceptuality. It is difficult to characterize briefly.

To attempt a summary: the underlying apocalyptic (millenarian) script of Paul is the story of God's sovereign faithfulness from creation to re-creation, whereby God will soon triumph throughout creation, signaled by the resurrection of the Messiah, himself victimized by the powers of darkness and death that are embodied by imperial Authority (1 Cor. 2:6–8). Whereas the creation was created good, it has suffered the entry of mysterious, created, yet rebellious powers which oppress

---

Press, 1989), 426–48. Hubmaier enters into the debate between Erasmus (*De libero arbitrio*, 1524) and Luther (*De servo arbitrio*, 1525), siding more with Erasmus. Some Mennonite confessions specially address the freedom of the will in specific articles: e.g., Thirty-three Articles (1617) and Ris Confession (1766; 1895).

[27] For instance, L. Berkhof, *Systematic Theology*, 248–50.

God's creation. Among these disparate but interrelated powers Paul includes, for instance, Error (Sin), Death, Law, Satan, Rulers, and Authorities. But beginning with and through the Messiah, in a kind of war of liberation, in which Messiah's people wage a kind of spiritual warfare in solidarity with Messiah's pathway of paradoxically weak and powerful suffering love, God is in the process of reclaiming all creation for God, including the transformation of all human beings toward the image of God in which they were first designed. Paul's script expresses this through the notion of the "age to come" versus the "age that now stands," a dualism that is at the same time cosmic (God vs. Satan, and their respective forces), anthropological (each individual embodies the tension, subject to forces that incapacitate and corrupt the individual), historical (the dualism has a *telos*, goal), and epistemological (God's wisdom vs. worldly wisdom). While human beings are subject to oppressive forces that corrupt within and without, they are still free and capable to choose the good, and are responsible for all their actions.[28] Paul can emphasize either side of this polarity on different occasions.

For Paul the primary imperatives for human living concern loyalty-faith in relation to God and justice-peace in social human life. But modalities of life in the present age are chiefly twofold: (1) Human beings are in the situation of "groaning," as a result of the inherent weakness, perishability, and suffering characteristic of life in the present age (Rom. 8:22–23, 26–28; 2 Cor. 4:17; 5:2–4); it is the whole person that "groans," not just the body (for the internal "groaning," see Rom. 8:26–28; 2 Cor. 2:13). Ultimately, it is Death, a cosmic power force that

---

[28] For a summative characterization of anthropology in Paul, see U. Schnelle, *Theology of the New Testament* (Grand Rapids: Baker, 2009), 282–83: "Paul intensively pursues the question of human identity: what constitutes, supports, and limits authentic human existence? His answers to these questions stand within the tradition of Old Testament faith in God the creator but also incorporate traditions from Hellenistic anthropology, which he combines into his own interpretation of what it means to be authentically human. Human beings cannot live out of themselves, from their own resources, for they always find themselves thrown into a contested arena, caught up in the conflicting influences of pre-existing powers. As creatures, human beings are not autonomous simply because they possess reason but are exposed to the powers that prevail in creation: God, and evil in the form of sin."

has entered the world, that is responsible for this condition. (2) Human beings are marked by an existential (phenomenologically experienced) tension between "willing" and "doing,"[29] such that the latter is constrained or rebellious relative to the former—that is, humans are beset by a kind of ethical inability, not because of their "original state," but because of the pervasive effect of the cosmic power of Error (Sin) in the arena of the "Flesh" (humans as natural, functioning beings, especially as morally incompetent). In the following century, however, Paul's apocalyptic anthropology was understood to mean an ontologically dualistic anthropology.

Interim Results. What these foregoing two themes reveal is that humans have a kind of two-sided condition. While some biblical texts emphasize one dimension (the inherent goodness and dignity of human beings; their freedom of choice and moral obligation; their capacity for good), other passages emphasize the degradation or incompetence of the human being in the present order of time. Thus, Christians have at different times and places often developed (or wavered between) either pessimistic or optimistic views of the capacity or potential of human beings in their relationship with God, in their enactment of God's will (toward justice-righteousness and peace), in the progress of history (humanity's ongoing collective movement and achievement through time), and (especially now) in their relationship with the world of God's increasingly degraded creation at the hands of humans.

Humanity in the Process of Re-creation, through Christ, Toward Justice-Righteousness and Life

We turn, finally, to the Bible's understanding of humanity through the lens of soteriology (how God delivers, restores, and heals). We should first note some key premises that are stressed in Mennonite confessions of faith (largely in line with other Christian confessions):

(1) God has taken initiative, through grace and mercy, in the person of Jesus and through his agency, to restore all creation and all humanity at the various levels of degradation: this includes the reconciliation between God and humanity through the forgiveness of sins and the defeat of the powers of Sin and Death in the world.

---

[29] Esp. Romans 7:7–25; Galatians 5:16–25; Philippians 2:12–13.

(2) This restoration will culminate ultimately in an act of re-creation in a new heaven and new earth. This will mean the reconciliation of all things, the coming of the age to come, the final defeat of Satan and Death, and the resurrection/transformation of the body.

(3) The blessings, gifts, and human transformations that will be fully realized in the age to come are already experienced in the present order of time, by the power of the Holy Spirit. Moreover, these proleptic transformations in the present are both personal and social (as the body of those who are transformed in Christ become a new humanity).

(4) As for what happens at death, the MC confession is silent on the matter.[30] The subsequent commentary adds: " The New Testament says much about the resurrection. It speaks much less frequently and clearly about the state of persons between the time of their deaths and the resurrection. Yet, we who are in Christ are assured that not even death can separate us from the love of God (Rom. 8:38–39)." The MB confession, however, explicitly affirms that "Christ's followers go to be with the Lord when they die."[31]

As pertains specifically to anthropology, the following elements can be found in both the MC and MB confessions:

(1) A human response is necessary in order to participate in and receive this salvation. This includes (a) "accepting God's forgiveness," "yielding to God's grace," "receiving Christ," (b) "repenting/turning from sin," (c) "faith," "placing trust in Christ," "placing full trust in God alone," "entrusting lives to God."

---

[30] The following Mennonite confessions also do not refer to an "intermediate state": Dordrecht, (1632); Prussian Confession, (1660); MB, (1902); Thirteen Articles (1626); Thirty-three Articles (1617) has nothing on an intermediate state, but confesses the soul's immortality. See Koop, *Confessions*, and Loewen, *One Lord*.

[31] The following Mennonite confessions refer explicitly to the human as made of body and soul, or highlight the glorified state of the righteous soul after death: Ris, (1766/1895); Waterlander, (1577); MB, (1975); MC, (1921); MC, (1963); MB, (1999). See Koop, *Confessions*, and Loewen, *One Lord*. Most Protestant Confessions stress that after death righteous souls are immediately glorified, while evil souls immediately suffer torment, contesting the Roman Catholic notion of a purgatory for in-between souls.

(2) And this response includes (or, leads further to) a moral expectation and calling: "following Christ in this life," "showing the obedience of faith in word and deed," "walking faithfully in the way of Christ," as those who are "called to love one another and live at peace with their neighbor."

(3) Fulfilling this high moral calling is made possible by the transformations made possible through Christ: (a) "delivered from the bondage of evil," (b) "empowered by the Holy Spirit," (c) they become "new creatures in Christ," as they "experience the new birth," and so "become more and more transformed into the image of Christ."[32]

The synergistic interconnection between (2) and (3), the correlation between human exertion and divine empowerment, is expressed well by a text in the writings of Paul: "work out your own salvation with fear and trembling, for it is God who is at work in (and among) you, enabling you both to will and to work (practice) for God's good pleasure" (Phil. 2:12–13). Especially for Paul, moral competence is restored in the new humanity through an infusion of God's Spirit under the power of Grace, not by tightening detailed legal commands or threats of punishment.

Finally, we should note the importance of the person of Christ for Christian anthropology. Christ is not only God's agent of salvation or the revealer of God's will. Further themes can also be found in the New Testament, as exemplified especially in the writings of Paul:

(1) In Christ, God has entered into solidarity with, and has identified with human suffering and pain (2 Cor. 1; Phil. 2).[33]

---

[32] Compare, however, differing assumptions among denominations as to how effectual this may become in the life of the believer, not merely imputed. Thus, for instance, in Lutheran understanding, the high demands of Jesus' Sermon on the Mount, including loving enemies, cannot be realized in practice, and is meant only to show humans how they can never measure up to God's standards, causing them to claim only God's mercy and grace. Anabaptists (and Mennonites), however, have assumed that these directives represent the will of God, and represent what those transformed in Christ are expected to practice. Jesus' command, "Be perfect, as your Father in heaven is perfect" (Matthew 5:48), was meant to be taken as a real moral demand, not an excessive one that only revealed the moral inability of humankind.

[33] On this, see Jürgen Moltmann, cited in n. 1 above.

(2) As the New/Second/Last Adam, Christ is the prototype and paradigm for a new transformed humanity: "We believe that the image of God in all its fullness has been revealed and restored in Jesus Christ, in whom we find our true humanity 2 Cor. 4:4; Col. 1:15" [MC, Art 6]; "As fully human and tempted as we are, yet without sin, he is the model human being" (Heb. 4:15; Rom. 5:14-21; 1 Pet. 2:21) [MC, Art 2]. While the Gospels use the imagery of "following Jesus," Paul expresses the concept of "participating in Christ," or "imitating Christ" (e.g., Rom. 15:1-8; 1 Cor. 10:24-11:1; 2 Cor. 8:6-9; Phil. 2:5-11). The human transformation into what God has designed is thus described as matter of "Christ being formed in you" (Gal. 4:19).

(3) As the New/Second/Last Adam, Christ is also the progenitor and (thus genealogical) head of a new humanity (1 Cor. 15:45, 47; Col. 3:10; Eph. 4:24).[34] Just as Adam's sin became universally efficacious for all his descendants, so also Christ's act has become universally efficacious for all humanity. Thus, those who are absorbed into his restoring power, and sphere of influence, together become a "new humanity" (Col. 3:9-11; Gal. 3:26-28: Eph. 2:15). The redemptive anthropology of the New Testament is thus in this sense crucially social and political (in regard to its ecclesiology, but also its cosmic scope), not merely personal and individual. And especially in Paul, a theology of radical grace leads to a most optimistic and grand vision for the scope and outcome of God's reconciling work in creation, ultimately overcoming all the divisions (including identity formations) that beset humanity, including that of belief and unbelief, fidelity and infidelity.[35] Thus for Paul, more than any writer of the New Testament, humans must always regard one another not simply because of what is in the past or even in the present, but especially because of what will be when God's grace is finally

---

[34] People are included in this New Adamic genealogy through "adoption," by being reborn in Christ (Rom. 8:14-15; Gal. 3:26-28; Eph 1:5). Or, alternatively, Paul describes Christ as "first born among many brothers and sisters" (Rom. 8:29).

[35] See my "The relevance of Paul's eschatological ecclesiology for ecumenical relations," in *New Perspectives in Believers Church Ecclesiology*, A. Dueck, H. Harder, and K. Koop, ed. (Winnipeg: CMU Press, 2010), 30-47.

victorious over all human infidelity, and not simply (though inclusively so) because of our common humanity in the image of God.[36]

---

[36] Mennonite confessions of faith, however, highlight an eschatological vision that is a zero-sum game based on a notion of distributive justice wedded to a notion of redemptive scarcity (the believing righteous will enjoy eternal bliss, whereas the unbelieving unrighteous will suffer eternal torment), whereas Paul's eschatology is dominated by an expansive (even if asymmetric) notion of restorative justice, in which ultimately mercy transfigures distributive justice and conquers human infidelity, while still attempting to avoid any consequences of cheap grace.

In the Name of Allah, the Beneficent, the Merciful

THE PERFECT MAN IN ISLAMIC MYSTICISM

MOHAMMAD FANAEI ESHKEVARI

Islamic mysticism as a system of knowledge is a kind of ontology or world view obtained through mystical experiences via living a mystical way of life. In this view, the real being is the Absolute Being or the Almighty God, Who is one, infinite and absolutely perfect. The world with all its multiplicity is the manifestation of His names and attributes. Among the creatures of the world, the human being enjoys a special status. Human beings are composed of a physical body and an immaterial soul. With such a combination, human beings have all the merits that can be found in other creatures. Whatever exists in the world exists in human beings. For this reason the human being is known as the microcosm and the most universal being. The human being is the goal of creation and, thus, everything else is created for him. With such a creation, the human being has reason and free will from one side, and animal-like desires and impulses from the other side. The seed of human existence has both the potential for blossoming and growing, and the possibility for decay and fetidness. The perfect man is the one who has actualized all his potential in the best possible manner. He is the most perfect manifestation of God's names and attributes. He is the mediator for others to receive God's grace, the fruit of creation, and is the divine vicegerent in the world. He is the proof of God and enjoys the status of *wilayah* (divine authority).

Attention to human beings and to their status in Muslim tradition has its roots in Islamic teachings. Many verses of the Qur'an and quite a large number of hadith have touched on the status of the human being in general and the perfect man in particular. Muslim mystics (Sufis, 'urafa), perhaps more than any other group, have focused on this aspect of Islamic teachings and dealt with its different aspects. Since the ultimate goal of mysticism is to achieve the highest stages of perfection through purification of the heart, knowledge of the real nature of man, including his dimensions and ultimate perfection, has fundamental importance. Hence, anthropology and mystical psychology enjoy a focal attention in Islamic mystical literature. Knowing the status of the perfect man, in so far as he shows the direction of the mystical journey and the ultimate goal of mystical life, is particularly significant.

The expression "perfect man" (*al-insan al-kamil*) can be seen in the works of Attar Nishabury, and Ibn Arabi in the seventh Islamic century. Ibn Arabi, more than anyone else, has systematically discussed the status of the perfect man in his theoretical mysticism (*al-'irfan al-nadari*), especially in the first chapter of his *Fusus al-Hikam* (*The Bezels of Wisdom*). All commentators on the *Fusus* have elaborated on the nature of the perfect man in the interpretation of this chapter. After Ibn Arabi, his followers such as Sadr al-Din Qunawi, Fanari, Shabistari, Nasafi, Jilli, Ibn Turkah, Tabataba'i, Imam Khomeini, and Mutahhari have discussed different aspects of the perfect man in their works.

Discussions related to the human being in Islamic literature are of various kinds:

a. philosophical psychology discusses the nature of man in general, as a species;
b. theoretical mysticism discusses the idea of the perfect man;
c. practical mysticism as a discipline deals with the soul in so far as it has an impact on one's behaviour and life;
d. an individual's self-knowledge as the gate to purification of the heart is emphasized in actual mystical training.

This paper focuses on the second type of Islamic anthropology, which elaborates the status of the perfect man from the viewpoint of theoretical Islamic mysticism.

Divine Manifestation

From the viewpoint of Islamic mysticism, real being and genuine reality is God, and the rest of the world consists of the manifestations of His names and attributes. God is infinite perfection. His one and simple essence contains all perfections in an infinite manner. Each name and attribute of God indicates one of His perfections. God knows Himself and sees Himself in Himself and does not need anyone else. However, since His perfection is absolute and His grace is eternal and never ending, the world manifests Him and He discloses Himself in the world and thus sees Himself in the world. Hence, God created the world in order to see His face in the mirrors of His manifestations.

In this view, God's names and attributes have consequences that are called immutable archetypes (*al-a'ayan al-thabitah*, eternal essences/fixed entities). They are intellectual correlates of things (*wujud al-'ilmi lil ashya*) in the knowledge of God. These archetypes that are essences of things are created by the most holy emanation of God (*al-fayd al-aqdas*). Realities of the world are external consequences of God's names and attributes and objective existences of those essences. Each objective being is the manifestation of one or some of God's names and the reflection of some of God's perfections. These realities came into existence by God's holy emanation (*al-fayd al-muqaddas*). Thus, the real being is God and the rest are manifestations of His names and attributes. Each reality is like a mirror in which some of God's perfections are reflected. And the world in its totality is the exhibition in which God's perfection is explicitly manifested. Each being reflects God's perfection according to its capacity.[1]

The Greatest Manifestation

Although the realities of the world are manifestations of God's names, and the whole world can show all His names, before the creation of the human being there was no single creature that was capable of being the manifestation of all God's names. God wants to create something that can alone show all His names so God can see Himself with all His names in this mirror. The only thing in the world that has such a capacity is the human being.[2] Even celestial beings, angels, and

---

[1] See Imam Khomeini, *Misbah al-Hidayah ila al-Khilafati wal Wilayah* (Tehran: Mu'assessah Tandhim va Nashr-e Athar-e Imam Khomeini, 1372/1993), 44.

[2] See Ibn Arabi, *Fusus al-Hikam* (Beirut: Dar al-Kitab, 1400/1980), 48.

intellects do not have this capacity. Therefore, God created the human being as His greatest manifestation and the most perfect theophany.³ Since the name "Allah" is the most comprehensive name of God, the perfect man is the manifestation of this name. "The perfect man is the manifestation of God's most comprehensive name (*al-ism al-jami'*) and the mirror for the disclosure of his greatest name (*al-ism al-a'zam*)."⁴ Therefore, we can say that manifestation of God takes place both explicitly in the multiplicity of the world, and implicitly in a unitary way of appearing in the perfect man.

It is noteworthy that the human being is a species; and thus all its individuals potentially have this capacity; however, its actualization depends on one's own free efforts, and thus, in the end, only some individuals enjoy this status. These individuals are in fact described as the perfect man (*al-insan al-kamil*), divine great manifestations, microcosms, and the most universal being. These are prophets and saints (*anbiya wa awliya*). They are not all at the same level; rather, their perfection has degrees. Highest of all is the status of the seal of prophets: Muhammad (s).⁵ Other people, depending on the spiritual status that they earn, enjoy some degrees of this perfection.

Creation of the Human Being

The difference between human beings and other creatures has its roots in the creation of the human being. Human beings, like other material beings, have a physical dimension, and, like other living beings in nature, have biological life. The Qur'an explicitly mentions the origin of human natural life and stages of development from the embryo to death:

> If you are in doubt about the resurrection, (consider that) We indeed created you from dust, then from a drop of [seminal] fluid, then from a clinging mass, then from a fleshy tissue ... then We bring you forth as an infant. (22:5)

---

[3] Imam Khomeini, *Sharh Du'a al-Sahar* (Tehran: Kav 'Ilmi va Farhangi, 1362/1983), 159.

[4] Imam Khomeini, *Sharhe Chehel Hadith* (Tehran: Raja, 1368/1989), 635.

[5] See Abdulkarim Jili, *al-Insan al-Kamil* (Cairo: al-Halabi, 1390/1970), Second part, 71.

In chapter 23, it is written:

> Certainly We created man from an extract of clay. Then We made him a drop of [seminal] fluid ... Then We created the drop of fluid as a clinging mass. Then We created the clinging mass as a fleshy tissue. Then We created the fleshy tissue as bones. Then We clothed the bones with flesh. (23:12–14)

But according to the Qur'an, human life is not restricted to its natural biological life as previous verse the Qur'an continues and ends:

> Then We produced him as [yet] another creature. So blessed is Allah, the best of creators! (23:14)

This means that after its corporeal and biological creation, God bestowed on man another creation. Thus, besides its physical nature, the human being has a nature of a different and higher kind which is its immaterial nature. In another verse, the Qur'an elaborates it more explicitly:

> When your Lord said to the angels, 'Indeed I am going to create a human out of a dry clay [drawn] from an aging mud. So when I have proportioned him and breathed into him of My Spirit, then fall down in prostration before him. (15:28–29)

The human being has a substance that makes him different from others and makes him closer to God. He enjoys a divine soul. A famous hadith says that God created man in His own image.[6] Although there are some controversial discussions about the authenticity and the interpretation of this hadith, many mystics agree that the hadith means that God created man in His own image. This is in accord with the overall mystical view of the status of human being as the best manifestation of God and His vicegerent. Some verses of the Qur'an also support this idea. For example, God says that He gave the human being the best form:

---

[6] Majlisi, *Bihar al-Anwar* (Beirut: Dar al-Turath al-'Arabi, 1403/1983), vol. 4:14.

He created the heavens and the earth with the truth, and He formed you and perfected your forms, and toward Him is the destination. (64:3)

We certainly created man in the best of forms. (95:4)

Value and Dignity of the Human Being
No doubt, from the Qur'anic view, the human being has a special status in the world. This is the human being that has a different creation, enjoys reason and free will, is the most perfect creature, and is created in the image of God. Thus, the human has the highest value, honour and dignity among all creatures. The Qur'an states:

Certainly We have honored the Children of Adam, and carried them over land and sea, and provided them with all good things, and given them an advantage over many of those We have created with a complete preference. (17:70)

The human being enjoys such a noble status that God commands the angles to prostrate before him. Because he has a divine soul, he deserves to be honoured:

So when I have proportioned him and breathed into him of My Spirit, then fall down in prostration before him. (15:29)

As we can see, from the Islamic perspective, the human's value totally depends on his relation to God. He is not autonomous. Because he is the best manifestation of God, has a divine soul, and is created in the image of God, he has the highest value among the creatures. For God is the only source of value, dignity, and honour. At the same time, we can say that human dignity is essential, not accidental, for his relation to God is in his very essence and existence. And this is the difference between Islam and humanism, liberalism, and other secular schools of thought with regard to human value. We must also add that since human value has its roots in human existence itself, the value of individuals is genuine and not dependent on their status in society.

In this view, the value of the human being is not merely static and predetermined; rather man has two types of value: first, the essential value of the human species, which has its root in his creation and, therefore, is common to all individual humans; and second, the dynamic dimension of value and perfection that each individual acquires by his own free will. This value depends on each individual's knowledge/faith and practice/piety and therefore is different from one person to another. The Qur'an says:

> O mankind! Indeed We created you from a male and a female, and made you nations and tribes that you may identify with one another. Indeed the noblest of you in the sight of Allah is the most God-wary among you. (46:13)

The first part of the verse refers to the common value of all people; the second part refers to the acquired and therefore different values of individuals. This value depends solely on piety (*taqwā*), which is the natural combination of faith and good deeds. Knowing God, loving God, and obeying God are three essential elements of the way to perfection. Whoever goes further along this way reaches the higher stages of perfection.

It must be noted that according to Islamic mysticism, there is no ending point in human perfection. Whatever stage one reaches one can go further and further toward the infinite. This is another merit of human beings over other creatures.

The Other Side of the Coin

Because of man's combination of material and spiritual substances, and because of his conflicting desires on one hand, and his free will on the other hand, man's final destiny depends on his own choice. He himself decides his future destiny. He can ascend upward to heaven or descend downward to hell. He can go beyond the angels or below the beasts.

> We certainly created man in the best of forms; then We relegated him to the lowest of the low, except those who have faith and do righteous deeds. There will be an everlasting reward for them. (95:4–6)

Man in his nature has a tendency toward the good; however, he has selfish desires, too. The Qur'an says that the example of one who denies the truth while he knows it, "is that of an ass carrying books" (62:5). Elsewhere the Qur'an compares those who follow their selfish desires and turn their backs toward the truth to dogs.

> Had We wished, We would have surely raised him by their means, but he clung to the earth and followed his [base] desires. So his parable is that of a dog: if you make for it, it lolls out its tongue, and if you let it alone, it lolls out its tongue. Such is the parable of the people who deny Our signs. (7:176)

Those who are slaves of their desires and do not benefit from their reason are lower than all creatures.

> Indeed the worst of beasts in Allah's sight are the deaf and the dumb who do not apply reason. (8:22)

Hell is the consequence of the behaviour of those who so indulge in the lower pleasures that they neglect the truth. They are no longer human beings.

> Certainly We have created for hell many of the jinn and humans: they have hearts with which they do not understand, they have eyes with which they do not see, they have ears with which they do not hear. They are like cattle; rather they are more astray. It is they who are heedless. (7:179)

Thus, although man can fly toward light and happiness by the two wings of faith and good deeds, if his selfish desires overcome his reason, he will be imprisoned in darkness and misfortune. The Qur'an says:

> By Time! Indeed man is at a loss, except those who have faith and do righteous deeds. (103:1–3)

The Most Universal Being

In Islamic mysticism, the human being is not merely a creature besides other creatures; rather, he is a comprehensive being who contains within himself all beings. Since man is the greatest manifestation of God, the world in its totality is summarized in him. In other words, since man reflects all names of God, he encompasses everything and is present in all worlds.

In this view, man is not only a species among others; rather he is a world that contains all other worlds. Mystics recognize four stages of worlds: the world of fixed entities (*'alam al-a'yan al-thabitah*), the world of intellects (*'alam al-'uqul*) the imaginary world (*'alam al-mithal*), the world of nature (*'alam al-tabi'ah*) and the world of most universal being or the world of human being (*'alam al-insani*).[7]

Since the human being in his arc of descent (*al-qaws al-nuzuli*) has crossed all worlds and contains and comprehends all, he has a kind of unity with all worlds.[8] The unity of the perfect man with the world and his presence in all stages of the world is likened to the unity and presence of the soul with and in its faculties.[9] Hence, Ibn Arabi says that the perfect man is the spirit of the world and the world is his body. The world without the perfect man is like a body without soul, i.e., a dead body.[10] Therefore, the perfect human being is called the minor world or the microcosm (*al-'alam al-saghir*) and the world is called the greater human (*al-insan al-kabir*). This description is according to the outward form, however, in reality, the human being is the macrocosm and the world is microcosm.[11]

Since the human being represents both God and the world, knowing the human is the key to knowing God and the world. As a prophetic

---

[7] See Muhammad Dawud Qaysari Rumi, *Sharh Fusus al-Hikam*, ed. S. J. Ashtiyani (Tehran: Entesharat 'Ilmi va Farhangi, 1375/1996).

[8] This idea is confirmed by some hadith from the Imams; for example, see Muhammad ibn Ya'qub al-Kulayni *Al-Kafi* (Tehran: Haydari, 1378/1999).

[9] Imam Khomeini, *Misbah al-Hidayah ila al-Khilafati wal Wilayah*, 18.

[10] Ibn Arabi, *al-Futuhat al-Makkiyyah* (Beirut: Dar al-Sadir, n.d., ca. 1970), vol. 2:67.

[11] See 'Abd al-Rahman Jami, *Naqd al-Nusus fi sharhi naqsh al-fusus*, ed. William Chittick (Tehran: Iranian Academy of Philosophy, 1977), 91; also Jalal al-Din Rumi, *Mathnavi* (Tehran: Ququnus, 1376/1997), the Fifth Book, line 521.

hadith says, "One who knows himself knows his Lord" or, knowing the self is the most beneficiary knowledge and the key to all knowledge.[12]

Man as Vicegerent of God

As mentioned above, the human being is the best manifestation of God and the closest of creatures to Him. Because of this status, God has chosen the human as His vicegerent in the world. We can understand from the Qur'an that God created the human being in order to be His vicegerent.

> When your Lord said to the angels, "Indeed I am going to set a viceroy on the earth," they said, "Will You set in it someone who will cause corruption in it, and shed blood, while we celebrate Your praise and proclaim Your sanctity?" He said, "Indeed I know what you do not know." And He taught Adam the Names, all of them; then presented them to the angels and said, "Tell me the names of these, if you are truthful." They said, "Immaculate are You! We have no knowledge except what You have taught us. Indeed You are the All-knowing, the All-wise." He said, "O Adam, inform them of their names," and when he had informed them of their names, He said "Did I not tell you that I indeed know the Unseen in the heaven and the earth, and that I know whatever you disclose and whatever you were concealing?" (2:30–33)

According to these verses, the position of vicegerency is related to man's knowledge of names. It is explicitly mentioned that since Adam knows the names, he is chosen as God's vicegerent. He knows all names because he is the manifestation of all names. When he knows himself he knows all names. But other creatures, even angels, do not reflect in themselves all names; therefore, they do not know them. Consequently, they cannot have the position of vicegerency and must prostrate before Adam. And so they did:

> And when We said to the angels, "Prostrate before Adam," they prostrated, except Iblis: he refused and acted arrogantly, and he was one of the faithless. (2:34)

---

[12] Imam Khomeini, *Ta'liqat 'ala Fusus al-Hikam* (Qom: Pasdare Islam, 1406/1986), 59.

In the same line, the Qur'an talks about a trust that all creatures refused to carry but the human being:

> Indeed We presented the Trust to the heavens and the earth and the mountains, but they refused to bear it; and were apprehensive of it; but man undertook it. (33:72)

Perfect Man as the Mediator for Creation and Sustainment of the World

The perfect man is the first creature emanated from God and the mediator for the creation of the rest of the world. God's grace reaches the world via the perfect man. He is the isthmus between necessity and contingency, a mediator between the Creator and creatures. He is the guardian and cause of the continuity of the world. Without him the world could not receive the grace of God, and thus could not exist.[13] As Qaysari states, "The perfect man is the intermediary cause of the world's creation, sustention, and perfection."[14] Therefore, although formally and apparently he is posterior to all, spiritually he has priority to all.

It must be emphasized that this position of the perfect man does not mean that he is like a partner of God. The perfect man achieves this position through obedience to God. According to Islamic mysticism, the perfect man par excellence is the Prophet Muhammad (s) whose most distinguished quality is "the servant" (al-'abd). The human being through obedience and purification of the soul can reach a point to become the mediator between God and the world, God's vicegerent and lord of the world.[15] His lordship is the shadow of God's lordship, and his intervention is by the permission of God (bi idhnillah). He is God's agent. In fact, his heart is the mirror of God and reflects His lordship.

The Perfect Man as the Goal of Creation

Before the creation of the perfect man, the world is incomplete and the goal of creation has not yet been achieved. Only by the appearance of

---

[13] 'Abd al-Rahman Jami, *Naqd al-Nusus fi sharhi naqsh al-fusus*, 97.

[14] Muhammad Dawud Qaysari Rumi, *Sharh Fusus al-Hikam*, 71.

[15] See Avicenna, *The Metaphysics of The Healing*, ed. Michael E. Marmura (Provo: Brigham Young University Press, 2005), 378.

the perfect man is the goal of creation met, for the ultimate goal of creation is God's complete manifestation. Only the perfect man can reflect all God's names and attributes. Therefore, without the perfect man, the purpose of creation cannot be met.[16] As previously said, the perfect man is the intermediary cause of creation; but he is also the final cause of creation. The final cause has priority over the effect of the knowledge and will of the efficient cause, though its existence follows the existence of the effect. As Jalal al-Din Mawlavi (Rumi) says, "although in the appearance the fruit comes out of the tree, but in reality the fruit is the cause for planting the tree."[17]

It follows that without the existence of the perfect man, the world would cease to exist. When the last perfect man dies, the resurrection will commence. This is in accordance with some Shi'i hadith which say that without a *hujjah* (the proof/the perfect man), the earth and its dwellers will vanish.[18] If the perfect man is the channel of God's grace to the world, the guardian of the world and its final cause and if the world is created for him, it follows that the world cannot exist without the presence of the perfect man.

Nabi, Rasul and *Wali*

Each name of God has a requirement in God's explicit knowledge which is called a fixed entity. The name "Allah" which is the most comprehensive name has a reflective eternal fixed entity that is called *al-haqiqah al-Muhammadiyyah* (the reality of Muhammad). The external manifestation of this reality in each period of history is one of the prophets. Its most perfect manifestation is in the person of the Prophet Muhammad (s). Therefore, all prophets, and thus all their messages, originated from the same source and are different reflections of the same light.

Here, we should distinguish between three connected concepts: *al-nabi* (the prophet), *al-rasul* (the messenger), and *al-wali* (the saint, the friend of God). One person may accumulate in himself all three concepts as the great prophets, such as Moses, Jesus, and Mohammad,

---

[16] Jandi, *Shrah Fusus al-Hikam* (Mashhad: Mashhad University Press, 1361/1982), 151.

[17] Jalal al-Din Rumi, *Mathnavi*, the Fourth Book, line 524.

[18] Muhammad ibn Ya'qub al-Kulayni *Al-Kafi*, vol. 1, 179.

do. Each of these concepts constitutes one dimension of a prophet's spiritual personality. *Wali* is the one who has a direct relation to God; his acts, qualities, and essence are annihilated in God. *Nabi* is the one who receives the message from God via a medium like an angel. And *rasul* is the messenger who has a *shari'ah* and is obliged to deliver God's message to the people. The *wilayah* of a *nabi* is the inner dimension of his prophethood and thus is higher than his prophethood. Every *rasul* is a *nabi* and a *wali*. Every *nabi* also is a *wali*, but not every *wali* is a *nabi* or *rasul*. *Nubuwwah* (prophethood) and *risalah* (messengerhood) are not eternal. After the last prophet there will not be any *nabi* or *rasul*; however, *wilayah* is eternal and the world will never be without a *wali*. For the word "*al-wali*" is one of the names of God which requires a manifestation, unlike "*nabi*" and "*rasul*."[19] According to Shi'ite doctrine, after Prophet Muhammad, each of the twelve Imams of his household are *wali*.

Beside the cosmic roles that prophets and sages play as the perfect men, they are masters and guides for the religious and mystical life. They are gates to salvation. Without following their teachings and examples, the spiritual journey of the mystics would not be complete. Therefore, knowing the *wali* and following him is essential. As the Qur'an says:

> [O Muhammad] Say, "If you love Allah, then follow me; Allah will love you and forgive you your sins, and Allah is All-forgiving, All-merciful." (3:31)

Conclusion

According to Islamic mysticism, the essence of God is absolutely hidden and cannot be comprehended. We know God through His names and attributes. The names and attributes emerge from the essence and the world emerges from God's names and attributes. God first discloses Himself in His names, and then with the mediation of His names in the world. The highest discloser and manifestation is in the human being which is the most universal being and capable of reflecting all God's names. This is due to the nature of the human being

---

[19] Muhammad Dawud Qaysari Rumi, *Sharh Fusus al-Hikam*, ch. 12.

which is composed of substances that are both physical and spiritual, both earthly and heavenly, and both material and immaterial. The human has reason and a tendency toward the good, but at the same time it has selfish desires too. Since he has free will, man can go in any direction. He can achieve the highest stages of perfection just as he can fall into the lowest pit of deficiency. The perfect man is the one who fully actualizes his potential for perfection. He is the vicegerent of God, the microcosm, the bearer of God's trust, the intermediary cause of creation, the ultimate goal of the world, the channel for sustaining the world and the guardian of the world, the friend of God, the mirror through which one can see God, the master, the guide and perfect example in the journey toward God, the prophet, and the Imam.

PART II

PERFECTION

THE WAY OF PERFECTION IN THE CHRISTIAN TRADITION

JO-ANN A. BRANT

Saint Augustine, the fifth-century North African bishop wrote, "This is the very perfection of a man, to find out his own imperfections." Nevertheless, many Christians feel a tug, as though drawn by gravity toward some exquisite standard most appropriately described as divine glory. If it is proper to speak of the way of perfection for a believer within the Christian tradition, that discourse must be tempered with the paradox that we are creatures, subject both to decay and the ignorance that comes with being located in time and space. Perfection itself is a divine attribute, but insofar as God allows us to participate in a divine reality, we can speak of God's ways that we are called to imitate and the means that God offers us by which we can sit in God's presence as the way of perfection.

The phrase "the way of perfection" is not found on the lips of many Christians. "The Way of the Cross," "The Way of Salvation," for example, are more common terms. The phrase "the way of perfection" is used by Theresa of Avila, a sixteenth century Spanish Carmelite nun and mystic, as the title of a book in which she describes a method of making progress through prayer, meditation, quiet, and repose. The perfection that she describes is the perfect union with God. In the following discussion, I will leave aside the mystical tradition for something more commonplace. While I lay out a somewhat broader path than the monastic life delineated by Theresa of Avila, I trust that if she were to read this paper she would recognize that the same principles of charity and humility and a similar reading of Christian scripture inform my analysis.

In order to appropriate the language of perfection in modern theological discourse, we must first disentangle it from the concept of perfection that dominates in current usage. Perfection in the modern context often refers to such things as precision instruments or to the performance of a task without error. For example, someone can score 100 percent on a mathematics exam or a musician can aspire to perform a piece of music flawlessly. The following line from British playwright Tom Stoppard's *Arcadia* is an astute critique of the modern notion of perfection: "Don't confuse progress with perfectibility."[1] The perfection to which Christian discourse refers is a form of harmony in which one's actions conform to the will of God. As human beings we belong to the realm of constant change. Consequently, the way of perfection calls us at each point to reject the idea that our actions, done in imitation of God, have met the mark, that we can reckon ourselves adequate facsimiles of the divine. Each act of imitation calls for the next.

In order to provide structure to this discussion, I will focus on passages from the New Testament, trace some of the relevant strands of Christian discourse in general and Anabaptist discourse in particular, and then identify the strain that modernity and secular culture places upon fulfillment of scripture. Through my reading of the Gospel of Matthew and the Letter to the Hebrews, I isolate three themes: 1) perfection through imitation of divine generosity, 2) perfection through the endurance of suffering, and 3) perfection through sanctification or holy living as children of God. This sanctification is a form of ordination. The members of the community can approach God because they have entered into the vocation appointed to them. They are perfect insofar as they fulfill their purpose. While I anticipate that my Muslim dialogue partners will disagree with the claim that baptism in Christ and a life of Christian discipleship is the path to perfection, we may find room for agreement that perfection lies in submitting to the path that God offers and, in doing so, receiving God's stamp of approval.

Perfection through Imitation of Divine Generosity
Matthew 5:48 and the Sermon on the Mount. The place to begin is with the passage that stands at the heart of Christian discourse on perfection.

---

[1] Tom Stoppard *Arcadia* (New York: Samuel French, 1993), 2.5. *Arcadia* examines the relationship between past and present, between order and disorder, and the certainty or uncertainty of knowledge. The line appears in a dialogue about scientific progress.

In the Sermon on the Mount, Jesus issues the following instruction: "Be perfect, therefore, as your heavenly Father is perfect" (Matt. 5:48). The conjunction "therefore" requires the exegete to place this command within the context of the verses that precede it. The broad context is the Sermon on the Mount in which Jesus lays out an ethic for his disciples that sets them apart from conventional notions of justice, piety, security, and honour. The command's immediate context is the call to love our enemies and pray for those who persecute us:

> You have heard that it was said, "You shall love your neighbour and hate your enemy." But I say to you, "Love your enemies and pray for those who persecute you, so that you may be children of your Father in heaven; for he makes his sun rise on the evil and on the good, and sends rain on the righteous and on the unrighteous. For if you love those who love you, what reward do you have? Do not even the tax collectors do the same? And if you greet only your brothers and sisters, what more are you doing than others? Do not even the Gentiles do the same? Be perfect, therefore, as your heavenly Father is perfect." (Matt. 5:43–48)[2]

Jesus explains that, just as our Father in heaven makes the sun to rise and the rain to fall on the righteous and the unrighteous, we are to love those who do not return our love. He prefaces the section of the Sermon on the Mount, which this call to perfection concludes, within a call for a righteousness that exceeds the generally accepted standard set by the Pharisees (Matt. 5:17–20). The Pharisees sought a sort of technical perfection in their observance of such things as the Sabbath, tithing, and ritual purity. They seem to have attempted to make God's commandments an exhaustive code of behaviour by which one would be able to know with confidence that he or she satisfied the demands of righteousness. Jesus leaves his disciples with a standard that cannot be codified. We are left with a demand that is without measure. Perfection entails more than giving one tenth; it calls for more than abstaining from certain activities. Perfection is, in part, a way of life marked by

---

[2] All quotations from the Bible are taken from the New Revised Standard Version translation.

endless giving. Perhaps the Apostle Paul correctly interprets this teaching of Jesus at the end of his letter to the Galatians when he characterizes the covenant of Moses as a set of restrictions upon one's actions, designed to keep one from sin (Gal. 3:23–24), and the covenant with Christ as the freedom to love and to express kindness and generosity, designed to break through the realm of sin (Gal. 5:22–26). The New Testament concept of perfection defies an Aristotelian metaphysic that insists that perfection is finite. Divine perfection is, as St. Thomas Aquinas puts it, an infinite perfection.[3]

The habit of generosity becomes one of the defining features of Early Christianity. Tertullian, known as the father of Latin Christianity, wrote a defense of Christianity in 197 CE in which he describes how the Church lived out this call to perfection by using its funds not to pay for feasts, as pagan religious societies did, but for the support and burial of the poor, for providing for orphans, the aged, and those in prisons, exile, or forced labour. He also describes how Christians were ridiculed for their charity:

> Even if we have a kind of treasury, this is not filled up from a sense of obligation, as of a hired religion. Each member adds a small sum once a month, or when he pleases, and only if he is willing and able; for no one is forced, but each contributes of his own free will. These are the deposits as it were made by devotion. For that sum is disbursed not on banquets nor drinking bouts nor unwillingly on eating-houses, but on the supporting and burying of the poor, and on boys and girls deprived of property and parents, and on aged servants of the house, also on shipwrecked persons, and any who are in the mines or on islands or in prisons, provided it be for the cause of God's religion, who thus become pensioners of their confession. But the working of that kind of love most of all brands us with a mark of blame in the eyes of some. "See," they say, "how they love one another;" for they themselves hate one another; and "how they are ready to die for one another;" for they will be more ready to kill one another.[4]

---

[3] Thomas Aquinas, *Summa Theologica*, 1a.7.1, 9.1, and 19.4.
[4] Tertullian, *Apology* 39; trans. Alexander Souter (1917).

The pagan satirist Lucian of Samosata (130-200 CE), a contemporary of Tertullian, mocked Christians for being prey to charlatans and tricksters who became wealthy by soliciting donations from followers of "the crucified sophist":

> Furthermore, their first lawgiver persuaded them that they are all brothers of one another after they have transgressed once, for all by denying the Greek gods and by worshipping that crucified sophist himself and living under his laws. Therefore they despise all things indiscriminately and consider them common property, receiving such doctrines traditionally without any definite evidence. So if any charlatan and trickster, able to profit by occasions, comes among them, he quickly acquires sudden wealth by imposing upon simple folk.[5]

Ancient Greco-Roman authors often criticize the public support of the disabled and beggars. Aristotle writes, "there should certainly be a law to prevent the rearing of deformed children."[6] In the comedy *Trinummus*, Plautus places platitudes of Roman virtues such as the following on the lips of Philto, the father of the protagonist: "You do a beggar bad service by giving him food and drink; you lose what you give and prolong his life for more misery."[7] They advocated charity but only to the deserving, those who were good or capable of contributing to society.[8] As Seneca puts it, "To some I shall not give although they are in need, because, even if I should give, they would still be in need."[9] John Chrysostom (fourth-century church father and Archbishop of Constantinople), in contrast, thought that Christians should give to any poor person who asked and let the poor determine if help is needed or not.[10]

---

[5] Lucian of Samosata, *The Passing of Peregrinus* 13; trans. A.M. Harmon (1936).
[6] Aristotle, *Politics* 1335b; trans. E. Barker (1998).
[7] Plautus, *Trinummus* 339, trans. Nixon (1938).
[8] See Isocrates, *Demon.* 29; Cicero, *Off.* 2.54.
[9] Seneca, *Vit. beat.* 24.1, trans. Basore (1958).
[10] John Chrysostom, *Quatr. Laz.* 2.5.

Insofar as the way of perfection is through the imitation of God, the Christian call to perfection is qualified. We are not to imitate God in all respects. There are actions that belong to God alone. Vengeance belongs to God. Judgment belongs to God. Later in the Sermon on the Mount, Jesus warns, "Do not judge, so that you may not be judged. For with the judgment you make you will be judged, and the measure you give will be the measure you get" (Matt. 7:1–2). The call to perfection entails trusting that God will provide for one's needs and that God will see that justice is done.

Topics in Christian Discourse. This call to imitate God through acts of charity transforms the understanding of wealth within the Greco-Roman world. To the Greco-Roman mind only those at the top of the socio-economic pyramid were granted the privilege of acting as patrons within society. Within the Christian context, anyone who had more than enough for their immediate needs was encouraged to think of him or herself as wealthy and was free to give, as formerly only those with extreme excess were allowed to give. As a result, the church became a wealthy institution. One of the recurring topics of discourse then becomes whether it is appropriate for the church to spend its money upon its own infrastructure or whether the church itself must continually give from its abundance rather than accumulating wealth. Throughout Christian history, individuals and groups arise who try to return to the sort of simplicity reflected in Jesus' own ministry. Many of these have been monastic orders, such as the one established by Francis of Assisi in the thirteenth century, that call for those who are admitted to give all their wealth to the poor and then to devote their work, not to filling their own purse, but to the care of others. The Anabaptist tradition began with a critique of the wealth of the church but in the course of its own history has struggled with the wealth of its own members. Discussion on the topic has resulted, on occasion, in the formation of smaller communities that have tried to fulfill the demands of divine charitable perfection. The most successful and enduring of these has been the Hutterites who hold all property in common. Unlike monastic communities, these associations have been comprised of families, and as a result, have had to struggle with the competing demands of securing the future needs of a family and fulfilling the present needs of others.

Those who engage in charitable activity have persistently grappled with a number of questions. J. Lawrence Burkholder, one of the more beloved presidents of Goshen College flew relief missions in China from 1944-48. In an essay entitled "The Limits of Perfection," he describes the dilemma that Christians face when trying to fulfill the demands of perfection.[11] Because there are always more people in need than one's abundance can satisfy, Christians are forced to choose between one demand and another. Moreover, the distribution of abundance requires the development of flawed institutions and sometimes engagement with secular political, economic, and even military agencies. Mennonites try to balance the perfection to which we are called with the necessity of working within imperfect institutions in an imperfect world.

Tensions with Secular Society. The call to give without qualification requires that one look at material wealth in a way that is counter to the prevailing tendencies of our modern age. Walter Brueggemann, one of the most respected contemporary Old Testament scholars in North America, describes the economy of the Bible as an ideology of abundance whereas the world tends to embrace an ideology of scarcity.[12] In this way, the present tension with the secular world is not different than the tensions that the Church faced with the pagan world. It is simply enshrined in different institutions. The modern science of economics seeks to fulfill the self-interest of individuals in a competition over scare resources. Our political economies turn extending food and shelter to an enemy into a crime against the state.

Perfection through the Endurance of Suffering
The Letter to the Hebrews. Teresa of Avila's work *The Way of Perfection*

---

[11] See *The Limits of Perfection: A Conversation with J. Lawrence Burkholder*, ed. Rodney J. Sawatsky and Scott Holland (Waterloo ON: Institute of Anabaptist-Mennonite Studies, 1993), 1-54.

[12] Walter Brueggemann, *Theology of the Old Testament: Testimony, Dispute, Advocacy* (Minneapolis: Augsburg Fortress, 1997), 559.

stands within an ascetic tradition in Christianity informed in part by the notion of righteousness in which one renounces personal wealth for a life of generosity and service and places one's trust in God alone rather than in one's material wealth. Her plan for perfection also entailed inflicting pain upon her own body as a means of spiritual union with the suffering body of Christ.[13] Although such practices as self-flagellation are means of penance within the Roman Catholic tradition, Christian suffering, even self-mortification, is not always about punishment of a sinful body. It is informed by the understanding that Jesus' death on the cross signifies perfect obedience to God's will and that through his humiliation Jesus achieves the reconciliation of the world with God. At the heart of Christian thought stands a paradox insofar as the way to perfection entails suffering the realities of our imperfect bodies.

Several passages in the Letter to the Hebrews (a thirteen chapter exhortation to Christians to preserve in the face of persecution) make the claim that Jesus is made perfect through suffering. The anonymous author calls Jesus the pioneer and perfecter of our faith through his endurance on the cross (Heb. 2:9–10 and 12:2). Jesus' suffering was of course physical, but it also included a psychological or social dimension. Crucifixion was a shameful death and signified Jesus' humiliating defeat as an enemy of Rome. The author of The Letter to the Hebrews subverts the opinions of the ancient Mediterranean world by treating Jesus' suffering metaphorically as the pain endured by a victorious athlete. Jesus is "crowned with glory and honour because of the suffering of death" (2:9). This is not a kingly coronation, but rather the conferring of a laurel wreath, the prize of an athletic competition. There are two aspects of this victory that I wish to explore. The second of the two is a pronounced theme of Christian discourse, the sanctification brought by Jesus' death. But first, I wish to explore the valuation of suffering that the Christian tradition brings to the Greco-Roman world because it is tied to the understanding of perfection in Matthew 5:48.

---

[13] See Teresa of Avila, *The Way of Perfection*, trans. E. Allison Peters (London: Sheed and Ward, 1999), esp. ch. 7.

Studies of the representation of suffering in Early Christianity indicate that mortification of the body was not about purifying the soul, but about equating oneself with the poor and afflicted, those in need of divine generosity. In the Letter to the Hebrews, we find several passages that point in this direction:

> Because he [Jesus] himself was tested by what he suffered, he is able to help those who are being tested. (Heb. 2:14–18)

> [W]e do not have a high priest who is unable to sympathize with our weaknesses, but we have one who in every respect has been tested as we are, yet without sin. (Heb. 4:14–16)

Judith Perkins demonstrates how, in the early imperial period, Christian writers joined with some non-Christian authors in a new representation of what it means to be human.[14] The Hellenic world stretching back to the fifth century BCE understood the self to be comprised of a soul within a rational mind. The self was then housed within a body. The needs and desires of that body hampered the quest for perfection of the self through participation in the rational order of the cosmos. While people of all social strata suffered in the classical period, literary representation of what it meant to be human tended to draw a sharp line between the bodies of those they called the *honores*, people with honour, and those of the *humiliories*, people of the servile classes. Only the latter were represented as having bodies that suffered. In the early Roman imperial period, another concept of the self begins to surface in which the body comes to be considered part of the self and

---

[14] Judith Perkins, *The Suffering Self: Pain and Narrative Representation in the Early Christian Era* (London: Routledge, 1995), 3. Daniel was a fifth century saint from upper Mesopotamia who lived on a pillar for thirty-three years relying upon God alone. These are his parting words to his disciples: "Hold fast humility, practice obedience, exercise hospitality, keep the fasts, observe the vigils, love poverty, and above all maintain charity, which is the first and great commandment; keep closely bound to all that regards piety, avoid the tares of the heretics. Separate never from the Church your Mother; if you do these things your righteousness shall be perfect" (John M. Robertson, *A Short History of Christianity*, vol. 2 [Whitefish, MT: Kessinger, 2004], 274).

its needs, something to which the rational mind should attend. Just as the church altered the conception of where to draw the line between the rich and the poor, it also participated in altering the representation of the bodies of those to whom it sought to serve.

Perkins points out that the early church was not alone in representing the body of all classes as something that experienced pain. She observes a trend in pagan literature informed in part by developments in medical science. For example, in Galen's narratives the bodies of slaves and emperors, men and women all shared equally in the need for external help.[15] Christianity makes suffering a virtue not because those who are martyred experience something extraordinary, but because, as Perkins puts it, "they graphically convey the similarity between the saint's physical condition and that of all others depicted in the Lives [of the martyrs] who suffer from grievous physical ailments."[16] For example, Daniel the Stylite becomes "a miracle worker who is as physically maimed as those he healed."[17]

Perkins examines the third-century story *The Martyrdom of Perpetua* at length. Perpetua is a wellborn matron with a nursing baby who is imprisoned and eventually martyred in Carthage. The story is told as a first person narrative. Perpetua recounts a prophetic dream in which her martyrdom becomes a wrestling match in which she prevails over her opponent:

> My opponent tried to get hold of my feet, but I kept striking him in the face with my heels. Then I was raised up into the air and I began to pummel him without as it were treading on the ground. Then ... I put my two hands together linking the fingers of one hand with those of the other and thus I got hold of his head. He fell flat on his face and I stepped on his head.[18]

Like the author of The Letter to the Hebrews, she represents her suffering as though it were an athletic competition. Her death becomes a victory. We find a similar depiction of the martyrdom of the aged

---

[15] Perkins, *Suffering Self*, 169.
[16] Ibid., 206.
[17] Ibid., 207.
[18] *The Martyrdom of Perpetua*, 10.10–11; trans. Musucilla (1972).

Polycarp, the second-century bishop of Smyrna who was burned at the stake. The author of *The Martyrdom of Polycarp* writes, "He was crowned with the crown of immortality, and had carried off the unspeakable prize."[19]

As Perkins points out, the purpose of renunciation of wealth, of persecution and suffering, is not about asceticism but redistribution. These martyr stories do not encourage the imitation of suffering as an end in itself but elevate those who suffer to the status of those deserving of honour. When the church holds up the suffering of God, it invites the rich and powerful to become aware of all human suffering. The Christian response to this suffering was to embrace the new medical sciences pioneered by pagans such as Galen and to provide care for the afflicted.[20]

Topics in Christian Discourse. John C. Cavadini identifies two strands of reflection upon the value of suffering within the Christian tradition.[21] He traces the first to Irenaeus of Lyon who wrote in response to intense persecution of Christians and the Gnostic dismissal of Christ's suffering as only apparent rather than real. For Irenaeus, who upheld the goodness of creation, the endurance of suffering is a way of growing into perfection, a way of maturing in the face of sin.[22] Several passages in the Letter to the Hebrews suggest that its author shared some of Irenaeus' understanding. Hebrews 5:8 states that, "Although he was a Son, he [Jesus] learned obedience through what he suffered." Hebrews 12:7–11 compares the endurance of persecution to the discipline that a parent uses for the child's good:

> Endure trials for the sake of discipline. God is treating you as children; for what child is there whom a parent does not discipline? If you do not have that discipline in which all children

---

[19] *The Martyrdom of Polycarp*, 17.1; trans. Kirsopp Lake (1912).

[20] Gary B. Ferngren, (*Medicine and Health Care in the Early Church* [Baltimore MD: Johns Hopkins University Press, 2009] 198), describes how in response to a Carthage plague in 252 CE all members of the congregation adopting the role of medical attendant to both Christians and pagans.

[21] John C. Cavadini, *Augustine through the Ages: An encyclopedia.* (Grand Rapids: Eerdmans 1999) 422–23.

[22] See Irenaeus, *Against Heresies* 4.38.3.

share, then you are illegitimate and not his children. Moreover, we had human parents to discipline us, and we respected them. Should we not be even more willing to be subject to the Father of spirits and live? For they disciplined us for a short time as seemed best to them, but he disciplines us for our good, in order that we may share his holiness. Now, discipline always seems painful rather than pleasant at the time, but later it yields the peaceful fruit of righteousness to those who have been trained by it.[23]

Irenaeus contends that suffering may be inflicted upon us by evil; we can find within it a good. Augustine presents us with another strand. He does not attempt to redeem suffering as a good but observes that suffering calls forth patient endurance and charity, expressions of faith in Christ that are good. In the face of suffering, we live lives of healing, virtue, and love.[24]

Tensions with Secular Society. The emphasis upon suffering has become less pronounced in Christian discourse in the modern age. Modernity has come once again to treat the suffering body as a failure, as something about which to be ashamed. We look to physical fitness to stave off decay and medical science to keep us pain-free. The existence of suffering has become a theological problem and the excuse for rejecting faith in God. That God would permit Christ to suffer strikes some as a sign of God's imperfect love and the suffering of the world as a sign of God's limitations.

Perfection as a Divinely Appointed Vocation

The Letter to the Hebrews Continued. For the early Anabaptists, suffering was a sign of the true church. They believed that persecution was inevitable if one followed the teachings of Jesus. The world for which Christ suffered resists submitting to the reign of God. This brings me to the final theme within Christian discourse about perfection, the concept of sanctification, the means by which God sets the church apart from the world to fulfill God's purpose. In the Letter to the Hebrews,

---

[23] See also 2 Cor. 12:7–10.

[24] See Augustine's treatise *Patience*.

Jesus through his suffering is the perfecter of the Christian faith. This means that he brings God's plan to completion, that is, to its intended end. This is the way that the verb τελείω is most often used in classical Greek literature.[25] The Septuagint (the third-century BCE Greek translation of Hebrew Scriptures) retains the classical usage but also uses the language of perfection to refer to "entirety and wholeness in a divine relationship." The Greek translators used the verb τελειόω to mean "to consecrate or sanctify."[26]

The author of The Letter to the Hebrews does not disparage the faith of the Israelites and the Jews who preceded Christ. He shares enough of a similar perspective with the Apostle Paul that the letter is often attributed to Paul. In his Letter to the Galatians, Paul compares the covenant of Sinai to a *paidagogos*, a slave who is charged with the task of disciplining the schoolboy (Gal. 3:23–25). Paul saw this period of the Sinai covenant as necessary to prevent the Israelites from becoming assimilated into the pagan world and, thereby, forgetting their relation to the one true God. The author of The Letter to the Hebrews, like Paul, contends that within the covenant of Christ, the community acts out of maturity, out of the status of the adult, prepared to move "on toward perfection" (Heb. 5:11–6:1). Perfection allows one to enter into a temple that is not bound by physical laws of purity but the heavenly temple that has no need of purification (Heb. 9:23–24). Hebrews describes God's people from Abraham through the Hebrew prophets as witnesses to a race being run by those being persecuted for their faith (Heb. 12:1–2). Once more the suffering of persecution is translated into the pain of an athletic competition. The prize at the end of the race is the receipt of the promise made by God to bless the nations through Abraham's seed, understood here to mean Jesus. Heb. 12:14–16 calls its audience to "pursue peace with everyone" and to see that "no one fails to obtain the grace of God" (Heb. 12:14–16). The nations' receipt of this blessing then perfects, that is, brings to fulfillment, the faith of that cloud of witnesses.

---

[25] David Peterson, *Hebrews and Perfection: An Examination of the Concept of Perfection in the Epistle to the Hebrews* (Cambridge: Cambridge University Press, 1992), 21–23.

[26] Ibid., 29.

Christians believe that we are made perfect—acceptable to stand in God's presence—through the sanctification granted by Jesus. I cannot do complete justice to the complexity of the concept of perfection in The Letter to the Hebrews. I will limit my focus to the emphasis in the letter on the participation in Christ's glory through following Christ's leadership. David Peterson concludes in his doctoral dissertation that the perfection to which Hebrews refers is in the end a vocational perfection. Jesus is perfect in his qualifications for the role to which he has been assigned, and we are perfect insofar as we fulfill God's intended purpose for us as the covenanted people of God, the community that we refer to as the Church.[27] Although the author of The Letter to the Hebrews does not use Matthean language of discipleship, he seems to share a similar vision of the vocation of discipleship when he writes that we are to leave the city with its temple and risk abuse in order to worship God by words of praise and acts of generosity (Heb. 13:12–15).

Topics in Christian Discourse. Whereas the Sinai covenant includes a set of commandments that provide visible boundaries to the covenanted community, obedience to the covenant of Christ required, as we have discussed, unbounded love expressed in such things as forgiveness and charity. Like the Sinai covenant, the covenant in Christ is marked by its unity, purity, and holiness; as Paul puts it, the church is to be "without spot or wrinkle" (Eph. 5:27), but the New Testament does not delineate cultic practices other than baptism and participating in the Lord's Supper, by which this purity can be maintained and unity can be made visible. It should come as no surprise then that later Christian discourse becomes dominated by the question of what doctrines and rituals the church should use to maintain its holiness and manifest its unity.

In the context of the sixteenth century reformation, when criticism of the Church practices without biblical foundation comes to the fore, a concept attributed to Augustine arises that the visible church, filled with members who confess belief but are not always true to their confession, is not the true church. The true church, without errors and

---

[27] Ibid., 67–73.

flaws, is the invisible Church. Philip Melanchthon, sixteenth century German reformer and collaborator with Martin Luther, explains:

> We are not dreaming about some Platonic republic, as has been slanderously alleged, but we teach that this church actually exists, made up of the believers and righteous men scattered throughout the world. And we add marks, the pure teaching of the Gospel and the sacraments.[28]

The Anabaptists rejected this idea of the invisible church and sought instead to live up to a vision of a visible church "without spot or wrinkle."[29] This has led to the inaccurate accusation that Anabaptism is a renewal of a sixth-century heresy known as Pelagianism, the heresy that purportedly claimed that a person can fulfill God's commandments by exercising free will and attain moral perfection without God's assistance. Instead, the Anabaptists sought to be the visible church by refusing to participate in activities that they deemed to be "outside the perfection of Christ." This included military service and public offices. Baptism was to be voluntary and an adult decision that entailed active expression of one's faith through good works. In this quest for evident perfection, for most of its history, Anabaptism has exercised strict community discipline including exercise of the ban (cf. Mat. 18:15–20) to exclude anyone whose disobedience was willful.

Tensions with Secular Society. Once more we find the modern context not conducive to this sort of discourse. Many people in Western society bristle at church order. Our secular culture encourages us to seek fulfillment by expressing our individuality. Many question the authority of the church to impose restrictions that seem to be unreasonable or the accidental products of tradition or culture. The church's emphasis upon maintaining unity and order has led to criticism of the church for being uncharitable to its own members and for sacrificing one kind of

---

[28] *Apology of the Augsburg Confession, 1530* trans. and ed. Theodore Garhardt Tappert (Philadelphia: Fortress, 1959), 171.

[29] See J.C. Wenger ed., *The Complete Writings of Menno Simons c 1496–1561* (trans. Leonard Verduin (Scottdale PA: Herald Press, 1956), 724.

perfection, the unbounded love of God, for another sort of perfection, unity of form.

In his major study of the theme of perfection in Western thought, John Passmore describes the consequence of a sect of Christianity that strives for a perfect order. He writes, "Their relationship with . . . outsiders must be maintained at an impersonal level; the 'chosen ones' can be charitable towards outsiders, relieving their sufferings, but they cannot enter into tender relationships with them as friends."[30] Perhaps the desire for a meaningful dialogue with devout Muslims explains why many in the Mennonite tradition have loosened their insistence upon perfection of church discipline. In looking back at the book of Hebrews and Paul's epistles, we find a call to trust that God is present within the gestures of friendship towards those with whom we disagree on points of doctrine and discipline. We have found that our vocation to which we are called, discipleship, requires that we manifest the purity of the Church by showing hospitality to strangers, for, as the author of The Letter to the Hebrews puts it, "By doing so some have entertained angels without knowing it" (Heb. 13:2).

Conclusion

The concept of perfection in the New Testament is about neither the perfectibility of individual gifts nor the individual achievement of a moral perfection. Instead, it is the way by which we, as God's creatures, can participate in God's perfection at God's invitation within the context of an imperfect world. The aspect of God's perfection that we are called to imitate is God's unbounded goodness or love. At the heart of the Christian understanding of perfection lies a paradox: God's glory is made manifest most clearly within imperfection, either through the suffering that one endures in faithfulness to God's will or in the suffering that one tries to comfort through one's vocation as a disciple of Christ. When we participate in the fulfillment of God's plan for the world by living lives true to our vocation, then we follow the way of perfection. From time to time, Western philosophers and social theorists have tried to delineate the form of a utopian society in which human beings can achieve perfection. In the twentieth century, we have

---

[30] John Passmore, *The Perfectibility of Man*, 3d ed. (Indianapolis: Liberty Fund, 1970), 455.

seen how utopian visions can give rise to dystopias. Christianity offers a paradox. It asserts that it is within the dystopian disorder of human societies that we can seek perfection. It is within this imperfect world that we can fulfill our vocation and express our faithfulness through the endurance of suffering and through the care of those who suffer.

In the Name of Allah, the Beneficent, the Merciful

PERFECTION ACCORDING TO THE QUR'AN

Aboulhassan Haghani

We are all familiar with divine religions, and every scholar of theology has sufficient knowledge of the divine religions, particularly one's own religion, for it to be clear that every religion has explained factors for man's perfection in order to enable him to approach perfection by observing these factors and following the religion's instructions. Islam is no exception.

Different sects, schools, religions, and cultures have always focused on knowing man and his existential dimensions. The famous aphorism inscribed at the Temple of Delphi, "Know yourself," which also has been attributed to Socrates, has been central to much thought before him and is also emphasized in the works and thoughts after him with different meanings. Knowing man and his position in the hierarchy of the system of being has been of great importance in different schools and religions, ranging from various Indian schools and different religions and sects to the philosophy of Greece and Rome, from the thoughts of medieval Christian thinkers to thoughts found in authentic Islamic traditions, and from the Renaissance to the modern age. All systems of thought, doctrines, religions, and sects have paid attention to and discussed the aim and end of man's creation, his life and activities, virtues, attributes and characteristics, with different degrees.[1]

Over the course of history, man has always sought the perfect man and, perhaps in the course of this search, has sometimes considered

---

[1] Muhammad Nasiri, "Insan-e kamel dar 'irfan-e islami" [The Perfect Man in Islamic Mysticism], *Andisheh Novin Dini* (Summer 1384/2005), no 1, 68.

metaphysical beings and goddesses, sometimes mythological and apocryphal heroes, and sometimes prominent historical figures as instances of the perfect man. We can find traces of the perfect man in all cultures, doctrines, philosophical schools, creeds, and religions: Confucius, Zoroaster, Jesus Christ (on whom be God's blessings and peace), and Prophet Mohammad (may the blessings and peace of Allah be upon him and his progeny). Western philosophers and contemporary psychologists have talked about the perfect or ideal man.[2] Man's desire to reach the perfect human being may be traced back to his instinctive desire for perfection and the avoidance of imperfection.

Man

Anthropology has various dimensions. Among the issues that have been discussed and investigated in anthropology are: the concept of anthropology itself, its methods, the origins of man, his position in the system of being, his capacities and abilities, merits and characteristics, the limits and obstacles to his growth and transcendence, his desires, and needs, and beliefs about his eternity and immortality. In this regard, the most important question is: "What are the conditions to be a perfect man?" In other words, "Who is a perfect man?"

Man is the only being that is separable from himself; that is, for example, there is no stone without having the characteristics of a stone or there is no apple without having the characteristics of an apple. In contrast, only man lacks the characteristics of being a man and must obtain these characteristics; and being a man is not related to material and physical properties, rather it is something beyond physical characteristics.[3]

Islam believes that man is the lord of all creatures, dominates all phenomena, has an unlimited soul, and his perfection and happiness rely on knowing and developing all his divine values and

---

[2] Mas'ud Azarbaijani, "Insan-e kamel (matlub) az didgah-e islam va ravanshenasi" [*The Perfect (Ideal) Man According to Islam and Psychology*], *Hawzah va Daneshgah* (Winter 1375/1996), no. 9, 17.

[3] Morteza Motahhari, *Insan-e kamel* (*Perfect Man*) (Qom: Sadra, 1370/1991), 155-156.

characteristics, and realizing his capacities in order to draw near to God. To be sure, this aim cannot be achieved without the guidance and instructions from the prophets who have been sent by God. Therefore, the aim of sending prophets and revealing holy books is to guide and nurture man and to prepare the grounds for the realization of his capacities, and finally to bring him to the height of glory and eternal perfection. It is clear that neglecting man's real capacities and getting away from God's aim, i.e., drawing near to God, will cause man's downfall and destruction.

According to Islam, the perfect man is not comparable with any other being. Everything is under his domination; all phenomena enjoy existence and evolution due to man's existence. Therefore, man's happiness and development differs from other creatures' development. Let us give an explanation in this regard.

The creatures of the world of creation are divided into four general groups:

1. Inanimate bodies or inanimate things like different kinds of stones, gases, and liquids, which have certain existential effects.

2. Vegetation or flora, which have higher qualities and existential effects than inanimate bodies. They grow and flourish, feed, and breed.

3. Animals, which have more merits and existential effects than inanimate bodies and vegetation. They possess common sense and will. They work and function, mate and nest, have sexual desires, and anger. They have sentiments and emotions. Some of them have a social life and some of them have virtues such as loyalty.

4. Man. He is not an inanimate body, vegetable, or mere animal because man is the lord of all creatures. Man has common existential effects with the other kinds of creatures. However, common features among the creatures of the world cannot be considered as distinctive merits or cause for superiority. Therefore, something other than the existential qualities of these

three groups is the cause of man's humanity and superiority over other creatures. Man's real superiority relies on superiority in the reality of humanity and this is the effect and virtue which is exclusive to man and does not exist in inanimate bodies, vegetation, or animals.[4]

Therefore, accepting man's superiority over other creatures means that he has virtue or virtues which other creatures do not have. These virtues are not the same as common virtues among creatures; otherwise, superiority and nobility would be meaningless.

Now the question arises about who is man. As already noted, man has certain characteristics that other creatures do not have.

1. Man is a two-dimensional being: first there is man's physical and animal dimension, and, second, the spiritual and human dimension:

> (And remember)When thy Lord said unto the angels: lo! I am about to create a mortal out of mire, and when I have fashioned him and breathed into him of My spirit, then fall down before him prostrate. (38:72)

Man's animal dimension is called nature and his human dimension is called his innate disposition (fitrat). There is an everlasting struggle and conflict between these two forces in man, and the result determines man's personality and fate. In other words, if nature dominates man, he will be inclined only towards animal and vegetative values. As a result, he will have an animal life:

> They have hearts wherewith they understand not, and having eyes wherewith they see not, and having ears wherewith they hear not. These are as the cattle, nay, but they are worse! These are the neglectful. (7:179)

---

[4] Of course there are other beings called jinn and angels, but they are not relevant to the current discussion which is of the creatures found in the natural world.

If the innate disposition dominates man, he will seek values beyond those of the animal and vegetable, the exercise of his virtues will go along with his innate disposition, and his nature will serve his innate disposition. As a result, he will have a human life and will be the lord of and superior to all creatures:

> Verily, We have honored the children of Adam. We carry them on the land and the sea [on mounts and ships], and have made provision of good things for them, and have preferred them above many of those whom We created with a marked preferment. (17:70)

Man's physical dimension is the source of his nature and animal desires, and his divine dimension is the source of his innate disposition and super-animal desires. Hence, man's divine dimension grants him a position which obliges the angels to prostrate before him:

> And when We said unto the angels: Prostrate yourselves before Adam, they fell prostrate, all save Iblis. He demurred through pride, and so became a disbeliever. (2:34)

2. By enjoying divine spirit, man can have unlimited, scientific and educational ability, to the extent that he can create and establish divine attributes and qualities in himself, follow the hierarchical degrees of perfection and draw near to God, one step after another, and become a complete manifestation and embodiment of divine attributes. This is the very position of God's vicegerent on His earth, which man is created to achieve:

> And when thy Lord said unto the angels: Lo! I am about to place a viceroy [representative] in the earth, they said: wilt Thou place therein one who will do harm therein and will shed blood [because other earthly beings before man did harm and shed blood. If the aim of creation of this man is to worship], while we, we hymn Thy praise and sanctify Thee? He said: Surely I know that which ye know not. (2:30)

3. Man is a free being who can voluntarily choose his path and aim, and move towards it:

> Lo! We have shown him the way, whether he be grateful [and accept] or disbelieving! (76:3)

4. Man has the ability of cognition, intellect, and reflection. He can recognize realities and develop materially and spiritually.

5. Another characteristic of man is that he enjoys revelation, God's message, and guidance by the prophets:

> O mankind! Now hath a proof from your Lord come unto you, and We have sent down unto you a clear light. (4:174)

> O mankind! There hath come unto you an exhortation from your Lord, a balm for that which is in the breasts [a treatment for your hearts], guidance and a mercy for believers. (10:57)

In short, man can be differentiated from other beings by two characteristics, cognition and will. He seeks perfection based on vision and cognition, using his will and choice. If his cognition is realized, his perfection will be realized, too. If his cognition is not realized, or while knowing the real perfection he does not recognize the true path, he will never achieve real perfection.

Perfection

Perfection is an existential attribute which is defined proportionate to every being and its end; therefore, the perfection of every kind of being must be defined separately. A perfect man differs from a perfect animal and from a perfect angel; it can be said that perfection is the realization of capacities and abilities.

Vegetables follow their path of perfection according to their natural requirements. Animals, inspired by instinct, follow their path to perfection, as well. Contrary to vegetation and animals, man acquires his perfection and moves to achieve his perfection, using his capacities and abilities, and according to his choice and cognition.

The stages of perfection for these three groups are different. If we evaluate different objects or aims, we will find that an aim may be a stage of perfection for some, while for others not only is it not a stage of perfection, but also sometimes it is an imperfection. Sweetness, for example, is a stage of perfection for some fruits, while for others it is not (rather sourness will be the perfection). The reason is that every being has a special essence and will be another entity and its essence will change, if it is to have another kind of perfection.

Difference between Perfection and Completeness
The two terms perfection and completeness are not synonyms, although their common antonym is imperfection. Completeness is applied when an entity has all the attributes that all entities of the same kind should have. For example, if a building has all necessary components of a building, it is complete. However, in the case of perfection, we evaluate every entity according to its aims and ends, and perfection is a status to be achieved only after its completeness. In fact, perfection is applied when an object, after being complete, can have a higher position, and after that another higher position, and so on.

Real perfection
If man wants to achieve real perfection, he must endow himself with the attributes of the origin of real perfection, and real perfection is following a path which leads him to Absolute Perfection, i.e., God. In fact, all paths but the path of real and absolute perfection are wrong ways and will never lead to man's main aim. Therefore, Satan tries to lead man astray from the true and main path of perfection and perhaps shows a wrong way, using seductive words:

Lo! Satan is for man an open foe. (12:5)

If man follows the real path of perfection, he will achieve a position that is called the position of God's viceroy. If man is able to be God's viceroy, it is necessary for him to have divine attributes and to become as similar to Him as possible in order to approach Absolute Perfection. That is why the Noble Prophet (s) says:

Endow yourselves with divine attributes.[5]

The Commander of Faithful, Imam Ali ('a), says:

One who endows himself with the attributes of God, Almighty and Glorious; He will lead him to eternal salvation.[6]

According to Shi'ite sources, Jesus Christ, Son of Mary ('a), addressing his disciples, said:

Become perfect as surely your Lord, God, in the heaven is perfect.[7]

At this point three subjects should be mentioned:

1. It is clear that drawing near to God does not mean spatiotemporal nearness. Spatiotemporal nearness is exclusive to physical entities. Rather, it means that man becomes more transcendent due to good works originated from faith, so that he consciously knows himself by intuitive knowledge, and consciously knows God by intuition of his soul and his absolute and complete dependence on God.

2. Man cannot endow himself with those attributes that are exclusive to God. Being a necessary or a simple existent are attributes exclusive to God, but man can acquire other attributes.[8] However,

---

[5] Muhammad Taqi Majlisi, *Bihar Al-Anwar* (Tehran: Dar al-Kutub Islami, 1362/1983), 58:132.

[6] Majlisi, 89: 214.

[7] Mawla Muhammad Salih Mazandarani, *Sharh-e Usul al-Kafi* (Beirut: Dar Ihiya al-Turath al-'Arabi, 1421/2000), 9:372.

[8] Perhaps there are some divine attributes that are divine perfections, but would be undesirable in a human being, such as pride.

even in these there is a difference, that is, God's attributes are essential attributes, while those attributes acquired by man are acquired attributes and cannot be essential attributes. Man can acquire such attributes as bravery, power, mercy, kindness, truthfulness, justice, benevolence, gratitude, and in this way can move to draw near to God, which is man's perfection. For example, on benevolence and goodness, God says:

Be thou kind even as Allah hath been kind to thee. (28:77)

3. If we want to draw near to God and achieve perfection by being similar to Him (considering the aforementioned meaning of similarity), we must pay attention to man's servitude and God's divinity. If God advises us to take the Noble Prophet (s) as our model and exemplar, the same God introduces the Prophet as His servant and slave:

He it is Who sendeth down clear revelations unto His slave [Muhammad], that He may bring you forth from darkness unto light; and lo! For you, Allah is Full of Pity, Merciful. (57:9)

The Perfect Man According to Islam

The Glorious Qur'an has explained man's final perfection with such expressions as triumph, felicity, and salvation.

He will adjust your works for you and will forgive you your sins. Whosoever obeyeth Allah and His messenger, he verily hath gained a single victory [and salvation]. (33:71)

These depend on guidance from their Lord. These are the successful. (2:5)

And as for those who will be glad (that day) they will be in the Garden, abiding there. (11:108)

According to the aforementioned verses, being in the service of God will result in salvation and happiness. In other words, faith and good works will make man achieve happiness. And since perfection has degrees, and since every man who has acquired a degree of perfection can acquire another degree, so his scale of perfection depends on his efforts to achieve perfection. Perhaps the highest degree of perfection is to draw near to God's mercy:

> Lo! The righteous will dwell among gardens and rivers, Firmly established in the favor of a Mighty King! (54:54-55)

> As for those who believe in Allah, and hold fast unto Him [and to this divine book], them He will cause to enter into His mercy and grace, and will guide them unto Him by a straight road. (4:175)

Existential Dimensions of the Perfect Man

The perfect man is one whose human values grow together and are in harmony. Here we will discuss some of the existential dimensions of the perfect man according to the Qur'ān:

Greatness and Honour

> Verily, We have honored the children of Adam. We carry them on the land and the sea [on mounts and ships], and have made provision of good things for them, and have preferred them above many of those whom We created with a marked preferment. (17:70)

God, the Most High, has given man a high rank which is innate to him, in addition to the goods of this world which are his hopes, drives, wishes, and lusts. Worldly rank is precisely the animal rank, and a higher rank is the very greatness and honour of man which is of great value and causes transcendent values. Professor Mutahhari says that honour, dignity, and greatness brims in the traditions narrated from Imam Husayn ('a). The reason that these traditions are narrated more from Imam Husayn than any other of the Fourteen Infallibles is that

Karbala was a context for Imam Husayn to manifest himself through these attributes.[9]

Rest of Heart through Remembrance of Allah

> Who have believed and whose hearts have rest in the remembrance of Allah. Verily in the remembrance of Allah do hearts find rest! (13:28)

If man's soul always obeys Allah, his submission to Allah will be stable and permanent, so that he will never be overcome by satanic temptations and his soul will be set at rest and tranquility. One who has intuitive faith in Allah, whose heart is set at rest because of this faith, and is satisfied with the Decree of Allah, has achieved the position of peace and tranquility. Allah says:

> But ah! Thou soul at peace! Return unto thy Lord, content in His good pleasure! (89:27-28)

This soul is the noblest soul.

The Station of Submission to Allah

> O My slaves! For you there is no fear this day, nor is it ye who grieve. (43:67)

The Commander of Faithful, Imam Ali ('a), supplicates Allah in one of his prayers as follows:

> O My God, the glory suffices me that I am your servant and the honor suffices me that You are my Lord.[10]

The Noble Prophet (s), who is the master of all creatures, says:

> For myself I have no power to benefit, nor power to hurt, save that which Allah willeth. (7:188)

---

[9] Morteza Mutahhari, *Majmu'eh-ye Athar, Collected Works* (Qom: Sadra, 1368/1989), 22:406.

[10] Majlisi, 42:402.

As a servant and slave of God, I do not control benefit or harm for my own soul and everything is under His command.

The Station of Contentment

But ah! Thou soul at peace! Return unto thy Lord, content in His good pleasure! Enter thou among My [special] bondmen! Enter thou My [special] Garden! (89:27-30)

In the hadith of the mi'raj (ascension), after explaining the features of the station of contentment, God says to the Noble Prophet (s):

I will accompany three virtues with whoever acts on My consent: 1. I will teach him a thanksgiving which is not accompanied with gratefulness. 2. I will teach him an invocation which is never forgotten. 3. I will grant him with a love, so that he will never prefer love of creatures over My love. When he loves Me, I love him and make him beloved of My servants.[11]

The station of contentment is higher than the station of patience. Those in the station of contentment endure and are contented with pain, grief, and troubles, and never complain in their hearts, because they consider them to be from God.[12]

Contentment is a spiritual characteristic of the believer who submits to the decree and ordinance of God and does not complain or get angry about his fate and things that dominate him (uncontrollable things).

But nay, by thy Lord, they will not believe (in truth) until they make thee judge of what is in dispute between them and find within themselves no dislike of that which thou decidest, and submit with full submission. (4:65)

Purity and the Good Life

Whosoever doeth right, whether male or female, and is a believer, him verily We shall quicken with a good life, and We shall pay

---

[11] Majlisi, 74:29.

[12] Muhammad Taqi Misbah Yazdi, *Bar dargah-e dust* (*At the sublime court of the Friend*) (Qom: Mu'assessah Amuzeshi va Pazhuheshi Imam Khomeini, 1380/2001), 262.

them a recompense in proportion to the best of what they used to do. (97:16)

What is meant here by "a good life" is a pure life that includes purity and goodness in all the aspects of human life, including the physical, cognitive, moral, social, economic, and political. It is an essential attribute which, in fact, is an ideal for the believer and could (and must) be part of one's personality. Such purity will be achieved through submission to divine orders and decrees (submission to God and His apostle) and will grow and increase in transcendence through stages.[13]

---

[13] Masʿud Azarbaijani, "Insan-e kamel (matlub) az didgah-e islam va ravanshenasi," 8.

PART III

CULTURE

Sin and Grace in Christian Perspective

Harry J. Huebner

"For by grace you have been saved through faith, and this is not your own doing; it is the gift of God—not the result of works, so that no one may boast. For we are what he has made us, created in Christ Jesus for good works, which God prepared beforehand to be our way of life." (Apostle Paul in a letter to the Ephesians 2:8-10)

"Grace does not destroy nature but perfects it."[1]

"Cheap grace is the deadly enemy of the church. We are fighting today for costly grace."[2]

The Christian understanding of human nature is unintelligible apart from the concepts of sin and grace. If it were not for sin in this world grace may well not be necessary; if it were not for grace, human beings would be damned. This is the Christian teaching of sin and grace in a nutshell. But saying it this way does not settle much for practical human well-being. Moreover, in the Christian tradition, sin and grace have been in danger of breaking apart. This has

---

[1] Thomas Aquinas, *Summa Theologica*, trans. Fathers of the English Dominican Province (New York: Benziger Bros. 1947-1948), 1, q. 1, a. 8, reply objection 2.

[2] Dietrich Bonhoeffer, *The Cost of Discipleship* (New York: MacMillan, 1974), 45.

resulted in the belief that human beings are totally depraved with little value themselves and nothing good can come from them—their only hope is the grace of God; or, on the other hand, it has resulted in the notion that all we can do is the best that lies within us and we should not be held responsible for failings we cannot control.

The challenges of presenting a Christian understanding of sin and grace in one short essay are enormous. The history of the church is filled with variations on the subject, how sin and grace are defined,[3] what has been named sin and what has not,[4] and so on. Moreover, the different churches sometimes have their origins in the controversy of what counts as sin, and on how sin and grace are properly related. This essay cannot possibly do justice to that history and so will limit its scope. My focal question will be: how do the Christian concepts of sin and grace help to inform a Christian view of human nature? Even at that I will choose only a few themes.

There is also the matter of speaking from a Mennonite perspective. I will not do that narrowly as if all that needs to be said on our topic has already been said by Mennonite scholars; for that is not the case. Moreover, Mennonite theology is only helpful if it is sound theology. So while I confess a deep embrace of my own theological tradition, it too must be brought before a higher standard of good theology.

---

[3] From the *Westminster Shorter Catechism*: "Sin is any want of conformity unto, or transgression of, the law of God." Available at: http://www.reformed.org/documents/WSC_frames.html. See also *The Catechism of the Catholic Church* at http://www.catholic. pages.com/morality/sin.asp, which says: "Sin is an offence against reason, truth, and right conscience; it is a failure in genuine love for God and neighbour caused by a perverse attachment to certain goods.... It has been defined [by St Augustine] as "an utterance, a deed, or a desire contrary to the eternal law." Sin is an offence against God.... Sin sets itself against God's love for us and turns our hearts away from it. Like the first sin, it is disobedience, a revolt against God through the will to become "like gods," knowing and determining good and evil. Sin is thus "love of oneself even to the contempt of God."

[4] For example, the Christian tradition sometimes speaks of the seven deadly sins: anger, greed, sloth, pride, lust, envy, and gluttony. These are only the official ones, and they remain largely undefined. When one asks what greed is, or what lust is, it of course gets complicated.

If we begin with an enquiry into a definition of sin, we see some uniformity among the various Christian traditions but also some variety. Some will speak of sin as breaking God's laws, others will use the language of covenant-breaking, some will speak of turning from God to the world or to self, and still others will speak of thwarting the will or end (the kingdom) that God is bringing about in history. While these are not necessarily incompatible languages, they do represent different emphases and often different traditions.

I begin by citing the article on sin from the confession of faith of my own church:

> We confess that, beginning with Adam and Eve, humanity has disobeyed God, given way to the tempter, and chosen to sin. Because of sin, all have fallen short of the Creator's intent, marred the image of God in which they were created, disrupted order in the world, and limited their love for others. Because of sin, humanity has been given over to the enslaving powers of evil and death. Sin is turning away from God and making gods of creation and of ourselves. We sin by making individual and group choices to do unrighteousness and injustice. We sin by omitting to do good and neglecting to give God the glory due our Creator and Redeemer. In sinning, we become unfaithful to the covenant with God and with God's people, destroy right relationships, use power selfishly, do violence, and become separated from God. As a result, we are not able to worship God rightly.[5]

There is much in this short article that could be further discussed, but this is not the place for that. It is interesting that the *Confession of Faith in a Mennonite Perspective* does not have a separate article on grace. This does not mean that it has nothing to say on the subject, for it says much about grace under other articles, like salvation. But one might say that in its emphasis on discipleship (living as Jesus called us to live), it naturally guards against the view that good works (ethics) is less important than the grace of God. For both good works *and* the

---

[5] *Confession of Faith in a Mennonite Perspective,* available online at http://www.mcusa-archives.org/library/resolutions/1995/1995-7.html.

grace of God matter. At the same time, there are some Mennonite scholars and others who believe that Mennonite theologians sometimes present a view of the Christian life that over-emphasizes discipleship and thereby places too much emphasis on human achievement and good works, and not enough on the grace of God. This is one of the issues, namely, the relationship of grace and discipleship, that will be addressed later in this paper.

Bible Stories
There are of course many stories in the Bible that deal with sin and grace. Grace gets associated with sin very early in the Bible. We see it already in the creation story with the sin of Adam and Eve, and then in the story of Cain and Abel. After Cain murders his brother and the Lord curses him, Cain pleads with the Lord, saying,

> My punishment is greater than I can bear! Today you have driven me away from the soil, and I shall be hidden from your face; I shall be a fugitive and a wanderer on the earth, and anyone who meets me may kill me." Then the Lord said to him, "Not so! Whoever kills Cain will suffer a sevenfold vengeance." And the Lord put a mark on Cain, so that no one who came upon him would kill him" (Gen. 4:13-15).

In other words, the Lord had mercy on Cain (extended grace to him) and without God's grace Cain could not have survived. Clearly there were consequences of the horrible deed of killing his brother, and yet the road of life was not closed to him.

Another biblical story tells of King David's sin.[6] When David was on the roof of his house he saw the beautiful Bathsheba, the wife of Uriah the Hittite. He summoned her to his house, had sex with her, and she became pregnant. Then he arranged to have her husband killed in battle and he married her. The Lord sent the prophet Nathan to speak words of judgment to David and Nathan condemned him for what he had done. David admitted his sin, sincerely repented (see Ps, 51), and Nathan said to him, "Now the Lord has put away your sin; you shall not

---

[6] See 2 Sam. 11 and 12.

die. Nevertheless, because of this deed, you have utterly scorned the Lord, the child that is born to you shall die" (2 Sam. 12:13b-14). Again, while there were consequences of his sin, God's grace saved David from death.

There are many such stories where grace is extended to sinners and they live despite their sin; there are also stories where grace is not extended and sinners die. In other words, the Bible teaches no law-like necessity to the relationship of sin and grace. Grace is a free gift and so can be both extended and withheld.

A familiar story of sin and grace in the New Testament is a parable told by Jesus.[7] It is usually referred to as the Prodigal Son Parable. It is about a Father who had two sons. In the story they are cast as insider and outsider—faithful and unfaithful. But while it is clear to the listener at the beginning of the story who the outsider and insider are, at the end the insider becomes the outsider and the outsider becomes the insider.

The story in brief: There was a man who had two sons and the younger asked for his inheritance (as though he had a right to the gift—notice the un-grace-like act). He sought to leave Father and make it on his own. Kenneth Bailey suggests that this is an act of de-fathering; an act of declaring radical independence from Father-God in whom humans have their being.[8] This is the paradigmatic act of sin. In other words, it is an act of denying one's humanness as created and fulfilled by God. The Father would have had the right to punish his son, to cast him from the family; but he did not. Instead the Father gave him his share of the inheritance, and the son left for a far away country. There he lived the life of self-indulgence and soon spent the money that for a while sustained him. Then he became aware of what he had done and decided to return to his father's household. He prepared a speech designed to convince his Father to accept him back, not as a son, for he had squandered the right to son-ship; at most he could be a servant. And when he returned, the Father, who saw him from a distance,

---

[7] See Luke 15:11-32.

[8] See Kenneth E. Bailey, *The Cross and the Prodigal: The 15th Chapter of Luke seen Through the Eyes of Middle Eastern Peasants* (St. Louis, MO: Concordia Publishing House, 1973).

because he had been yearning for his return ever since he left, ran to meet him, kissed him, placed a robe on him, put the family ring on his finger, and prepared for him a great feast of welcome. And the Father said, "For this son of mine was dead and is alive again; he was lost and is found" (Luke 15:24). Conveniently the son forgot about his speech. In other words, the way back into the household of the Father is via the Father's grace.

The elder son, when he heard the news that his younger brother had returned, refused to join the celebration. His Father pleaded with him to come to the table of the feast, but the elder son refused. He did not extend the grace of the household to his own brother. For that he became the outsider at the end of the story.

The understanding of grace in this story suggests a double movement: it is the free unmerited gift extending full restoration to humanity with God; and it is also to govern the behaviour of those in the household of faith. That is, when we open ourselves to God's grace we are empowered, enabled, and obligated to be gracious to others.

There is a parallel double movement with sin: it separates people from God and it separates one person from another. Sin leads to death since life without God cannot be sustained; grace opens the pathway to life with Father-God and it opens up possibilities of reunion and community with other people.

The biblical tradition suggests that we see ourselves properly, not as individuals but as participants in each other, and most formatively as participants in Christ, even in God. In Matthew 25, Jesus tells another parable that points to an understanding of how we should see ourselves in relation to others and God. It is a parable about the last judgement of the nations. He speaks of the final judgement on the basis of those who, having received grace, extend it to others who are hungry, thirsty, strangers, naked, and imprisoned, and those who do not extend the grace they received to others. The judge says to those who have opened themselves to the needy: "Truly I tell you, just as you did it to one of the least of these, who are members of my family, you did it to me" (Matt. 25:40). To those who have not opened themselves to the pain of others, he says, "Truly I tell you, just as you did not do it to one of the least of these, who are members of my family, you did not do it to me" (Matt.

25:45). The latter will receive eternal punishment and the former will inherit the kingdom.

What is especially interesting in the Matthew 25 parable for our discussion is the notion of human identity. That is, separation from brother and sister and separation from God are linked; and union with God and union with brother and sister are linked. God's hospitality to us (grace) and our hospitality to strangers are but two sides of the same coin of being. Grace is the act of openness to the other—ultimately to God; sin is the rejection of the other—ultimately of God.

The Apostle Paul's Theology of Sin and Grace
One of Paul's comments on sin and grace comes from his letter to the Romans where he says,

> Therefore, do not let sin exercise dominion in your mortal bodies, to make you obey their passions. No longer present your members to sin as instruments of wickedness, but present yourselves to God as those who have been brought from death to life, and present your members to God as instruments of righteousness. For sin will have no dominion over you, since you are not under law but under grace. (Rom. 6:12-14)

For Paul, sin was a power that could be given allegiance, and the way to curb that power was through an alternative allegiance to Jesus Christ. For Paul something very significant changed with the coming of Messiah. Sin could no longer be equated with disobeying the law. He saw the law (Torah) as a provisional arrangement which was to govern the life of Yahweh worshippers while they were waiting for Messiah. Now that Messiah had come, things changed. It was not that the law was no longer relevant, but good works were now interpreted through the life, death, and resurrection of Jesus Christ. So he could say to the Ephesians:

> For by grace you have been saved through faith, and this is not your own doing; it is the gift of God—not the result of works, so that no one may boast. *For we are what he has made us,* created in

Christ Jesus for good works, which God prepared beforehand to be our way of life (Eph. 2:8-10, emphasis mine).

Paul's anthropology is made complex by Jesus Christ. As he implies here and makes clear elsewhere (Romans 5), with Jesus' coming we are no longer best understood through sinful Adam, but who we are now flows through Jesus Christ. And the way he unpacks this is to say that life is now not best seen via the law which enslaves us to obedience, but through Christ who sets us free for God. This is further expounded when he talks about the new obedience to Christ as a participation in the body of Christ, which is the church. What this means is that the new person in Christ is not merely a new individual with a new loyalty, but a new person in community—where, when one person suffers, all suffer, and when one person rejoices all rejoice.[9] This is the new life of grace in relation to the other and it picks up the language of human identity from Matthew 25. Hence, the freedom Christians find in Christ (grace) is not a freedom *from* good works, but a freedom *for* good works.

For Paul, sin gets refocused in at least two ways: one in relation to Jesus and the other in relation to the powers of the world. His own life got turned around while he was persecuting Christians. Through his encounter with Jesus Christ he came to see that his sin was that he had not recognized that in Jesus Messiah had come. Second, sin had to do with more than personal disobedience. Sin was embodied within the world through "cosmic powers of darkness" that are vying for our loyalties. Sin was associated with the "passions of the flesh," and the "powers and principalities" that killed Jesus. And these same powers are seeking our allegiance. Only our "participation in Christ" can save us from the false promises of the powers.

What this means is that for Christians sin cannot be understood apart from Jesus and his teaching. For Jesus, sin was not something that could be easily defined and described, like breaking the law or covenant; instead he pointed to how pious people could sin by keeping the law, and by how, if the intent behind the law was not fulfilled, it was itself of little help for the righteousness he called people to. He makes this clear in Matthew 5 where he speaks about how the law was clearly

---

[9] See Rom. 12:15.

named in the tradition, yet he calls his followers to a greater righteousness which made keeping the old law inadequate. Hence for the early Christians, who saw themselves as disciples, the new standard was not an abstract law, but a person, Jesus Christ. Sin was measured by faithfulness to Jesus Christ, and this not by rote imitation, which could also fall short of the new righteousness, but by a "participation" in the very nature of Jesus Christ—by embodying the same spirit.

Sin as Pride: The history of theological thought on sin and grace, of course, is rich and takes many turns. I will touch on only a few issues very briefly. Early church theologian, Augustine (354-430), is sometimes read as so preoccupied with sin as rooted in the physical—flesh and sexuality—that the only alternative was an escape from this world to radical otherness—God. On this reading, to love God means that we must hate everything about our own lives. But Augustine's theology goes much deeper than that. While it is true that Augustine is overwhelmed with the horrors of sin, and believes that if left on its own the world is damned, it is precisely the redemptive and gracious ways of God that he believes can rescue the world from damnation. For the world is not hopelessly lost; that is, evil has no substance of its own as the ancient Manicheans thought. Hence, evil is not something extant, not something *that* we choice, but it has to do with *how* we choose; that is, it has to do with the will.

Augustine names pride as the basic human sin; when pride governs our choice we sin. His concept of pride is, however, difficult for the twenty-first century mind to grasp properly. We tend to think of pride as high self-esteem and positive self-worth and therefore its opposite is low self-esteem and even self-loathing. This was not Augustine's view. For him pride was properly paired with humility, which is a proper assessment of who we are under God. Humility invites us to value ourselves—both our failures and our achievements—under the knowledge that we are creaturely beings; ones who have been given life by a generous and gracious Creator. Kim Paffenroth helps us understand Augustine's view of pride and humility. She says:

> The sinful sense of "pride," then, is the opposite of the virtue of humility. Internally or personally, it is the ultimate disorder in

one's soul, inaccurately and irrationally valuing oneself above all else, instead of putting oneself in the right relation of humility toward God and other people.[10]

For Augustine pride and humility both name objects of hope; pride places hope in the self and humility opens space for hope in God. To say this differently, humility opens the possibility of redemption beyond the capacity of what humans are capable of and so requires hope. As Augustine puts it:

> . . . let us walk in hope, and let us by the spirit mortify the flesh, and so make progress day by day. For "the Lord knoweth them that are his;" and "as many as are led by the spirit of God, they are sons of God," but by grace, not by nature.[11]

Humility, for Augustine, is a stance of openness to God, accepting the soul's natural desire for God. Yet such openness does not suppose passivity on the part of the human will; instead it orients the will. This means that the life of humility requires that we train ourselves in humility—in spiritual exercises of prayer, fasting, worship, contemplation, and living in the expectation of God's blessing. These are all necessary in order to hope and desire properly. To walk in humility is to acknowledge that the kingdom grows by the grace of God and ours is the invitation to participate in the ways of God. God is creator and we are the created; we have wandered away from God as lost children and are invited back through God's grace. We human beings are only properly understood in light of our return to God who made us and in whom we have our true meaning.

Augustine believed that sin was "original" in the sense that after Adam's sin, sin was transmitted to all of humanity simply by virtue of being human. In other words, human nature is weakened in its power

---

[10] Kim Pattenroth, *The Heart Set Free: Sin and Redemption in the Gospels, Augustine, Dante, and Flannery O'Connor* (New York: Continuum, 2005), 37.

[11] Augustine, "The City of God," in *Nicene and Post-Nicene Fathers of the Christian Church*, ed. Philip Schaff (Grand Rapids, MI: Eerdmans, 1977), Bk XXI, chap. 15, 2:464-465.

to resist evil and hence it cannot be perfected on the basis of free will alone. This was part of his controversy with Pelagius.

The doctrine of original sin has a long and controversial history in the Christian church, especially on how it gets transmitted from generation to generation, but this is not the place to endeavour to sort this out. Suffice it to say here that the Christian church has generally accepted a view of sin which is not only voluntary but an insidious power and no one gets to escape its effects.

Nature and Grace
The late medieval understanding of nature and its relationship to grace is important because it helps us to see the natural world, humanity included, through the category of God's grace. And, especially through the writings of Thomas Aquinas (1225-1274), we learn that although the natural order is fallen and the power of sin is real, through God's grace it is constantly being perfected and restored.

To understand the medieval view of nature it is helpful to consider how transcendence was viewed in late medieval Christian thought. The word "transcendence" designated something else than "being in a different realm than time and space." Transcendence in the ancient sense was seen as beyond being itself. That is, it was not in the realm of being. Catherine Pickstock, Cambridge University theologian, says:

> Transcendence is beyond all understanding of things . . . for example as having boundaries, as having a place, as having a certain kind of temporality. Transcendence is beyond all of those things, it is beyond here and there, near and far, limit and unlimit. Transcendence is simply beyond every definition, which isn't to say it is formless . . . it is unity itself but unity perceived as beyond being.[12]

What this means is that God is not a being among other beings, but beyond being itself. At the same time, in medieval theology reality was viewed as hierarchical, with transcendence at the top and everything

---

[12] Catherine Pickstock, "" Radical Orthodoxy," in an interview on *Ideas*, CBC Radio, June 1, 2008. This interview is available as a podcast on the internet.

else underneath. Trees, buildings, animals, humans, insects, tables and chairs, everything in this earth is simultaneously below transcendence and yet transcendence is also present in everything. It is present in material objects, in human souls, and even in ants! Pickstock says, "Transcendence is both at the top and the bottom; there simply is no place that transcendence cannot be because it is beyond all limit."[13] To say this in another way, all of reality is infused with the divine. Yet, the divine is both present and beyond all our reach.

Given that all reality mysteriously participates in the divine, there is something about everything that eludes us. Nothing is only as it appears to be, and everything finds its fulfilment in its perfection. Again Pickstock, "If we apprehend a tree as participating in God we don't see the tree as an end in itself, and as somehow laid out as a given thing that we can manipulate. We now receive it as more than itself, and as somehow mysterious. It is not a given itself, but arrives."[14] This view of the world suggests that all that is, is properly received as gift from God (grace) and understood as participating in a beyond which gives it worth and a meaningful place, and that nothing is fully understood merely in reference to itself.

What does this have to do with sin and grace? It means that on the medieval view "fallen" creation participates in the grace of God and can be perfected through it. As Aquinas says it, "Grace does not destroy nature but perfects it."[15] Yet it must be said that today this theological view of the world is no longer dominant, not even in the Christian imagination, although there are those who would like to revive it.[16] Much internal debate has taken place on the topic of nature and grace since the late medieval era. Martin Luther (1483-1546) found it necessary to leave the Catholic Church over his understanding of the

---

[13] Ibid.

[14] Ibid.

[15] Thomas Aquinas, *Summa Theologica*, 1, q. 1, a. 8, reply objection 2, trans. Fathers of the English Dominican Province (New York: Benziger Bros., 1947-1948).

[16] One effort to re-empower medieval orthodoxy is the group of theologians associated with "Radical Orthodoxy," which includes Catherine Pickstock. See John Milbank, Graham Ward, and Catherine Pickstock, eds., *Radical Orthodoxy: A New Theology* (London: Routledge, 1999).

gospel of grace; the Radical Reformers (Anabaptists) found it important not to let the theology of *Sola gratia* (grace alone) trump the gospel emphasis on discipleship. And perhaps nowhere has the debate on how to speak of the relation of nature and grace been more fierce than in the twentieth century between Protestant theologians Emil Brunner (1889-1966) and Karl Barth (1886-1968), and Catholic theologian Hans Urs von Balthasar (1905-1988).[17]

Discipleship and Grace

It is hard to know where to pick up the discussion of sin and grace in contemporary theology. My choice, admittedly somewhat arbitrary, is to explore further the topic of discipleship and grace. German theologian Dietrich Bonhoeffer (1906-1945) offers helpful insights in his book, *The Cost of Discipleship*. Bonhoeffer was a German Lutheran theologian who believed that the German Christians had lost their way because of a failure to understand the proper relationship between grace and sin. They had forgotten that sin was both personal and political, and for this reason they thought they could live in sin justified by grace. Bonhoeffer did not believe that it was Luther's theology that had cheapened grace because he believed that "the providence of God raised Martin Luther to restore the gospel of pure, costly grace."[18]

---

[17] In 1934, Karl Barth wrote a polemic against Emil Brunner's book, *Natur und Gnade* (Nature and Grace). Brunner had attempted to write a nuanced version of the relationship that was rather sympathetic to Thomas Aquinas' "natural theology," but Barth wanted nothing to do with it because he believed it to be in opposition to his own theology of revelation. He said, "We must learn again to understand revelation as grace and grace as revelation, and therefore turn away from all 'true' or 'false' *theologia naturalis*." Quoted from the website, "Introduction to Barth's *Nein*," *Karl Barth Society of Amherst* at http://barthamherst.blogspot.com/2007/05/introduction-to-barths-nein.html. Barth modified his strong reaction to "natural theology" somewhat over the years, especially when he was in dialogue with Catholic theologian Hans Urs von Balthasar, for he realized that the incarnation of Jesus Christ demanded analogical language that his strong separation of nature and grace tended to foreclose. For a summary of that dialogue, see Edward T. Oakes, *Pattern of Redemption: The Theology of Hans Urs von Balthasar* (New York: Continuum, 1994), 45-71.

[18] Dietrich Bonhoeffer, *The Cost of Discipleship*, trans. R. H. Fuller (New

Bonhoeffer's reading of Luther is instructive: Luther was a cloistered monk who had left everything he had to be a disciple living in absolute obedience to Christ. Monasticism was a living protest to the cheapening of grace. Monks knew that to follow Christ meant to take up the cross of Christ and bear the burdens of both rejecting the world and experiencing the world's rejection of them. But as far as the Roman Catholic Church was concerned, Bonhoeffer says, "Monasticism was represented as an individual achievement which the mass of the laity could not be expected to emulate."[19] Luther came to see the distinction between the two kinds of Christians, those with minimum commitment and those with maximum commitment, as the fatal error of the church and so he risked all in his declaration "that the following of Christ is not the achievement or merit of a select few, but the divine command to all Christians without distinction."[20] Hence, Luther's coming out of the cloister was driven by the same costly commitment of faithfulness to following Jesus Christ as his commitment to enter the cloister to begin with.

As Bonhoeffer saw it, the Lutheran church in Germany in the 1940s seriously misrepresented Luther's theology of grace. He puts it starkly, "We Lutherans have gathered like eagles round the carcase (sic) of cheap grace, and there we have drunk of the poison which has killed the life of following Christ."[21] Bonhoeffer's famous distinction between cheap and costly grace serves to highlight the meaning of Christian discipleship. Cheap grace is a grace without discipleship; cheap discipleship is discipleship without grace. Says Bonhoeffer,

> Cheap grace is the preaching of forgiveness without requiring repentance, baptism without church discipline, Communion without confession, absolution without personal confession. Cheap grace is grace without discipleship, grace without the cross, grace without Jesus Christ, living and incarnate.[22]

York: Macmillan Publishing Co., 1974), 50.

[19] Ibid., 49.
[20] Ibid., 50.
[21] Ibid., 57.
[22] Ibid., 47.

"Costly grace," on the other hand, "is the gospel which must be *sought* again and again, the gift which must be *asked* for, the door at which man must *knock*."[23] Costly grace was about following Jesus in his mission and his vision, and with his power. Jesus told his disciples to take up their cross and follow him. This meant that they should be aware of the potential for suffering that may result from their following Jesus. Costly grace is rooted in the knowledge that the faithfulness of Jesus cost him his life; and it stems from the faith that in being faithful to God, Jesus was graced with new life—resurrection. Herein lies the free gifted nature of grace. Hence, the fruit that is associated with grace cannot be grasped through the mechanism of cause and effect, as if we have handles on producing God's grace; instead it requires another paradigm altogether, one that exploits the image of faithfulness in openness to divine blessing (gift).

For Bonhoeffer, and for discipleship theologians like John Howard Yoder,[24] discipleship is possible because God is acting in this world to redeem (God's grace); we are invited to participate in this redeeming activity. This calls for an active training in openness to God's redemptive work, as well as an active reading of what is going on around us. Bonhoeffer's concern was that sin and grace had received narrow definitions which allowed Christians to justify their participation in social evil, convinced that this was the will of God. For Christians to open themselves to God requires the readiness to say no to powers that can kill them; that is why grace is costly.

I want to conclude by telling a story that highlights notions like enabling grace, forgiving grace, and discipleship, all in response to a grievous act of evil. I tell this story not because I believe it is *the perfect* model for how to deal with such things or because it offers solutions to all the problems around sin and grace; in fact it raises some difficult questions of its own. But I tell it because it is an effort to conscientiously embody grace and forgiveness by a Christian community that has for centuries disciplined itself to follow Jesus, and particularly to respond to sin with grace.

---

[23] Ibid., (emphasis in source).
[24] See John Howard Yoder, *The Politics of Jesus* (Grand Rapids, MI: Eerdmans, 1994).

Amish Grace

In October 2006, a horrific event took place that stunned everyone who heard about it. Five schoolgirls were brutally murdered and five more were injured by a gunman named Charles Carl Roberts IV in an Amish schoolhouse near Nickel Mines, Pennsylvania.[25] The Amish are close "theological cousins" to Mennonites in that we share sixteenth-century Anabaptist roots. The difference is that Mennonites are more assimilated to mainstream culture than the Amish. The Amish shun much (but not all) technology, drive with horse and buggy, and generally seek to resist the many forces they associate with the secular world. One might say that they see themselves as a disciplined community of character.

West Nickel Mines School was a small elementary school in Lancaster County with twenty-six children from ten different Amish homes. It was a typical Amish school and began each day with Bible-reading, singing, and a brief time of worship. Many Amish schools display on the school walls the acronym JOY—Jesus first, Others next, Yourself last.[26] The teacher was a twenty-year-old woman from the community who had two years of teaching experience. This was also a day when they had four adult visitors from the community, including the teacher's mother.

When Roberts came into the schoolhouse waving a gun it was evident that they were in serious danger. The teacher and her mother immediately ran for help and called the emergency operator. Roberts ordered the boys and adult women to leave. He told the remaining girls, "I am angry at God and I need to punish some Christian girls to get even with him."[27] When it became clear that he planned to kill them, the oldest girl (thirteen years old), volunteered to be the first to be shot, because she thought this might save the others. When the killing ended, with Roberts taking his own life, five girls were mortally wounded and five were in critical condition. This was a catastrophic tragedy in a

---

[25] I am relying on the story as told in the book by Donald B. Kraybill, Steven M. Nolt, and David L. Weaver-Zerche, eds. *Amish Grace: How Forgiveness Transcended Tragedy* (San Francisco, CA: Jossey-Bass, 2007).

[26] Ibid., 20.

[27] Ibid., 25.

normally quiet Amish community. The authors of *Amish Grace* surmise: "Perhaps it was the stories of the martyrs in her people's history that imbued the oldest girl with the courage on that terrifying day."[28]

What is of specific interest here for our topic is the embodiment of Amish grace in this tragic event. In some ways this event is too dramatic to help with theological nuancing but in other ways it is precisely the Amish response to sin that helps to highlight the dynamics of the sin-grace exchange.

There was an immediate outpouring of support and aid to the families of the victims. Of course, the Amish community drew much support from their identity as a Christian fellowship under Almighty God. Almost immediately, while still in shock of the event, the Amish community "forgave the killer and offered grace to his family."[29] Yet the work of forgiveness and grace is not easy in such situations. The Amish realized that Roberts' family members too had become victims; they had to bear humiliation and shame which was a different kind of suffering from their own, but nevertheless just as real. Within hours after the shooting an Amish Minister sought out Roberts' widow and children, and he later said of this meeting, ". . . we just talked with them for about ten minutes to express our sorrow and told them that we did not hold anything against them."[30] They did the same with the killer's father. When they were asked by the media how they were able to forgive so quickly, their response was "Through God's help." The Amish also invited Roberts' widow and children to the funeral of their daughters and then attended the funeral of the gunman. It is said that more than half the mourners at the gunman's funeral were Amish. Many Amish donated to a fund that was set up to help the Roberts family.

In the media the story soon moved from the killing itself to the surprise of Amish grace and forgiveness. Repeatedly they were asked why and how they could forgive so quickly. One Bishop explained, "It's

---

[28] Ibid., 28.
[29] Ibid., 43.
[30] Ibid., 44.

just what we do as non-resistant people. It was spontaneous. It was automatic. It was not a new kind of thing."[31] There were of course not only positive reactions of praise and admiration for the grace shown by the Amish. Some questioned the appropriateness of forgiveness in this case, arguing that there should be consequences of such horrific deeds. Some argued that hatred and anger are appropriate in extreme events like this. Others questioned the idea of the leaders forgiving on behalf of individuals in the community.

This story, in a vivid way, raises the question of what forgiving is. How does re-gracing a sinner (in this case a cold-blooded killer and especially his family) change anything? Distinctions need to be made. Forgiveness is not pardon; and forgiveness is not reconciliation. Yet forgiveness opens the doors to pardon and reconciliation, because forgiveness forgoes the impulse to vengeance.[32] It is instructive to remember that the Amish act of forgiveness and grace for the gunman and his family was followed by the activity of restoration of relationships with this family. This act of forgiveness was for them not merely an intellectual or attitudinal event, but hard work involving the right-making of broken relationships of sin. In other words, forgiveness is one thing, restoration is another.

Conclusion

It turns out that the logic of grace is rather strange logic and not fully within our intellectual grasp. For to understand grace is to place ourselves into a stance of openness to the other *expecting a surprise gift*. Now, that is a paradox because "expectant waiting" and "surprise" are at odds with each other. Yet it is within this paradox that grace happens since it is gift and "transcends."

In concluding summary, I list several theological affirmations that Christians might make arising from the conviction that sin and grace

---

[31] Ibid., 49.

[32] See ibid., xiv. See also Romans 12:19-21 "Beloved, never avenge yourselves, but leave room for the wrath of God; for it is written, 'Vengeance is mine, I will repay, says the Lord.' No, 'if your enemies are hungry, feed them; if they are thirsty, give them something to drink; for by doing this you will heap burning coals on their heads.' Do not be overcome by evil, but overcome evil with good."

form the dialectic through which we seek to understand ourselves and others as human beings.

1. Being human is impossible without an account of our failings; it is intolerable without the gift of grace. The life of grace includes a stance of hospitality and openness to the other, since in the household of God we are all brothers and sisters.

2. Sin is not inherent in creation itself (Manichaeism). Sin is unnatural; that is, it is a distortion of creation. Sin may make creation less than perfect but its perfectibility is not taken away.

3. It does not lie within the capacity of free human beings to lift themselves out of Sin's grasp (Pelagianism). We know no other kind of human being than the one who consistently and mysteriously goes against the Creator's intent for human existence.

4. Human fullness and well-being (salvation) rest in the grace of creator God made manifest in Jesus Christ who, when we repent, graciously forgives us our sins and calls us back to faithfulness when we go astray and who empowers us to resist the power of evil.

5. We cannot see our own nature best by looking within ourselves; we can see the fullness of who we are by looking to Jesus Christ.

6. Grace is rooted in God's covenant faithfulness toward sinful human beings. That is, God does not deal with us according to our actions but according to God's mercy and righteousness.

7. The answer to sin in this world is to undermine its power; alternatively, to resist being seduced by it. This was done concretely through the life, death, and resurrection of Jesus Christ and the invitation to his disciples to take up the cross and follow after him is an invitation to participate in that undermining.

8. The grace of Jesus Christ is not cheap because it demands that Christ followers be drawn into the pain of this world and there participate in the healing power of the holy love of God. That is, the costly grace of Christ is a call to work for peace and justice, which may produce suffering.

9. Forgiveness is an act of re-gracing the sinner. This re-gracing entails a concern for just relationships. When Jesus forgave sin, he sometimes added, "And go and sin no more" (e.g., John 8:11). Hence,

the act of forgiveness is but the beginning of the restoration of community, not the end.

10. Grace opens the door to forgiveness; forgiveness opens the door to reconciliation. All three are made possible through prayer and openness to God's re-creative spirit.

If we say that we have no sin, we deceive ourselves and the truth is not in us. (1 John 1:8)

May the grace of our Lord Jesus Christ be with your spirit, brothers and sisters. Amen. (Gal. 6:18)

In the Name of Allah, the Beneficent, the Merciful

Religion, Culture, and Social Well-Being from an Islamic Perspective

Ali Mesbah

The aim of social life is to secure human well-being and interest through cooperation and interaction between individuals on the one level, and between communities and societies on another. When people decide to live together in a society, individual freedoms collide and it is indispensible to determine the limits for individual freedom, and to decide about the responsibilities and duties of each individual toward others as well as their rights. Despite the necessity of balancing the two, it is not always easy to resolve the conflict between individual rights and social duties. To manage social relations, and to solve the dilemma of right and duty, a wide variety of social systems of values and legal systems have been developed throughout history. Different ways of managing social life and value systems are based on the way people understand the world in general and human life in particular, which together are the cornerstone of a culture.

Culture consists of different components such as beliefs, values, motivations, languages, arts, and a common heritage, whether it is national, domestic, or an ethnic one. But not all these elements are on the same footing. What shapes the bedrock of a culture and supports other cultural elements is the framework of meaning, or a world view. A world view is the way one understands the world, and the way one answers such basic questions as: What is the nature of being as a whole? Whence has it come? Where is it going? Answers to these questions by the people and their belief systems enables them to interpret all things and events within this framework and ascribe meaning to them.

Questions about the characteristics, beginning, and end of the human being are also part of this process of the human effort to make sense of the world and of oneself, and to seek proper answers to the most vital questions of life.

This mental framework gives rise to a system of values and morality that acts as a guideline for one's actions. Moral values, in turn, produce and reinforce proportionate motives in people, and finally lead to actions congruent with such values and intentions. This triad of "thought-value-motivation" systems is expressed in the form of symbols and languages which form other parts of a culture. Language, script, arts, and some symbolic rituals and ceremonies in different cultures are diverse reflections of the fundamental elements of those cultures, which make them understandable and presentable to others, and apt for cultural communication. Cultural foundations influence all aspects of one's life, including one's relation to God and spirituality, individual behaviour, family life, social interactions, and one's treatment of the environment; in a word, they shape all cultural manifestations.[1]

From one perspective, we may classify different world views into two major categories. On the one hand are divine world views, revolving around the notion of God, which present a view of the world as created by God and eventually returning to Him. Divine world views consider the human being as one of the creatures of God and think of human beatitude within the framework of following the plan of God in order to accomplish happiness and beatitude. On the contrary, are profane world views, looking at the world as a self-sufficient entity that comes out of nowhere, survives and develops according to laws of natural evolution, and eventually perishes into nothingness. They follow the same route when it comes to the question of the human

---

[1] See, for example, Ward H. Goodenrough, "Cultural Anthropology and Linguistics," in Paul Garvin, *report of the Seventh Annual Round Table Meeting in Linguistics and Language Study*, Monograph Series on Language and Linguistics, No. 9 (Washington, D.C.: Georgetown University Press, 1957), 167; and Clifford Geertz, *The Interpretation of Cultures* (New York: Basic Books, 1973), 12, quoted in Jacob Pandian, *Culture, Religion, and the Sacred Self: A Critical Introduction the Anthropological Study of Religion* (Princeton, NJ: Prentice-Hall, 1991), 3.

being, the way one has to live, and the problem of one's destiny. They think of the human being as a natural phenomenon whose best interest is to live freely and enjoy one's limited life in this world as much as one can, very much like other animals. This is why they give priority to individual freedom and liberty over against all other values.

This view of the human being is best described by the term "humanism," in the sense reflected in the various humanist manifestos. Unfortunately, such a view of humanity, especially when it comes to the issue of human social life, is not restricted to atheist world views. Most modern scholars follow a secular ideology, even if they have religious beliefs. They divide human life into a private sphere and a public one, completely separating them from each other. They privatize God and religion, leaving the social aspect of human life to human rationality and experiment. This attitude stems from the pivotal role the human being plays in the humanist infrastructure of secular ideology. According to this standpoint, the human being is the original decision-maker, and the ultimate judge in all affairs pertaining to oneself, to the environment, and to society; there is nothing superior to an individual's rights and desires that can delimit one's liberty and interests.

If one pushes this idea to its limits, its logical consequence would be lack of law, and therefore, lack of civilization, because absolute freedom of individuals has no better perspective than anarchy and a wild life in a lawless jungle. This is while civilization implies order and law, and law is something that determines restrictions for individual freedoms in society. People live in society, and in a society, the interests of people always clash. This is why there is a need for regulations to keep order and organize the relations between people. It is also necessary to pass laws which arrange the relations of different societies with each other within a specific framework. This is one of the social needs that human communities have recognized from very early times of human life on earth; and social systems, legal systems, and political systems have been developed to meet this need. These systems have evolved throughout history according to the increasing complexity of human societies. In this process, each and every group has chosen a different legal and political system for controlling these relations and managing social life. In a civilized society, there is also penal law, which determines the proper punishment for those who transgress law, and go beyond limits.

This is why absolute freedom has no room in civilizations, and even the most zealous humanists admit the necessity of some restrictions on individual freedom in order to benefit from the advantages of social life.

Theories about how to determine the law and implement it form a wide spectrum with two extremes. On the one extreme, there are some political thinkers who suggest that the only way out of this dilemma is that all people of a society should submit to the will of one person, so that he decides the law, and sets the limits for individual freedoms according to his own understanding and desires. This person may be the one who is physically the most powerful, or the most charismatic, or the inheritor of a monarchy. This type of government is called autocracy and dictatorship. Obviously, one person, without enjoying a divine knowledge, has very limited knowledge of what is the best for society in all areas of social needs, including the economic, political, educational, etc., and therefore, his decisions cannot be reliable. Also absolute power is corruptive for fallible people, and there is a high possibility that one may abuse power to secure one's own interests and give precedence to his or her personal, familial, or group advantage over against what is best for society. Hence, investing one person with all sources of power without a proper process of supervision is not rationally acceptable. Such a social system cannot be trusted and cannot guarantee individual rights and social justice, as well as the well-being of people.

The only alternative that secular scholars could think of was a system of decision-making, in which the knowledge and desires of all individuals contribute to the establishment of limits and to decisions about the rules governing social affairs. Their only criterion for drawing up the boundaries for individual freedom was the freedom of others. Theoretical and practical problems with this criterion notwithstanding (because they are not a matter of discussion here), it did not lead to a prosperous life either. The reason is that human beings dramatically differ on how to understand human happiness or felicity, as there is no consensus on how to arrive at them. Conflicting needs and interests and the complex relations that exist in human affairs make it very difficult, if not impossible, to determine priorities. Some schools of thought, such as liberalism, consider human freedom an absolute value, which overrides all other values. Still others, such as socialism, give priority to social justice and define it in terms of complete equality between all people, disregarding individual freedom along individual differences. There are of course some other thinkers who have tried, unsuccessfully, to balance these two extreme views in one way or another.

What is common in all these views, and (I think) the source of their failure, is their commitment to a secular ideology. They try to do without God and ignore the guidance of religion in the most vital aspects of human life. The humanistic approach to social problems defines them within its narrow understanding of the human being and the short span of human life which ends after living a few years in this temporal world. Human problems, accordingly, are those situations that hinder complete enjoyment of opportunities that happen to someone, and the solution lies in attempts to further the possibility of engagement in activities and participation in situations that maximize pleasure and utility "here and now." Even those who look for social justice and try to find ways for maximizing utility for the greatest number of people do not think of anything except material benefits and worldly pleasures. Those who give priority to social justice (in theory, of course) interpret it in materialistic terms, too.

Exactly for this reason, we see that the language they use for presenting their ideas regarding human interests, human rights, and the like, is a materialistic language. It tries to restrict humanity within the boundaries of this world and to define human prosperity in that framework alone. Let us look at some articles of the humanist manifestos in this regard, as a clear example of such mentality and attitude.

The Humanist Manifesto, signed and published in 1933 by thirty four, including John Dewey, the American pragmatist and educator, includes the following passages:

> Religions have always been *means* for realizing the highest values of life. Their end has been accomplished through the interpretation of the total environing situation (theology or world view), the sense of values resulting therefrom (goal or ideal), and the technique (cult), established for realizing the satisfactory life. A change in any of these factors results in alteration of the

outward forms of religion. This fact explains the *changefulness of religions* through the centuries.

FIRST: Religious humanists regard the universe as self-existing and not created.

SECOND: Humanism believes that man is a part of nature and that he has emerged as a result of a continuous process.

THIRD: Holding an organic view of life, humanists find that the traditional dualism of mind and body must be rejected.

FOURTH: Humanism recognizes that man's religious culture and civilization, as clearly depicted by anthropology and history, are the product of a gradual development due to his interaction with his natural environment and with his social heritage.

FIFTH: Humanism asserts that the nature of the universe depicted by modern science makes unacceptable any supernatural or cosmic guarantees of human values.

SIXTH: We are convinced that the time has passed for theism, deism, modernism, and the several varieties of "new thought".

SEVENTH: ... The distinction between the sacred and the secular can no longer be maintained.

EIGHTH: Religious Humanism considers the complete realization of human personality to be the end of man's life and seeks its development and fulfillment in the here and now. This is the explanation of the humanist's social passion.

NINTH: In the place of the old attitudes involved in worship and prayer the humanist finds his religious emotions expressed in a heightened sense of personal life and in a cooperative effort to promote social well-being.

TENTH: It follows that there will be no uniquely religious emotions and attitudes of the kind hitherto associated with belief in the supernatural. . . .

. . . Though we consider the religious forms and ideas of our fathers no longer adequate, the quest for the good life is still the central task for mankind.[2]

The second humanist manifesto, published forty years later, in 1973, was signed by more than 230 people. It is more socially oriented, and

---

[2] From http://www.americanhumanist.org/Who_We_Are/About_Humanism/Humanist_Manifesto_I.

critical of some modern developments, especially in areas of social justice. But still it remains within the confines of the materialistic world view and seeks justice here and now, within the same narrow understanding of reality and of the human being. It says in part:

> As in 1933, humanists still believe that traditional theism, especially faith in the prayer-hearing God, assumed to live and care for persons, to hear and understand their prayers, and to be able to do something about them, is an unproved and outmoded faith. Salvationism, based on mere affirmation, still appears as harmful, diverting people with false hopes of heaven hereafter. Reasonable minds look to other means for survival.
>
> We affirm a set of common principles that can serve as a basis for united action - positive principles relevant to the present human condition. They are a design for a secular society on a planetary scale.
>
> FIRST: . . . We believe, however, that traditional dogmatic or authoritarian religions that place revelation, God, ritual, or creed above human needs and experience do a disservice to the human species. . . . We find insufficient evidence for belief in the existence of a supernatural; it is either meaningless or irrelevant to the question of survival and fulfillment of the human race. As nontheists, we begin with humans not God, nature not deity. . . . we can discover no divine purpose or providence for the human species. While there is much that we do not know, humans are responsible for what we are or will become. No deity will save us; we must save ourselves.
>
> SECOND: Promises of immortal salvation or fear of eternal damnation are both illusory and harmful.
>
> THIRD: We affirm that moral values derive their source from human experience. Ethics is autonomous and situational needing no theological or ideological sanction. Ethics stems from human need and interest. To deny this distorts the whole basis of life.
>
> FOURTH: ... As science pushes back the boundary of the known, humankind's sense of wonder is continually renewed, and art,

poetry, and music find their places, along with religion and ethics.[3]

The Islamic View

Over against the materialistic belief system and the secular value system, Islam, as a divine religion, does not consider the human being coming out of nowhere, left to itself. By the way, all divine religions share these ideas with Islam. Islam introduces the human being as the most virtuous creature of the Wise Creator, created for ascending the highest levels of nearness to God. In the Islamic ontology, the relation between this world and the hereafter is very much like the relation of an embryonic stage of life to our life in this world. Whatever one does in this worldly life leaves its effect on his or her eternal life which begins after leaving this stage of life in this world. This fact is expressed in different ways in the Islamic holy texts. For instance, sometimes this relation is compared to the relation between cultivating plants on a farm in spring and harvesting them in autumn. It means that for having a prosperous life in the hereafter one has to prepare the conditions in this world. Sometimes the analogy is made between this relation and the kind that exists between a bridge and one's final destination. As crossing a bridge is a necessary, but preliminary, step to arrive at the destination, human life in this world is also a necessary prelude for reaching the final destination of human life in the hereafter. Moreover, the life after death is the most important part of human life, for which our life in this world is only a preparatory step. The Qur'an says:

> . . . and surely, the hereafter is the real life, if they understood. (29:65)

According to the Islamic teachings, it is only through one's own intentional activities in this world that one can achieve infinite beatitude or misery in the hereafter. Unintentional behaviours have no effect in this regard, because they cannot generate value or responsibility, and one cannot be praised or blamed for them, as no one is going to be rewarded or punished for what others have done.

---

[3] From http://www.americanhumanist.org/about/manifesto2.html.

Everyone is responsible for what one has acquired. (52:22)

No laborer is to burden another one's load; and nothing is to benefit a human being but what one has tried for it. And that man can have nothing but what He does (good or bad). (53:39-40)

These are some basic ideas in the Islamic world view and its view of the human being that shape the cultural foundations for an Islamic social system. Based on these fundamental principles, Islam suggests a paradigm for an Islamic society. It is inclusive of the various relations and interactions a member of a society may have, and gives criteria for the kind of relations and the way of life one should have with others. It covers one's relations with one's creator, with oneself, and with other creatures, where other creatures comprise the environment (i.e., non-animate things, plants, and animals), as well as fellow human beings. Here I will review some salient features of an ideal Islamic society as depicted in the Noble Qur'an and the teachings of the Infallibles.

The first and the most basic feature of a religious society from an Islamic point of view is an accurate understanding the citizens have of the origin of the world and of the human being. Part of the import of such a belief system lies in its determining effect on other features. According to Islam, as a divine religion, God is the creator of the world, and His attributes, beside His existence, include oneness, omnipotence, omniscience, justice, forgiveness, punishment, beneficence to all human beings, special compassion toward the faithful, and anger against the disbeliever. God is exalted from being effected by anyone or any act, and speaking of His wrath is to express His extreme dislike for those who deliberately ignore Him, and as a result make themselves prone to eternal wretchedness.

One of His attributes, and a sign of His all embracing benevolence, is His guidance of the human being in order to show them the right direction to their felicity. He relates to the human being through revelation to His messengers, and the human being should relate to Him through thanksgiving, piety, submission, prayer, and rituals. So, apart from belief in God and His attributes, people in the ideal society practically comply with His commands as the blueprint for an eternally prosperous life.

Second, people in an ideal Islamic society have a clear idea about the reality of themselves as human beings. As for their relation with God, they know God as their Lord and caretaker, and see themselves as His servants. They know that God has bestowed upon them a lot of capabilities, and equipped them with the most precious bounties (i.e., intellect and free will) that he has not given to any other creature. They know that they are the noblest creatures of God and that this puts a great burden and responsibility on them. They understand that carrying out the responsibility will result in big rewards, while failing to do so will lead them to great anguish and regret. So they try their best to comply with the commands and guidelines offered by God.

Third, such people would realize that all creatures are God's properties, and that human beings only act as His trustees and stewards; they have the responsibility to preserve God's possessions and to help them flourish, and to utilize them in the ways God has permitted. This is why, in dealing with the environment, they do not feel free to do whatever they desire, to waste God's creatures, to destroy plants and forests, or to kill animals without good rational reasons or clear authorization from God. They feel the responsibility to look after the environment as a religious duty.

It is He who has produced you from the earth and settled you therein. (11:62)

To carry out this responsibility, people have to enhance their knowledge of divine guidance, so that they know what kind of use is permitted and what kind is prohibited. They should develop their knowledge of God's laws in nature, so that they can employ them to improve natural development and use them in the best way to increase real human prosperity.

Fourth, people in an ideal Islamic society recognize other human beings as those who are very much like themselves, created by God for the sake of reaching the highest zenith of possible perfection. So, they have sympathy for them, try to do whatever is at their disposal to help them find the right path to nearness to God and avoid going astray.

Fifth, they consider society as a unique opportunity for accomplishing certain qualities and excellence that are otherwise impossible to attain. In the Islamic society, treatment of other human beings is based on two principles: justice and benevolence. Social relations are actualized in the form of social institutions such as the family, economy, state, law, and education. I will refer, rather briefly, to the characteristics of a religious society in these areas from an Islamic point of view.

Family

An Islamic society encourages, supports, and prepares the conditions for all members of the society to be able to marry according to the divine law and benefit from the multi-dimensional benefits of family life. It is geared toward the elimination of conditions that lead to unlawful and extramarital relations. It also tries to minimize the possibility of divorce, the most hated permissible act in Islam.

Economy

The economic system and financial relations in an ideal Islamic society rest on Islamic law, including the prohibition of "interest" in monetary affairs. Islamic society tries to elevate the economic status of the society so that people are well off and the society in general becomes powerful enough to preserve its independence and stature.

State and Government

In an ideal Islamic society, government not only has the normal duties of a government such as securing order, assuring security, supporting the legitimate freedom and rights of its citizens, and defending the integrity of the society against enemies (militarily, economically, culturally, politically, etc.); it also has a higher goal beyond all such duties, that is, providing the necessary conditions for members of the society to attain the highest possible level of nearness to God. It cannot pursue this goal through coercion, because this is not something to be achieved except through intentional free acts. So the government should perform this duty through education, as well as providing the proper socio-cultural milieu so that there is a minimum of obstacles for whoever wants to take the right path.

From another perspective, in an Islamic government, socially hierarchical positions are determined by virtue of at least three elements: (a) one's acquaintance with the necessary religious knowledge and skill; (b) one's piety and ethical devotion; and (c) one's expertise and practical experience. As the position goes higher, higher standards in all the three elements are needed, to the point that the leader of the society should enjoy the highest degree of religious knowledge, statesmanship, and piety.

Law

To manage all the three aforementioned dimensions, it is indispensible to have a system of law. In an Islamic society, the principles of law are given through revelation. It is the task of the specialists in Islamic law to find the right instances of general rules in various circumstances.

Education

Education is the most important institution in almost any society. In an Islamic society, all people are engaged in educating others in one form or another, formal or informal. At least four levels, or dimensions, of education can be differentiated:

First, teaching the basic foundations of faith, including the belief system and the value system of Islam;

Second, teaching the way of relating to God, dealing with oneself, treating the environment, and communicating with others;

Third, ethical training so that people are brought up as ethical and pious people; and

Fourth, social education, so that people are aware of the rights of others and observe them in their social interactions.

CULTURE AND FAITH IN A MENNONITE-CHRISTIAN PERSPECTIVE

DAVID W. SHENK

The fifth General Assembly of the World Council of Churches (WCC) convened in Nairobi, Kenya in 1975. I was living in Nairobi and participated. Enthusiasm swept across the vast audience when the African Israeli Church Nineveh was welcomed as a member. This was an independent church with no linkages to missionary Christianity. The bishop had dressed in a coat of colobus monkey skins. With drummers at his side, he danced exuberantly during the acceptance ritual. In dramatic contrast several of us met for prayer and Bible study with the Syrian Orthodox bishop. He wore a black robe, with a large cross on his chest and a dignified turban on his head. He said that he came from a church with 2,000 years of history wherein the Aramaic language of Jesus was used for worship and fellowship. Those two congregations dramatically revealed the cultural diversity within the global church. The 348 denominations from 120 countries that comprise the WCC are expressions of astonishing cultural diversity.

The Theological Dilemma: Christ and Culture
The relationship of the church to culture is a constant challenge. When I was in college over half a century ago a 1951 publication on the gospel and culture by Richard Niebuhr, a professor at Yale University, created a lot of debate. His book *Christ and Culture* was discussed in seminaries around the world. He described five approaches to culture: 1) Christ against culture; 2) The Christ of culture; 3) Christ above culture; 4) Christ and culture in paradox; 5) Christ the transformer of culture. The book created engaged interest among Anabaptists for Niebuhr asserted

that Mennonites represent the Christ against culture "attitude most purely."[1]

As a college student I remember an emerging young Mennonite theologian, John Howard Yoder, in a public forum sharply critiquing Niebuhr's assertion that authentic Anabaptism is Christ against culture. Yoder objected to the withdrawal from society that such a commitment requires. Some years later Yoder collaborated with other scholars in writing an alternative assessment of the Anabaptist approach to culture. The name of the book states the alternative very well: *Authentic Transformation, A New Vision of Christ and Culture*. Yoder centres his critique of Niebuhr's assessment of Anabaptists in the incarnation. Christ does not escape culture. Rather he demonstrates "full and genuine human and cultural existence."[2] Yoder argues that if genuine cultural existence is true of Christ, then followers of Christ should also participate in full and genuine existence within culture.

The Bible as Narrative of the People of God within Culture

The challenges of the people of faith engaging culture are central to God's call to people to worship only God and demonstrate their commitment to God by becoming a community in mission. The prophet Isaiah proclaimed that the people of God are a "light for the Gentiles."[3] Jesus said that his disciples are to be "the light of the world."[4] How are the people of faith to express that light? How do they relate to people and societies who, as Jesus put it, "loved darkness instead of light."[5] Niebuhr's five alternatives are quite authentic descriptions of alternative ways that the church, local as well as global, responds to the challenge of being a community of faith within our

---

[1] H. Richard Niebuhr, *Christ and Culture* (New York, Harper and Brothers, 1951), 56.

[2] Glen H. Stassen, D. M. Yeager, and John Howard Yoder, *Authentic Transformation: A New Vision of Christ and Culture* (Nashville: Abingdon, 1996), 68.

[3] Isaiah 42:6.

[4] Matthew 5:14.

[5] John 3:19.

respective contexts. My assignment is to especially focus on the Anabaptist commitment.

The Anabaptist movement was birthed as a Bible-loving movement in sixteenth-century Europe. We are a people of the Scriptures. I engage with Anabaptist churches around the world; whenever a question arises, a common response is to ask: What light does the Bible shed on this question? In this essay we are looking at what light the Bible sheds on the challenges of faith and culture. Actually, the essence of biblical revelation is about that question for the Bible is missionary scripture describing God calling people to be his covenant people within a world that rejects God and amidst cultures that are not in harmony with God's righteousness.

Culture and the Human Condition

We begin with Genesis 1-3 and I will comment on two aspects of the meaning of the human condition as described in these opening chapters of the Torah. First, Adam and Eve are created in God's image. God's first command to the parents of humankind was caring for and developing the good earth. Theologians refer to this command as the cultural mandate. All human societies develop cultures. Why? Because people are created in God's image. God communicates; we develop languages to facilitate communication. God creates; we make things. There is communion and fellowship within God; we also fellowship with one another. God sustains creation; we also have the responsibility to care for creation. All aspects of human culture are expressions of our being created in God's image.

The second observation is that sinfulness has characterized the human condition right from the beginning of human history. In various ways, all cultures reflect human sinfulness. So cultures mirror both signs of the image of God as well as sinfulness. One of the first expressions of the consequence of human sinfulness was Adam and Eve making clothing of fig leaves to cover their nakedness. A psychoanalyst, Paul Tournier, writes that a consequence of our sinfulness is that the leaves become attempts to cover our real selves and project only our cultural selves.⁶ However, God then clothed Adam and Eve with the more adequate clothing of the skins of animals. In that act God affirms our need for clothing. Clothing is an expression of our cultural selves.

However, the problem is that we evaluate one another based on culture rather than recognizing that each of us is equally created in God's image. Rather than celebrating our one humanity, we are inclined to look down on those who wear different cultural clothing. For example, we observe that she is an ignorant, illiterate peasant, but he has a PhD from Harvard. We evaluate the worth of people based on their educational fig leaves, ignoring the reality that we are one humanity. The divisions of cultures were epitomized in Cain, a farmer, killing his brother Abel, who was a herdsman.

Our differing languages are one way that these divisions are reinforced. The account of the tower of Babel in Genesis 11 describes God scattering people because of their arrogance; that scattering was exacerbated through diversities of language. In time each language group embraced their own god. So our ethnic divisions not only took on language differences, but different gods for each language group reinforced these ethnic divides.

Abraham Called to a Journey of Cultural Transformation

It is in that kind of culturally and ethnically divided world that God called Abraham to begin the journey of becoming God's covenant people who would become a blessing to all nations. That was a tremendous revolution. The gods of Mesopotamia, where Abraham lived, empowered their devotees to oppress others. But Abraham was called to leave these oppressive and ethnocentric cultures and gods in order to worship the one true God, thereby becoming a blessing to all people.⁷ From that time onward for about 2,000 years the biblical narrative and prophetic voices develop this vision of the covenant people becoming a blessing to all nations.

However, the journey to becoming a people of blessing was often a rocky road. Although Israel looked to Abraham as the father of their

---

⁶ Paul Tournier, *The Meaning of Persons* (San Francisco: Harper and Row, 1957), 73-83.

⁷ Genesis 12:1-3.

faith, the biblical accounts describe Israel as often engaged in genocidal conflict with surrounding people. However, the biblical prophets were also clear that destroying other societies was not God's ultimate intention for his covenant people. The prophets held forth a vision of the Messianic reign when weapons of war would be no more and the covenant people would indeed be the heralds of peace to all nations.[8]

Father Vincent Donovan in Tanzania described how revolutionary Abraham's call was for the Masaai warrior tribe of East Africa. Like the Cain and Abel conflict, the animal-herding Masaai had been in conflict with neighbouring agricultural tribes for many centuries. For a year Donovan met with Masaai in their hamlets walking through the Bible. They began with the call of Abraham, culminating in accounts of the life and ministry of Jesus. Finally Donovan told each hamlet that the time had now come for them to decide whether they would become followers of Jesus.

A week later Donovan returned to hear their decision. He was surprised to hear each hamlet say that the decision point revolved around this one question: will they cease their warrior culture and be reconciled to the tribes around them against whom they had fought for centuries. The heart of their decision for or against Jesus was whether they would lay aside their weapons and culture of warfare so as to seek peace with their historic enemies. All but one hamlet decided for Jesus; one hamlet decided to continue their warrior ways. Donovan described his very sad departure from that hamlet, as he followed the instructions of Jesus by shaking the dust from his shoes and saying that since they had clearly decided against Jesus, he would not return to them again.[9]

Jesus introduced the communion table to his disciples the night of his betrayal and crucifixion. The disciples partook of bread that Jesus broke, and wine that he served, as signs of his forthcoming crucifixion and resurrection. Donovan and the Masaai hamlets partook of the communion table regularly. The first such event shattered a taboo of many centuries, because among the Masaai, men and women never ate or drank together. They used beer instead of wine. As the beer was

---

[8] Zechariah 9:9-10.

[9] Vincent Donovan, *Christianity Rediscovered: An Epistle from the Masaai* (Notre Dame: Fides/Claretian, 1978).

passed from person to person with men and women sitting in the circle together, hands sometimes shook in awesome recognition that this event of drinking and eating together would transform their society forever. They were indeed becoming a new community in Christ. In that communion event, they had become a community that not only included men and women, but also reached out to include those who had formerly been their enemies. This was the church wherein there is neither male nor female, and in whom people from all tribes are united in the covenant love of God.

Jesus and the Church within Culture

With the coming of Jesus and the kingdom of God that he proclaimed and demonstrated, the vision of the people of God being a light and blessing to the nations was enormously expanded. The apostolic church as described in the New Testament was confident that what God did through Jesus and the emerging church was a revelation of God's grand plan of reconciling people from all nations to himself and with one another. I will linger on the church and its formation as I further consider the theme of faith and culture.

Jesus is the key. Christians confess that Jesus is "God with us." He is "the image of God." He is the one in whom "the Word became flesh and made his dwelling among us."[10] The first Adam sinned, and all of us participate in Adam's sinfulness. Jesus is the renewal of the image of God that was distorted and spoiled in Adam's sin. All of this happens within culture. In fact he lived within a specific culture, that of the Jewish people in Palestine of 2,000 years ago. Incarnation best describes the relation of Jesus to culture. He is God with us within a particular culture. He never escaped from that culture. He was disturbingly present and transformative. He both affirmed and confronted that culture, but always as one who was within the culture, yet not entrapped in it. For example, when in Jerusalem Jesus would participate in the temple worship just as all other Jews did. Yet he also confronted the unjust and ungodly practices in the temple. In the last prayer Jesus

---

[10] This is language from the Gospel of John.

had with his disciples he observed that they were living within the world although they were not of the world.[11]

In one of some thirteen resurrection appearances with his disciples, Jesus showed them the wounds on his body from the crucifixion, and then he commissioned them, "Peace be with you! As the Father has sent me, I am sending you. Receive the Holy Spirit."[12] These appearances continued for about forty days. Then he ascended into heaven from a hill in the presence of his disciples. He left no relics behind. Not a sandal. Not even a fingernail. But at his ascension Jesus commanded his disciples to wait in Jerusalem for the coming of the Holy Spirit. Ten days later that is exactly what happened. The Holy Spirit descended upon 120 of his disciples in tongues of fire and with a sound like a rushing mighty wind. The Holy Spirit alighted on the disciples as they were together in prayer ten days after the ascension. That happened on the Jewish feast of Pentecost, which was fifty days after the Jewish Passover. Pentecost was a feast celebrating the first fruits of the early summer harvest.

The Cultural Implications of the Ascension and Pentecost
The ascension of Jesus and the Pentecost coming of the Holy Spirit powerfully formed the faith and culture commitments of the early church. The ascension and Pentecost meant that for the apostolic church there were no relics and no sacred place. There was no tomb where pilgrims could gather to be near the body of Jesus. Before his crucifixion Jesus prophesied that even the temple would be destroyed, which did happen about three decades later. This means that in the Christian movement there is nothing analogous to the Ka'bah. There is no sacred place or building, for it is the people of God who are the temple of God. There is no geographical locus for the disciples of Jesus. The temple of God is whenever people meet together in Jesus' name.

The Pentecost coming of the Holy Spirit was also significant in beginning to bring down interethnic cultural walls. That was the beginning of the church. Luke, the historian, wrote that people were in Jerusalem from "every nation under heaven."[13] When the Holy Spirit

---

[11] John 17:14-16.
[12] John 20:21-22.
[13] Acts 2:5.

came like a rushing mighty wind, these people who were in Jerusalem from many nations ran to the place where the 120 were gathered to see what was happening. A miracle occurred! The onlookers exclaimed, "We hear them declaring the wonders of God in our own tongues."[14] Amazed and perplexed they asked one another, "What does this mean?"[15] One of the apostles named Peter preached the Gospel. People repented and on that day 3,000 were baptized into this new community that included language groups from many nations. Thirteen languages and communities are specifically mentioned.

At the tower of Babel people were scattered because of linguistic diversity. At the Pentecost birth of the church the divisions of Babel were reversed. Each person heard the Gospel in his or her own language. They were baptized into the new community of believers who came from every nation. There was a healing of the divisions of nation and language. Those who had repented and been baptized went from home to home sharing food and eating with one another.

This event planted within the church the conviction that every person should be privileged to hear the Gospel and to worship in her own mother tongue. It is for this reason that around the world the church in mission has translated the Bible or portions of the Bible into the languages of people everywhere. I grew up among the Zanaki language group in Tanzania. My parents were pioneer missionaries. The first priority for my father was to translate the Gospel of Matthew into the Zanaki language. That Zanaki Gospel account of Jesus was the first book published in Zanaki. In fact that is true across Africa. In hundreds of languages across Africa the first two books to be written in vernacular languages were Genesis and Matthew, the first books of the Old and New Testament. Today some 3,000 languages around the world have portions of the Bible available; that means that over 98 percent of the people on earth have potential access to the Bible in their mother tongue. The goal of Bible translators is that all language groups have at least portions of the Bible available in their native tongue; there are still 3,000 small language groups in need of the Bible.

---

[14] Acts 2:11, 12.
[15] Acts 9:12.

Bible Translation and the Transformation of Culture

Lamin Sanneh, whose origins are the Gambia in West Africa, describes the empowerment that the translation of the Bible brings into the experience of a people. The Zanaki people did not need to learn a strange language in order to become full members of the church. When I return to the village where I grew up, the church is always packed with eager worshippers—they sing and worship in Zanaki. Sanneh asserts that the Bible is empowerment. Zanaki is the language God uses to speak to them, and it is the language they use to worship God. This empowerment means several things.[16]

First, the newly emerging church is empowered to critique any cultural imperialism that the missionary is bringing with the Gospel. Sanneh's statement reminds me of an experience I had among the Kekchi people of Guatemala. The highest educated pastors in that rapidly growing church had not more than a third grade education. I was a visiting church leader with three degrees in my pocket. At a church conference I made a suggestion. The Kekchi leaders respectfully countered my comments by saying that their reading of the Bible shows them that my observations do not apply to them—my idea was an American idea quite different than what they surmise in the reading of the Bible. They were confidently empowered to critique my American assessment, because they had the Bible in their own language.

Second, not only does the Bible in the language of the people empower them to critique outside cultural imperialisms, but it also empowers the newly developing church to critique wrongful practices in their own culture. Here is another example from East Africa. Just over a century and a half ago, German Lutheran missionaries translated the Gospel of Matthew into the Chagga language. They decided that they would not seek to transform the Chagga culture in any way, and restrict their missionary work to preparing people for heaven. Then the missionaries went to Germany for a home leave. While they were gone, the Chagga, who had become disciples of Jesus the Messiah, studied the Gospel carefully. They determined that the Spirit of Jesus was calling them to undergo a cultural revolution. So they convened a meeting of

---

[16] Lamin Sanneh, *Translating the Message: The Missionary Impact on Culture* (Maryknoll: Orbis, 2009).

all Chagga leaders and made a covenant for a cultural transformation. They determined that they would abstain from alcohol, that no father would permit his daughter to be circumcised, that they would abandon polygamy, that men would desist from wife-beating, that they would abandon witchcraft, and that every Christian homestead would be characterized by cleanliness. When the missionaries returned they were astonished to discover a transformed Chagga culture.[17] The motivation for that change was the life and teachings of Jesus.

Third, the Bible in the vernacular helps to preserve local culture. An example is the work of William Carey, who was the forerunner of the Protestant missionary endeavour in India. He and his team translated at least portions of the Bible into forty-six Indian languages. The Hindus had no interest in putting vernacular languages into writing for they focused on Sanskrit. The Muslims were concerned with Arabic. But Carey believed that God speaks through the language of the heart, and that meant that everyone should have access to hearing the Bible in his mother tongue. Therefore, he and his team developed the Serampore Christian College which trained Indian teachers to teach people to read in their vernacular languages. The graduates started vernacular elementary schools across India. It is for this reason that Carey is recognized as the pioneer for the renaissance of Indian vernacular languages.[18]

Carey believed that each language is a precious gift, and therefore he and his team not only translated the Bible, but also a variety of Indian literature, including Hindu philosophical works. It is not just in India that vernacular Bibles have been the carriers of the renaissance and preservation of linguistic culture. In a quite remarkable diversity of cultures, the presence of the Bible in the vernacular has served as a carrier for the preservation or standardization of vernacular languages, such as Swahili in East Africa or Serbo-Croatian in the Balkans.

---

[17] W. B. Anderson, *The Church in East Africa 1840-1974* (Dodoma: Central Tanganyika Press, 1977), 98-99.

[18] S. K. Chatterjee, "William Carey and the Linguistic Renaissance in India" and Christopher Arangaden, "Carey's Legacy of Bible Translation," in *Carey's Obligation and India's Renaissance*, J. T. K. Daniel and R. E. Hedlund, eds. (Serampore, West Bengal, Council of Serampore College, 1993), 154-175, 176-186.

And all of that derives from the event of Pentecost when Luke describes peoples from multitudes of nations hearing the Word of God in their mother tongues. Jerusalem was the crossroads of the continents of Africa, Europe, and Asia. All who were present heard the Gospel in the language of the heart. That was a miracle. However, the miracle of hearing the Gospel in the idiom of specific language groups begins with Jesus.

The Gospel of John asserts that Jesus is the Word in human form. This is incarnation. The Word is clothed in human culture and language. The Pentecost miracle of people hearing the Gospel in their own languages was an extension of the Word becoming human within Jewish culture. The missionary movement believes that if the Word was incarnate in Christ within Jewish Palestine nearly 2,000 years ago, then the Word should also become incarnate in every culture. Translating the Bible into vernaculars is one way that happens.

Is Mission a Converting or Proselytizing Movement?
However, the incarnational character of the Gospel goes further than only scripture translation. Incarnation is also relevant to another key question of faith and culture, namely, should the Christian missionary movement be a proselytizing movement, or a conversion movement. What is the difference? Proselytizing means that the new believer needs to move from his culture into the Christian or Christianized culture. Conversion means that believers remain in their cultures, but with Christ as the centre.[19]

Cultures are like an onion. The culture core is the worldview. The next layer is the value system. Then as we move outward from the culture core we come to the practice layer of culture, and finally the outer skin is the artifacts, the things that people make. One can study all cultures with this four-layered onion. When the early church was birthed at Pentecost, all the apostolic leaders were Jewish, just as was Jesus. Their worldview and all the other layers of their culture system were formed by the Torah and the other prophetic writings of their scriptures. They assumed that if Gentile non-Jews wished to believe in

---

[19] Paul Hiebert, "Conversion in Cross-Cultural Perspective," in *Conversion: Doorway to Discipleship*, ed. Henry Schmidt (Hillsboro, KS: Board of Christian Literature, 1980), 88-106.

Jesus as the Messiah, those believers would need to become proselytes, that is, moving from their Gentile culture into the Jewish culture, which was formed by the Jewish scriptures and the teachings of the rabbis.

However, very soon the church confronted an enormous challenge to that proselytizing view. The problem was that in Antioch in Syria large numbers of Gentiles were believing in Jesus and were receiving the anointing of the Holy Spirit. Their lives were transformed. But they remained Gentiles. Some of their Jewish brothers were horrified. The key issues were diet and circumcision. Gentile men detested circumcision and the Gentiles loved their diet, which was critiqued by the Jewish scriptures. From Antioch the church was quickly spreading into other Gentile regions as well, so the issues around proselytizing were rapidly spreading.

The tensions were building, so elders from the church in Antioch went to Jerusalem to meet with the apostles. This is called the Jerusalem Conference, and is described in some detail in Acts 15. At that meeting missionaries such as the Apostle Paul, who had preached the Gospel among the Gentiles, shared what was happening among the Gentiles. They were being converted, and their lives were being transformed through the new life in Christ. So the big question was whether these Gentile believers in Christ needed to not only believe in Christ, but also to move into Jewish culture. In other words, would the Christian movement become a proselytizing movement or a converting movement? To be a proselyte into Judaism meant accepting the whole cultural onion, including dress and diet patterns. To be a converting movement meant that Christ of the Scriptures would occupy the worldview centre, thereby transforming the culture from within, but not requiring one to leave ones culture.

The decision at the Jerusalem conference was momentous. The gathering decided that Jews would remain Jews and Gentiles would remain Gentiles. The only requirement for the Gentiles was to refrain from sexual sin, worshiping idols, eating meat offered to idols, and from drinking blood. Otherwise, the Gentile believers were completely free to continue living as Gentiles. The decision was so momentous that the conference sent a respected delegation with a letter to the Gentile churches to explain the decision. There was rejoicing among the Gentile believers when they were informed that they did not need to leave their culture in order to be believers in Jesus the Messiah.[20]

This decision set the course for the Apostolic church. Anabaptist Mennonites in their global missions commitments return again and again to the decision of the Jerusalem Conference as modern churches multiplying around the world seek to determine how they should relate to their native culture as believers in Jesus the Christ.

One of my joys serving the church globally is attending the occasional Acts 15 conferences in which I am invited to participate. These are gatherings where emerging churches seek to discern the ways that their commitment to Christ will transform their culture and ways that Christ affirms their culture. There are several questions from the Jerusalem Conference that are pertinent at such conferences: 1) What is the Holy Spirit doing in the lives of the new believers? In other words, what are the signs of the new life in Christ? 2) What are the principles from the Scriptures that apply to the issues? 3) How can the emerging churches relate to more established, traditional churches in ways that preserve the unity of the church? 4) What is the discernment of the community of believers as guided by the counsel of the Holy Spirit? 5) Then make a decision on what can be affirmed in the culture of the emerging church and what needs to be transformed or abandoned. I am amazed by how consistently a clear decision is possible when the church meets in the spirit of humility, seeking the counsel of the Holy Spirit and one another. I am also amazed by the rich cultural diversity of the global church, while celebrating the unity of faith.

Nevertheless, the discernment process about what it means to be faithful to Christ within particular cultural contexts is ongoing. For example, Mennonites are historically pacifist. In the last decade the United States has gotten into several ongoing wars. Patriotism and militarism is strong in United States culture at present. I was recently in a large Mennonite church, preaching on the peace of Jesus. Several young men in that church have volunteered to enter the military because they believe this is what they should do as patriotic citizens. There were also several older men attending the church who are in the military. How does an Anabaptist church address that kind of

---

[20] Acts 15.

challenge? Many are concerned that in time Anabaptist Mennonites will lose their commitment to pacifism if military personnel are members of Mennonite churches. We have a Confession of Faith, which is helpful in nourishing faith within our worldview centre. But our culture challenges that centre.

Culture and the Gospel

Recently my wife and I were back in my country of birth, Tanzania. We were immersed within the life of a newly forming diocese of Mennonite churches in the Dodoma area. At the front of each church we visited there was ample space for dancing. As the congregation began singing, dancers often moved into that space. With exuberance they sang with drums and a variety of instruments, enhancing the joy-filled times of worship. Some in the congregations came from churches my parents had founded. My father's church membership in the United States was Millersville Mennonite in Pennsylvania. We never danced with joy in that church! The cultural differences between the two kinds of worship and practice were enormous. However, amidst the enormous diversity, both communities were united in their love and commitment to Christ.

The Gospel is God's gift to culture and culture is humankind's gift to the Gospel. The Gospel is not understood unless it is clothed in culture. There are many ways that church does this. Song is only one way that a people offer culture as a gift to the Gospel. Another astonishing gift is the awareness of and name for the creator God. One of the surprising ways that a society offers a gift to the Gospel is in the local name for God.[21]

When my wife and I served in Somalia, there were two names used for God by the Somali people. One was Allah, introduced by the Muslims. The other name was Waq, which was a pre-Islamic name for the creator God. So when Christian missionaries translated the Bible in Somali, they generally used Waq, which was the traditional Somali name. This was significant for it communicated to the Somali people that the God revealed in the Bible is the same God whom the Somali ancestors worshipped. In the 3,000 languages that have portions of the

---

[21] Lamin Sanneh, *Whose Religion is Christianity? The Gospel Beyond the West* (Grand Rapids: Eerdmans, 2003), 18.

Bible, the translators, with very few exceptions, have found local pre-Christian names for God. This means that within every culture there are signs of truth before there is any awareness of biblical revelation. The church in mission builds upon those signs as it seeks to communicate the Gospel in local idioms. The name for God is a preeminent example of those signs pointing toward the Gospel.

In conclusion, one of the most remarkable aspects of the global church is that it is both a local and global movement. The name for God is a preeminent example of the local nature of the church. In the church the universal God is recognized as the one whose name is local. Christians believe that the church is united across vastly different cultures in the common commitment to the One and only true God whose eternal Word has become human in Jesus the Messiah.

PART IV:

HUMAN RIGHTS

In the Name of Allah, the Beneficent, the Merciful

ISLAM AND HUMAN RIGHTS: EQUALITY AND JUSTICE

ABOLFAZL SAJEDI

What is Islamic view of human rights? Does Islam support or negate them? In the case of support, what are those rights? Looking at the Qur'an and hadith shows that we can talk of Islamic human rights because according to this religion, everyone has various rights, including the rights of equality, justice, freedom of thought, belief, expression, contribution, and welfare.[1] This article concentrates on two basic rights, equality and justice. What is the Islamic position on these rights? Are they purely conventional rights or are they connected to human nature and creation? What is the religious basis of these rights? What does the Qur'an say in this regard? What is the position of the Prophet and Imams? This article is an attempt to answer these questions and clarify the roots of the rights of equality and justice in Islamic sources.

The Meaning of "Right"[2]

The word for "right" in Arabic and Persian, *haqq*, has various meanings in different disciplines. In philosophy, its meanings include external being, necessary being, and being in accordance with fact, reason, or truth. In morality, it means good, justified, or acceptable action. In

---

[1] See Muhammad Taqi Ja'fari, *Huquq al-Insan fi al-Islam wa al-Gharb* (Qom: Ayin Ahmad, 2007), 17-120.

[2] See Ibn Sina, *Illahiyyat min al-Shifa ma'a ta'liqat Sadr al-Muta'allihin* [The Theology of the Healing with the Comments of Mulla Sadra] (Qom: Bidar, n.d.), 306.

jurisprudence, it has meanings such as any issued rulings from divine sources. In law, it is used sometimes as a privilege that is given to someone for particular action. What is considered in the following discussion is its usage in human rights, which is a subcategory of law.[3] So *right* here is a privilege held by a human being simply by virtue of being a human being. Every human person can benefit from these rights because he or she is a human being.

The Principle of Brotherhood and Sisterhood

Brotherhood is rooted in the Islamic view of the human family. According to the Qur'an, all men and women are from one and the same family. The unity of the family is the main basis for brotherhood and sisterhood, because this is a regular relation between the members of a family. The principle of brotherhood should be respected in a family. Therefore, the Islamic view of the human family is a basis for brotherhood and brotherhood is a basis for equality and the omission of any discrimination. Referring to the unity of the family among human beings, God says:

> O mankind! Be wary of your Lord who created you from a single soul, and created its mate from it, and, from the two of them, scattered numerous men and women. (4:1)

In another verse, we read:

> O mankind! Indeed we created you from a male and a female, and made you nations and tribes that you may identify yourselves with one another. Indeed the noblest of you in the sight of Allah is the most God wary among you. Indeed Allah is all-knowing, all-aware. (49:13)

According to this verse, variation of people in tribes and nations is for the possibility of differentiation between them. If all people were in the

---

[3] See Sayyed Mahmud Nabaviyan, *Haqq va Chahar Porsesh-e Bonyadin* [*Right and Four Fundamental Questions*] (Qom: Mu'assesseh Amuzeshi va Pazhuheshi Imam Khomeini, 1388/2009), 30-36.

same shape and group, how would it be possible to be differentiated and made ordered societies and groups?

At Mina, near Mecca, a place where Muslims gather during the ceremonies of the *hajj* pilgrimage, the holy Prophet addressed the people and said:

> Oh people! Be aware that your God is one and your father is one, the father of all of you is Adam, and he was created from clay. Indeed, the noblest of you in the sight of Allah is the most Godwary among you. And there is no superiority of the Arabs over non-Arabs except by virtue. Then he said: "Did I convey the divine commandment to you?" All who were present there replied, "Yes." Then the prophet said, "Convey this message to those who are absent."[4]

As you can see, the Prophet in this saying, at the very special place for gathering various tribes, nations, skin colours, and economic and cultural classes, emphasizes the principle of brotherhood and sisterhood. He rejects any kind of criteria for discrimination except virtue. The Prophet here connects the removal of discrimination to a natural reason, which is the unity in the family. We are all family because of our common ancestry from Adam.

According to another saying of the Prophet Mohammed:

> All people are from God's family, so, the most loveable people for God are those who are more beneficial for the members of this family and make them happy.[5]

This narration considers symbolically all human beings as members of God's family. Since we have one creator, He is like a father for all of us. So, we are from one family. Based on this saying, not only should we theoretically support equality among all nations but this idea should be observed practically. To be beneficial to all people in practice is a way to achieve God's love.

---

[4] Muhammad Taqi Majlisi, *Bihar Al-Anwar* (Tehran: Dar al-Kutub Islami, 1362/1983), 73:348.

[5] Majlisi (1362/1983), 74:339.

To serve people all around the world, to look upon all of them as equals and to bring equality into society—these are recommended by human rights organizations on the basis of conventions and declarations; but they are also recommended on the basis of human nature in the teachings of the Qur'an. Which one is deeper and more effective? It seems that the latter teachings are more convincing and effective. When we base the principle of equality on a natural root and a belief system, it will become more stable.

God's General Blessings
Another religious basis of equality in the Qur'an is God's general blessings to all human beings. The word *al-Rahman* (the beneficent, and in some translations, the all-beneficent) is a divine attribute that a Muslim uses to describe God frequently every day. The verse "In the name of God, the Beneficent, the Merciful" is the first verse of the Qur'an. Most Muslims repeat this verse at least twenty times a day in their prayers. All the chapters of the Qur'an, except the chapter *Tawbah* (repentance), start with this verse. We can say that this verse is a main mirror in which we can see the Islamic picture of God. The first attribute that is used in this verse is *Rahman* (all-beneficent). This is a divine attribute that indicates God's general blessings to everyone, regardless of religion and nation.

We can also see God's general blessing to all human beings in other verses of the Qur'an, for example, in the following:

Indeed Allah is most kind and merciful to mankind. (2:143; 22:65)

Indeed Allah is gracious to mankind, but most people do not give thanks. (2:243)[6]

After we accept that God is all-beneficent, then this will be a religious basis for Muslims to be kind to everyone. They will be encouraged to follow this way. According to Islam the most important goal of moral perfection is to be close to God. This means that Muslims

---

[6] Also see 10:60; 27:73.

should try to achieve divine attributes as much as is humanly possible. Indeed, as a human being, no one can reach to His level of being; but one can assume some of His attributes at a much lower level. One of His attributes is all-beneficence. So by striving to make this attribute a personal virtue, everyone may strive in the way of moral perfection and approximation to God.

The next Islamic basis of equality is the Prophet's general guidance for everyone. He is not the messenger for a particular nation, tribe, or social class. He is God's blessing for all human beings. The Qur'an describes him as a "mercy to all the nations."

> We did not send you but as a mercy to all the nations. (21:107)

Justice in Islamic Human Rights

Since Islamic human rights emphasizes brotherhood and equality, Islam supports justice and recommends Muslims to expand it in society. Justice is a result of equality. If brotherhood is valuable, justice should be respected, established, and supported. Based on Islamic human rights, we should remove any kind of oppression, with which justice cannot be established. According to the Noble Qur'an, one important reason for sending prophets to people is to maintain justice among them:

> Certainly we sent our apostles with manifest proofs, and we sent down with them the Book and the Balance, so that mankind may maintain justice. (57:25)

Maybe this is a reason that in another verse, God, addressing his messenger, says:

> Say, "My Lord has enjoined justice." (7:29)

Not only prophets but also all faithful Muslims are commanded to maintain justice:

> O you who have faith! Be maintainers of justice. (4:135)

God is a just creator and He loves this quality among His creatures:

Do justice. Indeed Allah loves the just. (49:9)

Since the prophets demanded justice, they were under the pressure of racists, wealthy people, and unjust rulers.

Equality of Men and Women
As mentioned above, Islamic teachings in support of justice reject all kinds of discrimination based on skin colour, nations, tribes, etc. One type of discrimination that is rejected by Islam relates to gender. If justice is a value, we cannot discriminate between man and woman in their human value.

The story of the creation of Adam and Eve in the Qur'an is different from what is in the Bible. This may lead to two different understandings related to human rights.

According to the Bible, first Satan tempted Eve to eat prohibited fruit, and she ate it; then she gave it to her husband to eat.[7] Referring to Eve's fault, God says to her, "What is this that you have done?" The woman says, "The serpent beguiled me, and I did eat."[8] Addressing God, Adam says, "The woman whom you gave to be with me, she gave me of the tree, and I did eat."[9] Then God punished Eve because of eating the prohibited fruit and Adam for listening to his wife.[10] So first Satan tempted Eve, and then she tempted Adam.

One may conclude from this story that man and woman do not have the same human and moral value in their nature, because first Satan tempted Eve and then she started to mislead Adam.

The Qur'an narrates the story in a different way. Based on this book, Adam and Eve, both, were tempted by Satan.

> [Then God said to Adam,] "O Adam, dwell with your mate in paradise, and eat thereof whence you wish; but do not approach this tree, lest you should be among the wrongdoers." Then Satan

---

[7] See Gen. 3:6.
[8] Gen. 3:13.
[9] Gen. 3:12.
[10] Gen. 3:14-17.

tempted them, to expose to them what was hidden from them of their nakedness, and he said, "Your Lord has only forbidden you from this tree lest you should become angels, or lest you become immortal." And he swore to them, "I am indeed your well-wisher." Thus he brought about their fall by deception. So when they tasted of the tree, their nakedness became exposed to them, and they began to stitch over themselves with the leaves of paradise. Their Lord called out to them, "Did I not forbid you from that tree, and tell you, that Satan is indeed your manifest enemy?" They said, "Our Lord, we have wronged ourselves! If you do not forgive us and have mercy upon us, we will surely be among the losers." (7:19-23)

In verse 7:19, God commands both Adam and Eve to stay in paradise and eat everything that they wish except the fruit from the prohibited tree. In verses 7:20-21 that talk about Satan's temptation, all pronouns are dual which refer to both Adam and Eve. There are ten pronouns in these verses that remove any kind of discrimination between men and women regarding human values and the root of evil-doing. Based on these verses, it is a misconception that we consider Eve the root of Adam's fault. So, according to these verses, both are equal in this regard, both were cheated by Satan, and both made a mistake. Therefore, we cannot consider woman as the first guilty person and the root of man's fault. Again, in verses 7:22-23, twenty pronouns are used to express their equality in this event. These verses provide a good religious basis for equality between men and women regarding their values in their nature.

No Bearer Shall Bear Another's Burden

According to the Qur'an's view of equality and justice, no one can be punished because of another's faults. Everyone's mistake is on his or her own shoulders. It is a kind of injustice to put one's sins on others' shoulders.

No soul does evil except against itself, and no bearer shall bear another's burden. (6:164)

One who goes astray, does so only to one's own detriment. No bearer shall bear another's burden. (17:15)[11]

This point is also different in the Qur'an and the Bible. Based on the story of Adam and Eve in the Bible, God punishes Eve and all other women for her fault. After her mistake, God says to her:

I will greatly multiply your sorrow and your conception; in sorrow you shall bring forth children; and your desire shall be for your husband, and he shall rule over you. (Gen. 3:16)

So the reason for women's great pains in childbirth and then being ruled by men is Eve's first fault. God also punishes Adam and all his offspring for his fault. God says to him:

Because you have heard the voice of your wife and have eaten of the tree, of which I commanded you, saying, "you shall not eat of it," cursed is the ground for your sake; in sorrow shall you eat of it all the days of your life; thorns also and thistles shall it bring forth to you; and you shall eat the herb of the field; in the sweat of your face shall you eat bread, till you return to the ground. (Gen. 3:17-19)

The story of the creation of Adam and Eve in the Qur'an does not include any verses that indicate that their offspring will suffer for the mistakes of the first parents. Moreover, as mentioned, there are verses that negate such an idea.

Conclusion

From an Islamic perspective, the right of equality is based on the principle of brotherhood and sisterhood, which are rooted in the nature of human beings and their family relations. According to the Qur'an, all human beings are from the same parents; and there is even a tradition that considers symbolically all human beings from God's family. The prophet Muhammad also emphasizes the unity of the human family.

---

[11] Three other verses also emphasize this point: 35:18, 39:7, and 53:38.

Another religious basis of equality in the Qur'an and Islamic tradition are God's general blessings and the Prophet's general guidance and grace to all human beings.

Islam emphasizes brotherhood and equality, and supports justice and the removal of any kind of oppression and unfair discrimination. One result of the right to equality and justice is to accept the equal value of man and woman and to reject any discrimination between them in this regard.

The story of the creation of Adam and Eve in the Qur'an and the Bible relates to two issues of human rights: (1) Equality or difference between man and woman in their human values; and (2) The role of the first mistake of Adam and Eve in the suffering of their descendants. The story of the creation of the first parents in the Qur'an is different from that of the Bible. This difference could lead to two understandings related to human rights.

Who Is My Neighbour? Human Rights and Acknowledgement

Peter Dula

A theological assessment of human rights language with a focus on the scriptures is challenging. The Bible rarely, if ever, mentions "rights." It is not like "sin and grace" or "the way of perfection" or many other topics about which there is ample material in both Christian and Muslim scriptures. Nor is it like assessing some other modes of philosophical discourse. If the topic were, for example, utilitarianism, deontology, or virtue ethics, I could find particular passages and writers who seem to deploy analogous modes of reasoning. But the topic of human rights is absent from both the Old and New Testaments. Moreover, it is not a neutral topic like "human nature" or "male and female," but is purported, at least by some, to be a secular concept. So it seems that the task at hand is to use one discourse, that of the Bible, to assess the other, human rights, and declare if they are compatible, mutually exclusive, mutually reinforcing, or even the same thing, just in different words. The problem with that is that the Christian scriptures are not one discourse. The Bible is a plurality of voices, some of them in tension and many of them using different idioms. I mention all this as a way of explaining why much of what is to follow is methodological. I will explore how, or more often how not, to read scripture, as much as I will actually read scripture. But let me begin with a story.

One evening in the fall of 2005 I was at a dinner party in Amman, Jordan at the home of some French aid workers. One of their Iraqi colleagues had been released from a Baghdad prison the day before and came immediately to Amman. They were throwing a party for him on the roof of their flat. When I arrived I took a seat in the empty space beside him. He started talking and didn't stop for an hour. He was arrested at 2 am by Iraqi security forces and taken to one of Saddam Hussein's old palaces that was being used as a prison. For twelve days he was in a large, crowded hall with a couple hundred others. (This was in Baghdad in the summer where temperatures reach 120 degrees Fahrenheit.) He never found out why he was there and never found out why he was released. He said there were drunks, mentally ill persons, and even teenagers among the prisoners. He said they beat the prisoners with cables and tortured them with electric shocks. He said he watched two of them die after they returned to the holding room. They staged photographs of them in front of piles of munitions. They taped forced confessions that they would air on TV. He got off because a friend on the outside was able to arrange a bribe ($1500 US).

A couple of the others joined the conversation. Some of the guests had just sponsored a conference gathering women's associations from Iraq, Palestine, and Lebanon for a discussion of women's rights. One of the Iraqi men there works for a child-protection group and so they started joking about all the talk about women's rights and children's rights. "What about men's rights?" they said. "When are you going to sponsor a conference on the rights of men?" Later my friend talked about a fellow prisoner who said if he ever got out he was going to live in a tent in the desert. But, they told him, they will find you even there. So my friend told the story of a shepherd who was in prison with him, taken from his flocks in the middle of the day, and who kept worrying about what had happened to his sheep and goats. The man from the child-protection agency asked, "Yeah, what about animal rights? We need a conference on that, too."

All these people work energetically for human rights in Iraq. That rights can become the butts of their jokes does not mean they will stop working for them. But what does it mean? Before that night on the roof, the last time I had seen my friend was over dinner the previous spring. I arrived at the restaurant late because I had been trying to finish up a paper on democracy in the work of John Howard Yoder, Stanley Hauerwas, Sheldon Wolin, and Jeffrey Stout.[1] He quizzed me about the

---

[1] Peter Dula and J. Alexander Sider, "Radical Democracy, Radical Ecclesiology," *Crosscurrents* (Winter 2006).

paper with genuine interest and only mild skepticism. That night at the party, the day after he got out of prison, the skepticism had intensified. "Quit writing about democracy,' he said bitterly. "Start writing about human rights. There is no hope for democracy, but maybe we can get some rights protected."

His statement knocked me off balance. I wasn't at all surprised by his bitterness. Nor was I surprised by his loss of hope in the prospects for a democratic Iraq. But I was not prepared for such a clear and straightforward severing of democracy and human rights.[2]

It turns out I should have been. There is a passage in Archbishop Rowan Williams' *Lost Icons* which I had underlined long before I ever met my Iraqi friend. There Williams says that the grievances addressed by rights are understood as "moral property." But, he argues,

> The loss in question is not moral property but moral *presence* as enacted in a true conversational relation. But if we are starting from this point, what "makes good" loss or injury will not be simply the enforcement of a claim and the restoration of property, but the creation of some possibility of speaking together.[3]

For Williams there is a contrast between turns to human rights and "some possibility of speaking together." That is, he contrasts it with the central component of democracy. Like my Iraqi friend, he suggests that rights discourse has become an alternative to democratic conversation. My Iraqi friend said to me, "I have lost any hope that we can sit down together as one people and deliberate honestly about the good. The best we can hope for is a minimalist framework of human rights to protect us against the arbitrary power of whatever form the new Iraqi tyranny is going to take."

---

[2] If I understood him correctly, he was expressing both skepticism about the emergence of a viable democratic state in Iraq and a well-founded worry that even if some kind of representative government did emerge, it would be characterized by Shi'a majoritarianism.

[3] *Lost Icons* (Edinburgh: T&T Clark, 2000), 114. (Emphasis in source.)

In this paper I want to push off from that into a conversation with Nicholas Wolterstorff's recent and highly regarded book *Justice: Rights and Wrongs*.[4] Wolterstorff seems like an appropriate interlocutor because he is arguably the most important and influential Protestant philosopher in North America. I will be somewhat ambivalent about rights discourse and critical of Wolterstorff's book, but since any criticism of rights these days is dangerous territory, I want to be clear about what I am not doing. In my ambivalence about rights discourse, I do not mean that I am against protecting the things that rights protect. Nor do I mean that such language should be stricken from our vocabulary. Instead I am worried about its *place* in our vocabulary, how it relates to other ways of talking about justice, and what it means for rights to become foundational or to take over the language of justice, to become, as it does for Wolterstorff, the *only* way to conceive of, and even talk about, justice.

Two Conceptions of Justice

Wolterstorff sets out to demonstrate that justice is constituted by inherent rights,[5] that a just society is one in which members enjoy the goods to which they have a right, and to ground those rights in a Christian theology. But as he set out to accomplish that task, he realized that he had to first contend with an opposing conception of justice— justice not as inherent rights but as right order. The first part of the book is devoted to sketching a historical counter-narrative to the right order narrative, a counter-narrative that goes all the way back to the Old Testament.

Right order theorists like Alasdair MacIntyre, C. B. Macpherson, Oliver and Joan O'Donovan, and Stanley Hauerwas argue that rights discourse is necessarily tangled up with possessive individualism. That is, older right order societies had an overarching vision of the common good. Conversations about justice and the conferral of rights were

---

[4] Nicholas Wolterstorff's, *Justice: Rights and Wrongs* (Princeton, NJ: Princeton University Press, 2008).

[5] Understood as "normative social bonds," such that others have a claim against me to certain goods, claims that trump all other interests, on the basis of their humanity alone.

conceptually dependent upon that notion of good. It wasn't that there were no rights, but that, for right order polities, rights were "an enhancement which accrues to the subject *from* an ordered and politically formed society."[6] With the emergence of modernity, however, the very possibility of a common good evaporates. Instead we tend to think in terms of autonomous individuals, each with their own competing accounts of the good. The common good cannot help but appear as an imposition of arbitrary power. In such societies individuals will be constantly under threat from other individuals and hence will need protection. The language for that protection is rights. "What is distinctive about the modern conception of rights, however, is that subjective rights are taken to be original, not derived. The fundamental reality is a plurality of competing, unreconciled rights, and the task of law is to harmonise them."[7] Moreover, those rights will adhere to them simply as human beings *qua* human beings which suggests to right order theorists the ability to isolate a "human as such," before or beneath any accidents of culture or history. But if that is impossible, if the human is historical all the way down and if nature and culture cannot be pried apart, then there can be no "human rights," only rights that are socially conferred in particular communities. This critique of rights discourse is grounded in a historical narrative which locates the emergence of rights alongside the emergence of individualism either in fourteenth-century nominalism or the Enlightenment. One way to summarize this would be to say that with the emergence of modernity we move from an anthropology which is basically cooperative to one that is competitive.[8]

Now Wolterstorff thinks that very little of this is true and that none of it is necessarily true. First, he argues that while it is true that rights language is often used in service of individualism, it needn't be so and

---

[6] "Oliver O'Donovan, *The Desire of Nations* (Cambridge: Cambridge University Press, 1996), 248 (emphasis mine).

[7] Ibid., 248.

[8] See Benjamin Nelson, *The Idea of Usury: From Tribal Brotherhood to Universal Otherhood*, 2nd ed. (Chicago: University of Chicago Press, 1969) and Lewis Hyde, *The Gift* (New York: Vintage, 1983). Both texts narrate this as a struggle between Luther and the Anabaptists.

rights discourse is too powerful and important to abandon just because it is occasionally misused. Second, following Brian Tierney and Charles Reid, he argues persuasively that, first, there is clear evidence of subjective rights language in twelfth-century canon law long before Ockham.[9] But he is not content to rest in the twelfth century. And so chapter three "continue[s] the counter-narrative by showing that inherent natural rights were assumed and recognized by the writers of the Hebrew and Christian scriptures."[10]

Hearing the Voices of Scripture
A central question for Wolterstorff is "How do we adequately listen to the voices of the wronged?" The first paragraph of *Justice: Rights and Wrongs* says,

> It was injustice that impelled me to think about justice, not the imperatives of some theoretical scheme or the duties of some academic position. Injustice in the form of the wronged, which is the form injustice always takes. The victims confronted me; I was not looking for them. I should have noticed them much earlier. The wronged are all around us.[11]

He then goes on to describe his experiences in the 1970s at conferences with South Africans and Palestinians where "the victims confronted me." *Justice: Rights and Wrongs* is an attempt to speak up for the wronged. More precisely, it is meant to "undermine those frameworks of conviction that prevent us from acknowledging that the other comes before us bearing a claim on us, and of offering an

---

[9] Wolterstorff, *Justice*, 53-55.

[10] Ibid., 65. It is worth noting that this is a very different task than the one Tierney and Reid take up with regard to rights in the twelfth and thirteenth centuries. Reid makes a detailed argument that what the Decretalists meant by *ius* is quite similar to what Wesley Hohfeld, one of the most important twentieth-century theorists of rights, meant by right. Wolterstorff is trying to do the same thing for the Bible and for the church fathers but with no equivalent usage.

[11] Ibid., vii.

alternative framework, one that opens us up to such acknowledgment."[12] That, it seems to me, is wonderfully phrased. The other does bear a claim on us and we are disturbingly adept at inventing ways to refuse to acknowledge that claim. But are rights actually the best framework for acknowledging such claims?[13] I want to approach that question through another question: Is the translation of the Bible (or of the church fathers) with its own specific languages of justice, into the language of rights, really an acknowledgement of the biblical authors' claim on us? Might it be an avoidance of that claim?

The obvious problem for Wolterstorff's attempt to find inherent rights in the Bible is that the Bible never uses that language.[14] But that doesn't seem to slow down Wolterstorff as much as it might slow down other thinkers. Robert Cover, for example, in an influential essay from a Jewish perspective, wrote that the central term in Jewish jurisprudence is *mitzvah*, commandment or obligation, and that that means something very different than "right" and is embedded in a very different narrative than rights. Rights are about autonomy while obligation is about heteronomy. Rights are about individuals while obligation is corporate.[15] But Wolterstorff dismisses Cover in a short sentence or two and moves on to his own reading of the Old Testament. He explains the lack of rights language this way: "These writers speak a great deal about what is just and unjust; every now and then they step

---

[12] Ibid., ix.

[13] That is, I am not arguing that there are no such things as inherent natural rights or that to believe such things is like believing in witches and unicorns (MacIntyre's language) or that they presuppose an agonistic, nominalist ontology. (Part of this is about just what it means to acknowledge a claim. One worry I have is that Wolterstorff sees claims as self-evident. The claims of the wronged come fully formed and demand to be righted. But most often what the claim *is* forms part of the content of the argument. The difficulty of moral argument is not just that we need to know how to respond to a particular action, we also need to discern just what the particular action was. Are rights a way of labeling actions in advance of that argument?)

[14] Actually, it depends upon the translation. The NRSV does occasionally use rights, but older translations do not.

[15] "Obligation: A Jewish Jurisprudence of the Social Order," *Journal of Law and Religion* 5/1 (1987): 65-74.

back a bit to speak about the role of justice in God's life and ours. What they do not do is step up to the meta-level and talk about how to think about justice. They do not articulate a conception of justice. We ourselves have to extract the underlying pattern of their thought from their testimony." [16] The underlying pattern Wolterstorff discovers is a "deep structure" of inherent rights.

There would be a number of questions to pursue with regard to Wolterstorff's strategy here. That one can take the claims made in those writings and find the language of rights "under" them seems entirely plausible. But why do it? That is, I am not wondering if it is possible or if that "deep structure" is really there. I am wondering if it is advisable. Assuming there is such an "underlying pattern," and that it is extractable (without sorting through "the bewildering mishmash of regulations"[17] of the rest of Old Testament Law) and that the extraction is advisable, it still seems strange to not first ask the obvious question, "If the 'surface' was good enough for them, why isn't it good enough for us? If in their own struggle for justice, the prophets, for example, did not feel the need for recourse to 'the meta-level,' why would we?"

I am not sure that Wolterstorff ever answers that question. He does have a section in his introduction arguing "Why We Need Rights Talk." There he claims that without rights talk we would lose "our ability to bring to speech one of the two fundamental dimensions of the moral order: the recipient dimension, the patient dimension."[18] But that answers a different question. Clearly he thinks that the Old Testament brings to speech the recipient dimension. He might also be read as suggesting that only rights discourse provides the kind of framework that "opens us up to acknowledgement." But that too isn't clear. Regarding his experiences with South Africans and Palestinians, he writes, "Their faces and their voices evoked my empathy. I now think it is above all empathy that energizes the struggle against injustice."[19] It is

---

[16] Wolterstorff, Justice, 67.

[17] Ibid., 83.

[18] Ibid., 7.

[19] Not so much in *Justice: Rights and Wrongs* but in "Why Social Justice Got to Me and Why It Never Left," *Journal of the American Academy of Religions* 76/3 (2008): 666.

the testimony of the victims, the cries of the Psalmist, the rage and sorrow of the prophets that provoke empathy, not theories of rights.

Why not instead investigate the differences in language to see what those differences tell us? Why not use the rich languages of the ancient world to enrich and enhance our understanding of justice rather than investigate them in order to show that they are, after all, saying the same thing, just in different words?[20] Why not end those chapters with the question, "Even if all I have said is true, why didn't they use that language?" Or "What does this language add now that we have it?"[21]

This isn't an argument about the validity of rights discourse; it is an argument about reading. (A Wolterstorffian way of saying it would be that it violates the Old Testament's rights to read it as about rights while ignoring the various questions I am raising.) That is, such reading practices become one of "those frameworks of conviction that prevent us from acknowledging that the other comes before us bearing a claim on us." Surely one of the most basic claims with which another confronts us is with the claim to be heard, in her own voice, on her own terms.

A compelling example of the kind of reading practice which truly does manage acknowledgment is Cora Diamond and Stephen Mulhall's

---

[20] Part III of Wolterstorff's book begins with "We now leave narrative behind and attend exclusively to theory," suggesting that the purpose of the narrative was merely counter-narrative. That is, it was necessary in order to show that the right order folks are wrong, not necessary in order to develop an account of justice.

[21] The method strikes me as analogous with "anonymous Christians" arguments. "Anonymous Christians" was Karl Rahner's term to describe those of other faiths who, though they may never have heard of Christianity, let alone accepted it, might, because of their exemplary lives, still find salvation in Christ. It was an influential attempt to skirt the Scylla of pluralism and the Charybdis of exclusivism. Yet it remains patronizing just insofar as the goodness of those others has to be framed in Christian terms.

Perhaps more pressing given Wolterstorff's own claim to be an advocate for international human rights, what about other religions? We know how this universal Christian doctrine of human rights interacts with secularism, but how about with Islam, Buddhism, Hinduism? Must we also locate a "deep structure" in the Qur'an and in the various texts and testimonies of Buddhism and Hinduism? If we can't, do rights now become part of the missionary task?

reading of J. M. Coetzee's *The Lives of Animals*. In 1997, Coetzee, the Nobel prize-winning South African novelist, gave the Tanner Lectures at Princeton. But Coetzee did not give conventional philosophical lectures. Instead he presented two short stories about an elderly Australian novelist named Elizabeth Costello invited to deliver the Gates Lectures at the fictional Appleton College.[22] Her lectures, transcriptions of which make up part of the stories, are emotional, convoluted, disturbing pleas for justice for animals, full of examples of the horror of what we do to animals every day in our laboratories and factory farms, as well as references to literature and philosophy.

Coetzee's lectures were then published along with several responses from philosophers and others as *The Lives of Animals*. Diamond, in "The Difficulty of Reality," and Mulhall, in *The Wounded Animal*, read Coetzee's interlocutors as captured by "frameworks of conviction" (one called "philosophy") that prevent them from acknowledging Costello's claim on them. Those interlocutors take her to be presenting (poorly) a series of conventional philosophical arguments in fictional dress. Moreover, they are arguments about wounded animals, not a presentation of herself as a wounded animal. Instead of engaging the wounded animal before them in all the specificity of her idiosyncratic language, they choose to extract an underlying pattern that they can then debate in conventional philosophical terms.[23] Only one of them has a specific interest in extracting rights (Peter Singer), so the point

---

[22] Mulhall astutely observes, "Since the Tanner Lectures generally take the form of philosophical essays or addresses, and an invitation to give them is seen as a mark of real distinction in the philosophical world, it is hard to see Coetzee's way of responding to that invitation as anything other than a deliberate attempt to reopen an issue that has marked—indeed, defined—philosophy from its inception among the ancient Greeks: the quarrel between philosophy and poetry." *The Wounded Animal* (Princeton, NJ: Princeton University Press, 2009), 1. I can't help but think that this ancient antagonism is partly at work in Wolterstorff's project of philosophical "extraction" from Hebrew literature.

[23] "The Difficulty of Reality and the Difficulty of Philosophy," in *Philosophy and Animal Life*, ed. Cary Wolfe (New York: Columbia University Press, 2008).

again is about the process of extraction and how that is what Williams called the "failure of some possibility of speaking together," of *listening* to these texts.

Human Rights and the Good Samaritan

It would be unfair to simply criticize Wolterstorff without presenting an alternative. But in order to provide a compelling alternative to Wolterstorff, I would have to be able to a make a more compelling reading of scripture on justice than Wolterstorff did, one that cultivates scripture's strangeness, not flattens it. I am not sure I can do that, and I won't even attempt to give an account of the Bible as a whole. I will simply try to read one brief story against the background of human rights.

Luke 10:25-37

Just then a lawyer stood up to test Jesus. "Teacher," he said, "what must I do to inherit eternal life?" He said to him, "What is written in the law? What do you read there?" He answered, "You shall love the Lord your God with all your heart, and with all your soul, and with all your strength, and with all your mind; and your neighbour as yourself." And he said to him, "You have given the right answer; do this, and you will live." But wanting to justify himself, he asked Jesus, "And who is my neighbour?" Jesus replied, "A man was going down from Jerusalem to Jericho, and fell into the hands of robbers, who stripped him, beat him, and went away, leaving him half dead. Now by chance a priest was going down that road; and when he saw him, he passed by on the other side. So likewise a Levite, when he came to the place and saw him, passed by on the other side. But a Samaritan while travelling came near him; and when he saw him, he was moved with pity. He went to him and bandaged his wounds, having poured oil and wine on them. Then he put him on his own animal, brought him to an inn, and took care of him. The next day he took out two denarii, gave them to the innkeeper, and said, "Take care of him; and when I come back, I will repay you whatever more you spend. Which of these three, do you think, was a neighbour to the man who fell into the hands of the robbers?" He said, "The one who showed him mercy." Jesus said to him, "Go and do likewise."

What do we discover in this text when we read it alongside human-rights discourse? Let me note just a couple things. First, the lawyer answers correctly, straight out of Deuteronomy: "Love the Lord your God . . . and love your neighbour as yourself." The story ought to end here. But the lawyer "seeking to justify himself" wants to continue (presumably to justify his failure to love his neighbour) and so asks, "Who is my neighbour?", a question which prompts Jesus to tell the story of the Good Samaritan. But, as you may have noticed, the Samaritan story doesn't answer the lawyer's question. The lawyer's question is, "Granted that my neighbour has a claim on me, how am I supposed to know just who among all the many people out there, counts as *my* neighbour? (Or is it "my *neighbour*"?) So one expects the moral of the story to be, "The man in the ditch is your neighbor. Go and love him as yourself." But instead the neighbor is identified as the Samaritan and the moral is, "Go and be like him."

One way to read this is that by shifting the terms of the conversation, Jesus makes it about obligation, not rights. The lawyer's question is a rights question: "Just who is it that holds rights against me? Point them out, and explain the basis on which they hold those rights, so I can know to whom I am responsible." But Jesus doesn't answer the question on those terms. If he had, the man in the ditch would have been identified as the neighbour. Instead, Jesus makes it a story about *mitzvah*, obligation. Moreover, the Samaritan's actions go far beyond any "right" the man may have against him. Even if the man does have a right to be helped, not just a right to not be molested on the road, the Samaritan's actions are described as extravagant.

But is it that simple? The second thing I want to highlight in this story concerns the man who was robbed.[24] Who is he? It strikes me as terribly significant that we don't know. One of the most important features of this story is that everyone else in the story has an identity: a

---

[24] I am grateful to Jack Marmorstein and his contribution to a Scriptural Reasoning session on this passage for provoking much of what follows.

lawyer, a Teacher, robbers, a priest, a Levite, a Samaritan, an innkeeper. We can place every character but one not just in a history and a culture, but in precise roles in that culture. That makes it all the more striking that the victim is simply "a man," stripped, beaten, half-dead. This is "the human-as-such," presented now not as a philosophical abstraction but as the suffering victim, the one identity we all fear most. Moreover, this is the one that is the topic of Hannah Arendt's well-known discussion of human rights. In *The Origins of Totalitarianism*, she famously pointed out the paradox that human rights, those rights that adhere to individuals purely by virtue of their humanity, are simply not protected as soon as they become merely human. In theory they are great; in practice they must be accompanied by citizenship.[25] This was brutally demonstrated by the Nazis who first took away the citizenship of the Jews. All eighteenth-century revolutionaries knew this. They may have said "The Rights of Man" but like later anti-colonialists, national self-determination was the first right. So we get the bitter irony that human-rights discourse emerges just when the numbers of those who would be happiest with civil rights—the Jews of pre-war Europe, the Palestinians in the camps in Lebanon, and many, many others—are increasing.

In that light, this reads to me like a humanitarian's story. Who takes on the task of showing mercy to all those who have lost their identity, deprived of home and nation, if not the kind of people who were in the story I began with, the representatives of agencies such as the Red Cross, Doctors Without Borders, Oxfam, even, I suppose, MCC? Who has told their story better than Human Rights Watch or Amnesty International? The task is to neighbour these people, to make them our neighbours.

But is it because they have rights? I am not against saying it that way if it is useful. But I am against saying it that way if it obscures reasons

---

[25] "Not the loss of specific rights, then, but the loss of a community willing and able to guarantee any rights whatsoever, has been the calamity which has befallen ever-increasing numbers of people. Man, it turns out, can lose all the so-called Rights of Man without losing his essential quality as man, his human dignity. Only the loss of a polity itself expels him from humanity." Hannah Arendt, *The Origins of Totalitarianism* (New York: Schocken Books, 1958), 297.

closer to the text. There is one final thing about this story, the most important thing. It is only secondarily about rights and Samaritans. First and foremost, it is about Jesus. Like in so many parables, Jesus is telling us about himself. He is the man in the ditch. In John's Gospel, at Jesus' trial, after he is whipped and crowned with thorns, Pilate brings him out and says, "Behold the man!" He has become humanity reduced to its naked, shivering nature. "Go and do likewise" because that is Jesus. Because whatever you have done to the least of these you have done to me.[26]

But it is also "Go and do likewise" because that is what I have done for you. The story is doubly autobiographical for Jesus is also the Good Samaritan, the one who loves us even though we despise and persecute him; the one who tends and bandages our wounds and spares no expense to save us. So it was misleading for me to suggest that Jesus doesn't answer the lawyer's question. He does. He says, I am your neighbour. I am the one who has neighboured you. And, of course, that transforms the man in the ditch from Hannah Arendt's stateless person into each one of us, neighbours who have fallen among thieves, unable to continue down the road. "Go and do likewise," when the neighbour is standing right in front of you telling you a story, means "follow me."

So where does that leave me with regard to rights language? I hope it is clear that I am not trying to rule out all use of rights language. I am trying to place it in the critical light of Wolterstorff's laudable wish to enable the acknowledgment of the claims of the victims. I think that sometimes rights discourse becomes a way of avoiding, not acknowledging, the other. The lawyer in Luke 10, like the philosophers in *The Lives of Animals,* seems like an example. Yet I also think it is highly plausible to read the story of the Samaritan as a humanitarian story. I can see no reason to argue that human-rights discourse is *always* a mode of avoiding the claim of the other, or always a mode of obscuring other, more primary, meanings of the text. What particular discourse, in what particular place, will best acknowledge the claims of the other upon me, or will best shed light on scripture, cannot be decided in advance.[27]

---

[26] See Matt. 25.

[27] Something like that is how John Howard Yoder taught us to do ethics. He was once asked to make the case for "Biblicism" in contrast to other

Reviewing Wolterstorff's book, Stanley Hauerwas concluded,

> What we need is not a theory of justice capable of universal application. Rather what we need is what we have. What we have is a people learning again to live in diaspora. And we are reminded that Israel's political vocation took the form of a politics of diaspora through which she becomes a blessing to all people. Such a political vocation has been given to the church insofar as she has been joined to Israel's Messiah, requiring her to be on pilgrimage to the ends of the world seeking reconciliation through the works of mercy. Such is the justice of God.[28]

My Iraqi friend urged me to quit writing about democracy and start writing about human rights. I have finally attempted to do what he told me, but I have only succeeded in betraying my own desire to keep writing about democracy. That is, I read Hauerwas to say here that the church is supposed to be the place where we don't need to give up hope on the possibility of deliberating together about the good; not just how to implement a good known prior to the deliberation, but about the good itself. And so while we support and appreciate minimalist frameworks of the good such as provided in accounts of human rights, we hold out for a maximalist account of the good embodied in Jesus Christ, the justice of God.

---

methodological options. He responded, "There is no such thing as 'biblicism'.... Skepticism about methodological reductionism and respect for the 'thick' reading of any real history, in which the Bible belongs, go naturally hand in hand. The Bible is itself, in its role as the common memory of the God movement, full of a multiplicity of styles of praising and blaming. It is the prototypical narrative ... of how a value-bound community exercises all kinds of moral discourse, missing and matching its modes rather than being concerned to please the philosopher for whom one idiom must be shown to be more acceptable than another." "Walk and Word: Alternatives to Methodologism," in *Theology Without Foundations*, Stanley Hauerwas, Nancy Murphy, Mark Nation, eds. (Nashville, TN: Abingdon, 1994), 87-88.

[28] Stanley Hauerwas, "Inherent Rights, Disability and the Justice of God," *Religion and Ethics*, (30 May 2011).

PART V:

GENDER

In the Name of Allah, the Beneficent, the Merciful

ISLAMIC WOMANOLOGY: TOWARD THE DEVELOPMENT OF ENGENDERED ISLAMIC CULTURE AND VALUES

ABBAS ALI SHAMELI

If anthropology is the study of man, meaning the study of human beings without regard to gender, there should be a subfield of anthropology for the study of woman. We may call this "womanology." An Islamic womanology will base itself on a theological perspective that draws on the Qur'an; but must also take into account modern discussions of culture and values. The development of a theory in womanology may begin with attempts to discover the main commonalities and differences between men and women in nature, capacities, potentialities, and opportunities for effective action. Differences between men and women appear at the level of cultural development and social change. The context of my study has been the society of the Islamic Republic of Iran. I have attempted to collect proper information about the nature of cultural development and social change in an Islamic society, the Islamic view of women, the ideal woman in an Islamic society, the impact of women's roles on the stability of the family, and the Islamic womanology according to the logic of nature. In this way, I have linked my theological discussion to a socio-cultural one and ultimately I have highlighted the vital role of education in this connection.

Women, Education, Cultural Development, and Social Change

Inspired by the central message of the 1995 Human Development Report,[1] which explicitly states that "Human development, if not engendered, is endangered," I assume that no discussion of the Islamic model of culture and values development can be undertaken in ignorance of gender issues. Despite his insistence on the necessity of rethinking women's issues in Islam and despite his vital impact in educating his sister Bint al-Huda as a Muslim woman thinker, Allamah Shahid Sayyid Muhammad Baqir Sadr never really had a chance to deal with the gender issue in his theory about culture and values development.[2] Relying on my own understanding of Sadr's model and considering the practical challenges of post-revolutionary Iran, I have elaborated on cultural development and gender in this paper from an Islamic point of view. Both theoretical and practical dimensions of an engendered Islamic model of cultural development are considered.

In what follows, a general portrayal of the Islamic view of women is provided; and then this view is considered in the context of post-revolutionary Iran.

Most of the scholars who have written about women in Iran during the post revolutionary era believe that not only the female education system but the educational system by and large aims at educating citizens with an explicit emphasis on Islamic values.[3] This, they argue, will compromise the possibility of developing highly skilled human resources. Other writers like Erika Friedl call the Iranian Islamic context a situation which exerts "extraordinary ideological pressure" on women.[4] I argue that the emphasis on Islamic values is characteristic of

---

[1] United Nations Development Programme [UNDP], The State of Human Development in *Gender and Human Development: Human Development Report 1995* (Oxford: Oxford University Press, 1995), 11-28.

[2] Muhammad Baqir al-Sadr, *Al-Islam Yaqud al-Hayat* [*Islam Guides the Human Life*] (Tehran: Vizarat al-Irshad al-Islami/The Ministry of Islamic Guidance, 1982), 203.

[3] See P. J. Higgins and P. Shoar-Ghaffari, "Women's Education in the Islamic Republic of Iran," in ed. M. Afkhami and E. Friedl, *In the Eye of the Storm: Women in Post-Revolutionary Iran* (Syracuse: Syracuse University Press, 1994), 19-43, 20.

[4] V. Moghadam, "Women, Work, and Ideology in the Islamic Republic," *International Journal of Middle East Studies* vol. 20 (1988): 221-243, 223.

an Islamic educational model. The reason behind it is to make the system Islamic-value-laden and protect those educated in this fashion from secularizing consequences. Another reason for this commitment is to create a feeling of independence and self-sufficiency in students. However, this does not mean that needed skills and expertise are compromised by a commitment to Islamic values. It is vital to build an educational system that encourages both knowledge and commitment. The secular system of education in Iran, like that in other colonized countries, was the legacy of Western colonization. It is reasonable to attempt to implement an Islamic model as another alternative.

Western ideas about education entered Iran during the nineteenth century along with the colonial movements of the time. The Western cultural invasion encompassed a combination of positive and negative values. This mixture created pessimistic and optimistic reactions. The exploitation that accompanied these invasions prevented colonized populations from trusting even positive modern values like equality, freedom, human rights, development, and social change.[5] This schizophrenic and opaque environment persuaded Shi'i scholars to oppose the modernizing efforts put forward by their own Western-oriented national governments. Women, like other segments of the population, had particular difficulty in keeping up with the modernizing process since it aimed at introducing a stereotyped Western model which was also anti-Islamic. The available Islamic model, however, could not be implemented since power was in the hands of those who were pro-West. The situation of women needed improvement in the sphere of Islamic values and sex education, in socio-political participation, in family welfare, and in other aspects. Steps towards improvement would have to have been inclusive but Islamically value-laden, yet little immediate consideration was given to these matters.

In the political domain, Iranian women won the right to vote in 1963 as an element of the Shah's White Revolution.[6] To what extent this right was translated into practice is a matter of debate. Certainly it was no more effective than similar rights granted after the Islamic Revolution. Women from higher levels of the society and the elite could

---

[5] Higgins and Shoar-Ghaffari, 9.
[6] Ibid., 11.

exercise their rights. Women from middle and lower-middle class urban backgrounds and those from rural areas could not. These rights were furthermore accompanied by other anti-Islamic values, which created a negative attitude towards the whole package of reforms offered by the White Revolution. Not only women, but the entire population remained suppressed because of the tension between pre-revolutionary development plans and Islamic ideals. Iran, as a Muslim country, had experienced Islam for centuries. Shi'i scholars, as the protectors of Islam, had played a vital role in mobilization of the people to work for social change. Ignorance of this factor led to the failure of the pre-revolutionary regime and provided the background to the Islamic Revolution of 1979. Post revolutionary Iran has attracted the attention of those who are looking to see what Islam can provide for women. This is indeed a situation where the Islamic view of women is put into practice. It is therefore important to evaluate the roots of the problems and assess future possibilities.

Reviewing the Islamic View of Women

Before describing some aspects of the status of women in Islam, it must be noted that the Islamic approach towards women features a number of characteristics. One should remember that this approach may or may not be compatible with other approaches, particularly some of the Western ones. The feminist movement within Western culture has a different history altogether. This movement stands opposed even to the metanarratives of Western male-oriented culture, let alone Islamic standards. Although feminists are not in touch with Islamic standards, there would be tension if they confronted Islamic womanology with its distinctive value system. To investigate an important issue like women's status, we need varying perspectives. Womanology will be more inclusive if we study it through a comparative perspective. In this project, I aim to provide a general picture of the Islamic approach in order to compare it later with other perspectives. We will be totally confused if we judge Islamic and other non-Western approaches in isolation from their cultural contexts. Islamic standards cannot be observed to function in a Western context as diversely as they do in Muslim cultures. Islamic ideology is a complete system. The functionality of each component depends on the functionality of other components of the whole system. However, it is worth bearing in mind various perspectives.

Women, who have made up more than half of the human population throughout history and in all nations, have been oppressed, violated, and discriminated against solely on account of their gender. Even within developed countries women have suffered from explicit and hidden types of tyranny. They have not been able to enjoy their rights to education and socio-political participation within the family, marriage, and society. Women are still victims of poverty, illiteracy, postwar crises, homelessness, and violence. Companies and commercial institutions in industrialized countries enlarge their interests through female exploitation. The existing discriminative status of women is more or less a norm in Muslim and non-Muslim societies. Aside from the type and form of discrimination, women are discriminated against in all societies. We need to revive or rebuild the status of women even in Islamic countries. One reason for the discriminatory treatment of women in Islamic societies is that Islamic instructions in these societies are misunderstood or mistranslated. Islamic standards usually are mingled with local cultural values and stereotyped expectations in Muslim nations.[7]

To understand fully the Islamic view of women we have always to keep in mind the explicit difference between the revealed doctrine of Islam and the actual practice in Muslim societies. Socio-political, economic, national, and global elements often force Muslim societies to mingle pure Islamic tenets with local customs and beliefs. Before looking at the realities of Muslim life in any one aspect, particularly the issues related to women, we must first refer to the main sources of Islamic knowledge. The reality is that neither in theory nor in practice can Muslim women ever fully realize their potential, understand themselves, or enjoy their rights. The Qur'an and the prophetic tradition, along with the narrated traditions from the infallible Imams (in Shi'i thought), constitute these sources. Although in referring to them we face the problem of conflicting interpretations, we may find a way to avoid misconceptions. As in understanding any text, the most

---

[7] M. Fanaei Eshkevari, *The Status of Women in the Islamic Thought* (Qom: The Imam Khomeini Education and Research Institute, 1998), 21-2.

reliable method is to turn to experts, in this case to Muslim scholars, who mostly agree upon the fundamental tenets. The reliance on experts in each branch of knowledge is a commonly accepted norm. Therefore, at the level of theoretical discussion, I prefer to turn to the main Islamic references.

According to Islamic teachings, value-laden differences between men and women are merely based on the acquired level of piety. Piety is the characteristic which shapes individual and collective behaviour to be God-laden. Rejecting any type of superiority claimed by one group over another, the Qur'an addresses all human beings:

> O you people! Surely We have created you of a male and a female, and made you tribes and families that you may know one another; surely the most honorable of you with Allah is the one among you most pious. (49:13)

The core message in this verse is that the characteristics that distinguish one person from the next are only means of knowing one another. Race, sex, class, geographical differences, age, and wealth should not provide the bases of superiority or power relationships. The only criterion of honour and superiority is piety, which eradicates any unjust and discriminative hierarchical relationship.

As the main source for issues related to women in Islam, the Qur'an discusses twelve well-known women in religious history and describes their lifestyles. It is also interesting to note that one whole chapter in the Qur'an is entitled the "Chapter of Women" (*Surat al-Nisa'*), which indicates the attention that the Qur'an pays to women.

The Ideal Woman in an Islamic Society

I would like to quote Jane I. Smith's words on the complexity of the position of women in Islam at both the theoretical and practical levels. She, interestingly enough, maintains:

> Like an intricate and complex geometric pattern on a Persian rug or a frieze decorating a mosque, the practices, roles, opportunities, prescriptions, hopes and frustrations of Islamic women are woven

together in a whole. The colors are sometimes bold and striking, at other times mute and subtle.[8]

A reason for this interrelatedness and complexity is that on the one hand, Muslims believe that Islamic law remains divine and immutable, while on the other, society has to find answers for the questions raised by women about their status, roles, and function in the context of a modern, but Islamic state.[9] The discussion of the ideal woman in Islam and attempts at defining her model behaviour become crucial when an Islamic society, like post revolutionary Iran, undergoes rapid development and encounters the problem of putting theories into practice. The contrast will be more explicit when, on the one hand, the society follows the Islamic values system, whereas on the other it is asked to follow the path towards the goals of development and modernization. Social change cannot be avoided. Muslim scholars therefore, are faced with finding feasible Islamic patterns. These two tasks will cause challenges in developmental and educational plans and policies. It should also be mentioned that the issue of women, education, and development in Iran is linked to Shi'i ideology, which has had a deep impact on social and individual lives. Since the central value in socio-educational change, as was pointed out earlier, is piety, the educational system aims at creating a pious and committed citizen, whether male or female. Piety, as a core characteristic, influences social and individual attitudes and behaviour. The Qur'anic educational teachings, therefore, are piety-centered. A key goal in formal education is accordingly to educate students for a pious life which is called in the language of the Qur'an the purified life (*hayat tayyibah*).

Educational teachings are more effective if they are accompanied with concrete, feasible models of piety. An important aspect of the Qur'anic educational teachings, as in other effective educational methods, is that they always provide feasible models. These educational

---

[8] J. I. Smith, "Islam," in *Women in World Religions*, ed. A. Sharma (Albany: State University of New York, 1987), 235-250, 248.

[9] S. Haeri, "Obedience versus Autonomy: Women and Fundamentalism in Iran and Pakistan," in *Fundamentalism and Society: Reclaiming the Sciences, the Family, and Education*, ed. M. E. Marty and R. S. Appleby (Chicago: University of Chicago Press, 1991), 181-213, 182.

models and ideals are not only masculine. In providing models of good and bad characters, the Qur'an offers examples of both male and female characters. In the following verse, the Qur'an reminds us of the wives of Prophets Lut and Noah who rejected the prophetic instructions and became disbelievers.

> Allah sets forth an example to those who disbelieve, the wife of Noah and the wife of Lut: they were both under (the teachings) of two of Our righteous servants, but they acted treacherously towards them so they availed them nothing from Allah. (66:10)

In the next verse, a female model, Pharaoh's wife, is provided as a concrete example for both men and women to challenge the motives of those who would try to indoctrinate them.

> And Allah sets forth an example to those who believe the wife of Pharaoh when she said: My Lord! Build for me a house with you in the garden and deliver me from Pharaoh and his doing and deliver me from the unjust people. (66:11)

Hence, in verse 10, the Qur'an talks about two women who disregarded the prophetic teachings, although they had access to prophetic instructions from within their family but decided instead to disbelieve in the religion of their times. Verse 11, on the contrary, provides the example of a woman who did not have direct access to the prophetic message. She was the wife of the emperor of ancient Egypt. However, she was able to reach a high level of piety. The Qur'an offers her example as a champion of piety and belief in God.[10]

It is important to note that Pharaoh's wife and the other two models provide all believers, both men and women, examples of those who acted against or along with the oppressing conditions of their times. Pharaoh's wife furthermore is a model of resistance to absolute power. Although she lived in a most worldly and oppressive environment, she was faithful in following the prophetic instructions of Moses. The other

---

[10] M. Mutahhari, *Nizam-i Huquq-i Zan Dar Islam* [*The System of Women's Rights in Islam*] (Tehran: Shirkat-i Ufsit Sahamiy-i 'Am, 1980), 117.

two, who lived in the most sublime of environments, nevertheless preferred to adapt a worldly lifestyle. The message is that the final choice is in our hands, regardless of our gender.

In other verses, Mary the mother of Jesus appears as a surprising model. She acts so piously that the prophet of her time is astonished.

> Whenever he [the Prophet Zakariyya] entered the sanctuary to [see] her [Mary], he found with her food! He said: "O Mary! whence comes this to you?" She said, "It is from Allah." There, Zakariyya asked Allah to grant him such a good offspring. (3:37)

This and other corresponding verses provide an illustration of the Islamic understanding about the ability of women to reach the sacred levels of perfectness. The female, according to the Qur'an, should be a model and champion of piety among males and other females.

In Islam, the ideal model in female education according to Shi'i belief is Fatima, the daughter of Prophet Muhammad, the wife of 'Ali, (the first Shi'i Imam), and the mother of the second and the third Imams, Hasan and Husayn. This conception is the reason why Women's Day in Iran is celebrated on the occasion of Fatima's birthday. Although Fatima was neither a prophet nor an Imam, her spiritual position is higher than that of her eleven descendents who were imams and also higher than the other prophets with the exception of her father.[11]

Khadija, the prophet Muhammad's first wife, and Zaynab, the Prophet's granddaughter, also played important roles in the sociopolitical events of their times, more so even than many Muslim men. Therefore, they are regarded as guiding and encouraging models in Islam. In Sunni Islam, Aisha's credentials and prophetic admiration for Umma Salama provide other examples of the honour given to women in Islam.

The first and the most important task of women in an Islamic society is to fulfill the sacred role of motherhood in order to preserve the sanctity and stability of the family. This, of course, does not mean that all burdens in the family should be placed on the shoulders of

---

[11] Mutahhari (1980), 117-18.

women or that they should be prevented from fulfilling other roles. The above-mentioned personages, though, played a decisive role in the establishment of Islam. Their family roles never obliged them to disregard their socio-political roles. Moreover, men are also expected to play a complementary role in domestic responsibilities. Pious mothers and fathers are both the first and the most effective educators in establishing the foundations of a life-long educational process. To play the role of a pious mother should not come at the expense of her socio-political and economic status. A mother, before being a mother or a wife, is herself. The elevated status of Fatima was not merely due to her relation to the Prophet Muhammad or the Imams. She was a champion in all aspects of life. Muslims should be proud of her because of her exemplary personality. A complete research is needed to show the individual qualifications of Lady Fatima in Islam. Ali Shari'ati, a famous Muslim intellectual who was active in Iran prior to the Islamic Revolution, has written a volume on this topic entitled *Fatima is Fatima*.[12]

It is necessary to provide women with educational opportunities both before and after marriage. If a woman has access to education she is able to invest in herself. This will give her the ability to play a more complete role both in the family and in society. She will be a better educator and mother if she receives more and higher levels of education. Family and social roles will be better conducted if society invested more in the education of women. Uneducated mothers not only lose their own rights but also are less likely to be good mothers and wives, as well as being deficient in other complementary roles.

Women's Roles in Family Stability

The family in an Islamic society is seen as the core and the key element of the society (Iranian Constitution, article 11). Efforts at Islamic socialization should begin with the family. Both men and women are expected to play complementary roles based on their different abilities and varying capabilities. Both sexes are endowed with different biological and psychological capabilities which help them fulfil different

---

[12] Ali Shari'ati, *Fatima is Fatima*, trans. Laleh Bakhtiar (Houston: FILINC, 1979).

needs. Explaining the importance of the family unit, the Qur'an maintains that God created humankind as male and female. His wise creation of humankind provided the foundations of the family unit.

> And among His signs is that He created mates for you from yourselves that you may find rest in them, and He put between you love and compassion. (30:21)

The implication of this verse is that the Qur'an views the family as a unit which includes both male and female. The Arabic term, *azwaj* (mates), in this verse applies to both sexes, men and women. Units with two female or male components are not considered families nor do these entail the expected consequences. Moreover, the family is regarded as a centre of love, compassion, and relaxation. These strong psychological relationships are the background of a lifelong companionship. This refers to the creation of a human condition that provides interpersonal reliance. Reliance on others, as R. W. Morris states, is a part of the human condition. People rely on one another for understanding, comfort, and love.[13]

Recent sociological and developmental findings support the idea that the family unit is the core of the socialization process and of human development for the entire society. Human interrelationships, informal education, and socialization begins and is constructed within the family.[14] The sexual-biological differences between men and women and the consequent roles that arise from these differences are not discriminative; rather they are a way of natural cooperation which joins men to women and maintains the human race on the earth. Sexual differences call men and women to play complementary roles within the institution of the family. Tensions, nonetheless, begin when we do not have a clear definition of "complementary roles." The main task is

---

[13] R. W. Morris, *Values in Sexuality Education: A Philosophical Study* (Lanham, MD: University Press of America, 1994), 40.

[14] See W. R. Avison and J. H. Kundel, "Socialization," in *Introduction to Sociology: A Canadian Focus,* ed. J. J. Teevan, 4th ed. (Scarborough: Prentice-Hall Canada, 1991), 55-89, 79; and A. E. Woolfolk, *Educational Psychology*, 6th ed. (Boston: Allyn & Bacon, 1995), 87.

to clarify the borderlines of "complementary roles" based on the fundamental differences.

My understanding of the above-mentioned verse is that the family unit begins with mutual love and affection between girls and boys. This key element along with the consequent sexual pleasure and attraction links both sexes, helping them to overcome the pressures of life cooperatively. Yet the sexual role of reproduction is different. While men play an instant role in the reproductive process, women undertake a long-lasting role that includes their crucial role in the postnatal period, as they feed and rear their infants in their early years.

It is also crucial to understand that the reproductive process is usually preceded, accompanied, and followed by pain, pressures, and indisposition, and possible side effects. Women need time to pass through this process and regain their normal health.[15] In promoting any productive opportunities for women, we have to consider the more vital role of women in reproduction.[16] This is why in Islam men are urged to support women financially and bear more of a burden in

---

[15] M. T. Misbah, "Women or Half of the Body of Society," in *Status of Women in Islam* (India: Sangam Books, 1990), 1-26, 6.

[16] Our approach to the twenty-first century is associated with some previously inconceivable developments. The growth of the women's movement and the gay and lesbian movements in the 1960s and 1970s has proposed new types of families in which parents play less traditional roles. The introduction of new reproductive technologies means that women no longer have to experience pregnancy or have sex with a man to have a child. Laboratory fertilization of women's eggs with men's sperm and the implantation of the embryo in a host womb is regarded as an alternative. See S. Golombok and R. Fivush, *Gender Development* (Cambridge: Cambridge University Press, 1995), chap. 9. My understanding from an Islamic point of view is that these technologies are, indeed, the result of human beings losing sight of divine instructions. I believe that the development of new reproductive technologies which remove women from their natural roles is nothing less than producing an artificial intelligence that has the same functions as the human brain. It is, in my view, like swimming against a current. The family unit, as the Qur'an suggests, is a male-female-cooperation place, a "team" (30:21). Reproduction is the natural function of a woman's autonomy (31:40; 46:15). Eradication of socio-culturally constructed stereotypes must not lead us to ignore the ultimate purpose of creation.

productive aspects. This, of course, does not mean to restrict the role of women in reproduction. Rather we have to take into consideration the fact that a long period of pregnancy, the side effects of delivery, and the postnatal recovery are reasons that women play the most essential roles in reproduction. They must therefore bear a lesser burden on the social level while they are dealing with human development. If within the newly proposed concept of development people are located at the centre of all development plans,[17] then the reproductive role of women should not be compromised by the value attached to producing goods and commodities. I do not think that a productive role at any level can be compared with the value of women's crucial role in reproduction. I assume that a significant aspect of social justice is to give primary value to reproduction for those women who decide to complete their role in this area. Reproduction or human development in its formative period requires experts in education and child psychology. It is therefore especially worthwhile to have skillful women who oversee the early stages of human development. To give more power to women and provide them with financial independence, we first need to reevaluate their reproductive value.

The reproductive task is usually misperceived. People always categorize reproduction with the unpaid and invisible productive roles of women in the family. In Islam, the complementary role of the woman in a family is reproduction, which I call "human development." Other invisible productive activities like housekeeping, laundry, cooking, cleaning, and even child-rearing which are usually conducted by women are remunerable tasks. Women can charge their husbands for performing these tasks. However, the Islamic legal system is accompanied by a moral system which discourages disputes which may disturb the marriage. In its familial instructions, Islam directs Muslims toward mutual love, compassion, and cooperation rather than mere economic competition. If, nonetheless, men and women decide to interpret strictly the legal nature of the marriage contract, claiming what each owes to the other, both have something to say about the economic value of their participation.[18]

---

[17] Suggested in UNDP, *Human Development Report* (1995), 11.
[18] Misbah (1990), 17.

If a society neglects the value of women's activities within the family, then social planners have to find ways to engage them in productive roles. I observe that social change can be effected by women if we reevaluate their reproductive and invisible productive roles. Reformulation of social norms can provide women with a deserved and independent position. This emphasis does not mean that women should always stay at home. Reproduction, particularly in the present when societies are confronted with the problem of the exploitation of population, does not cover the whole scope of women's lives. Once the family's foundations have been established and the children provided with stability, both the wife and husband are free to continue their out-of-home activities.

To give a higher value to family stability and to insist on the crucial role of women does not necessarily mean that a woman's role should be confined to domestic responsibilities. Val Moghadam opposes what she calls "the ideology of domesticity" in post-revolutionary Iran, but provides statistics that reveal a growth trend in Iranian women's participation in various sectors of the work force. She restricts herself to one specific interpretation of a particular prophetic tradition that she quotes from the women's journal *Zan-i Ruz* where it is written that the Prophet Muhammad said: "Domesticity is the woman's jihad." It is on this basis that she attempts to support her thesis of the ideology of domesticity.[19] I would observe that although this prophetic tradition is reported in various Islamic primary sources,[20] it could have alternative interpretations.

This tradition, with its specific Arabic phrase *husn al-taba' 'ul* (to have a good relationship with one's spouse), actually emphasizes the cooperative role that married women should play with their husbands. It never implies an ideology of domesticity where women should be prevented from taking on out-of-home responsibilities. Moreover, the late Ayatullah Muhammad Bihishti, the former vice-president of the Assembly of Experts, who was in charge of establishing the post-

---

[19] Moghadam (1988), 223.

[20] See Muhammad ibn Ya'qub Kulayni, *Al-Usul min al-Kafi* (Tehran: Dār al-Kitāb al-Islāmiyyah, 1954), vols. 5 and 9; also M. B. Majlis, *Bihār al-Anwār* (Beirut: al-Wafā, 1983), 10: 99; 18:106.

revolutionary constitution, has an interesting explanation for the role of women in the Muslim family. He has stated that the emphasis on the role of the woman at home in raising children and caring for the husband does not imply that women's work is 'maid's work'. The spirit of Islamic teachings, he points out, accords great importance to the mutual responsibilities of both parents within the family context.[21] It is incumbent on both of them to divide the responsibilities cooperatively. "Maid's work" is an example of a wrong translation of a prophetic tradition. As previously mentioned, according to Islamic law, domestic work is a kind of hidden, productive, and remunerable activity. This may be specified by women under the moral values of the marriage contract. Moreover, the cooperative and complementary roles of men and women are not confined to the family unit. Wives and husbands must agree upon cooperation in all aspects of their shared lives.

Women and Socio-Political Development

To discuss the equality of men and women in social participation, we have to discover whether their respective social roles go back only to the socialization process or whether they depend sometimes on socialization and occasionally on biological and psychological differences. If we hold the first opinion, the existing labour division based on the male-female criterion will be entirely discriminatory. If we follow the second criterion, we may accept a kind of labour division at the social level between male and female.

It seems that both men and women are capable of performing many social responsibilities. Therefore, the differences do not refer to their potentialities. Social role-playing then reflects the better compatibility of men or women for particular tasks. Men and women may have different degrees of ability to perform various social responsibilities.[22]

Besides those activities that both men and women are equally able to perform, there are some that are more compatible with one of the sexes. In many societies, both past and present, the harder or more difficult tasks were assigned to men, such as hunting, fighting, and mining.

---

[21] H. Esfandiari, "The Majles and Women's Issues in the Islamic Republic of Iran," in Afkhami and Friedl, *Eye of the Storm*, (1994), 61-79.

[22] Fanaei Eshkevari (1998), 17-20.

Women, on the contrary, were asked to take on softer and more secure social responsibilities. Despite this fact, exceptions can be found all over the world. In some societies women have been asked to perform hard and heavy work, such as construction. This, of course, does not mean that women did not suffer within their own domain of responsibilities. The reproductive process, postwar hardship, drought crises, and other examples hurt women more than men. Even when a nation is at war, while men serve on the front women have served as well by remaining at home to rear children and handle household duties. In cases where both men and women participated in national defense, women took care of nursing and support behind the lines. These examples of labour division are not discriminatory; rather they naturally fit with the varying abilities of men and women.

In Islam, reproduction and human development during the early years is a priority assigned to mothers. Mothers are regarded as the most compatible for this duty. They endure the pains of almost nine months of conception. In the postnatal period they also are endowed with a source of natural nutrition. The Qur'an reveals that these two tasks, bearing and nourishing, will last thirty months if mothers are willing to the fullest. To remind us of the importance of these responsibilities, it is stated in the Qur'an:

And We have charged humankind concerning his/her parents—his/her mother bore him/her in weakness upon weakness and his/her weaning occurs in two years. (31:40)

Another verse reemphasizes the same fact and asks people to treat their parents well, particularly their mothers:

We have enjoined on man kindness to His parents: In pain did His mother bear him, and in pain did she give Him birth. The carrying of the (child) to his weaning is (a period of) thirty months. At length, when he reaches the age of full strength and attains forty years, he says, "O My Lord! grant me that I may be grateful for Thy favour which Thou has bestowed upon me, and upon both My parents, and that I may work righteousness such as

Thou may approve; and be gracious to me in my issue. Truly have I turned to Thee and truly do I bow (to thee) in Islam." (46:15)

This reminds us of the difficulties that mothers suffer during pregnancy and delivery. Although men can also take part in postnatal responsibilities, mothers are regarded in the Qur'an as the most appropriate. They are the ones who naturally have the ability to conceive and breastfeed. These responsibilities are not, however, forced upon them. It is, after all, possible to set up daycare and have women work or to ask men to stay at home or take the children with them to work, but this makes things difficult if the parents wish to feed their child naturally. Needless to say, breastfeeding has a crucial psychological impact on a child.

I do not think that this labour division is unreasonable. What is most crucial is how and on what type of criteria we divide labour. Next, what is most important is the way in which we evaluate men's and women's participation. Social credit and financial reward have admittedly always been discriminatory. A solution for such treatment is to reconsider men's and women's capabilities and reevaluate their shares. Although in post-revolutionary Iran, women do not face impediments against working outside of their homes, in December 1983 a legislative measure was introduced ostensibly to ease the burdens on working mothers by encouraging part-time rather than full-time work.[23] Such legislation maintains two sides of the coin. It not only provides an opportunity for women to work but also leaves them enough time to look after their families. They can of course work full-time when they are free from family responsibilities.

Holding to the idea that the postnatal responsibilities of child-rearing require male-female cooperation, I cannot see how rearing by only one parent can result in healthy psychological development. Thus, it is clear that postnatal responsibilities are addressed to both parents. Fathers should also look out for the child's needs for education and affection during the postnatal period.

One might still argue that Islam has restricted women to performing only reproductive tasks and that they are deprived of other social

---

[23] Moghadam (1988), 227.

opportunities. The answer is that reproduction never fills all of a woman's lifespan. This is more understandable during the present age when the size of a family is much smaller than in the past. Moreover, women can still be engaged in productive tasks even within the reproductive period as long as they do not compromise the more important task of human development. Women have to participate in the workforce, not only to create economic independence for themselves but also to cope with the economic realities of everyday life. This, however, adds to the burden faced by women who have to struggle with maintaining a home along with the pressures of a job.

A dramatic point in Islam is that division of roles and responsibilities between men and women is not a question of higher or lower value. The core of spiritual and social values consists of piety and full participation in compatible tasks. The social value of each person, male or female, depends on his/her level of cooperative participation and the intentions behind it.

If one returns to the post-revolutionary context in Iran, it is clear that teaching at various levels has been an important area for the socio-educational participation of women. Following the return to Islamic values, the Council of the Cultural Revolution (1989) encouraged women to fill all needed teaching positions in female education. Despite this emphasis, female teachers still constituted only one-eighth of the total workforce in the educational sector by 1995.[24]

Women also receive military training as members of the female paramilitary forces. Started during the Iraq-Iran war, this program mobilizes women to receive military training on an extra-curricular basis. Women are also allowed to run for Parliament, and since the Islamic Revolution, there have been a number of notable women parliamentarians in Iran.

Equality of Men and Women: Difference or Discrimination?

The debate over the equality and freedom of human beings in social life has engaged minds for at least three centuries. The equality of men and

---

[24] M. Fallahi, *Foundations of Education in Iran and Education after the Cultural Revolution of 1980*, PhD Dissertation (Milwaukee: Marquette University, 1995), 136.

women was however only recognized internationally for the first time with the passage of the Universal Declaration of Human Rights by the United Nations in 1948. As human beings, both men and women enjoy many inborn and undeniable rights. The issue has likewise been debated in post-revolutionary Iran from the outset. Theoretical and practical solutions have been proposed ever since.

In an informative lecture addressed to Iranian women, Ayatollah Khamenei, the present leader of the Islamic Republic, maintains that women are not weaker than men in terms of mental and intellectual abilities, thinking, and emotions.[25] In some cases they are even stronger. However, throughout history men have oppressed women simply because they were taller, physically stronger, and had louder voices. The roots of this oppression lie either in the lack of a strong and supportive law, or the lack of strong psychological parameters like intense love, or the lack of a stable and clear religious faith.

Male-female relationships in the Iranian context must therefore be improved, according to Khamenei. These relationships must be re-established on the basis of the Islamic standards of justice and love. For him, blind imitation of the Western model, even in support of women's rights, would be nothing more than falling into a new trap. He observes that the Islamic attitude toward women represents a more appropriate path. He states his belief that the majority of ill-treatment of women comes from husbands. What is needed is a change in interrelationship patterns in order to avoid this sort of oppression. As a step towards women's development in post-revolutionary Iran, new efforts should be made to reform family patterns. Women need more protection and immunity against spousal abuse. Out-of-family limitations, I believe, are partly rooted in family oppression. This explains Khamenei's emphasis on family-pattern development.

To begin any reform we must have a clear understanding about men's and women's capabilities. Both sexes enjoy various capabilities due to femininity and masculinity. Sex differences dictate the respective potentials that men and women bring to collective life within the family and at the social level. Muslim thinkers insist that to eradicate pressures on and mistreatment of women we should not place new burdens on

---

[25] *Electronic Hamshahri* 1375/1996, No. 1113.

women's shoulders in the name of equality. They assert that men and women are equal but not similar in their experience of human rights.[26] Similar treatment, they argue, is another kind of tyranny over men and women.

Muslim thinkers believe that Islam does not support the idea of a similarity between men and women, but that this does not lead to any discrimination against women. They insist that Islam is opposed to discrimination both in terms of sex and similarity of the sexes. A woman's nature is not deemed to be inferior to a man's, but neither is it the same. The two complete and complement each other.[27]

As men and women are born with different potentialities, they are different in that they deserve different rights.[28] Undeniable differences are, indeed, a tool for linking men to women in the demanding situation of shared and collective life. As women suffer from menstruation, a long period of conception, difficulties with delivering babies, and breast-feeding during the first two years, they need men's protection, fewer responsibilities, and more rights.[29] According to the Qur'an, men and women are looked upon as two complementary members of both the family and society. In an interesting statement, the Qur'an refers to the mutual protective roles of men and women. The Qur'an states:

> They (women) are an apparel for you (men) and you are an apparel for them. (2:187)

This statement comes in the context of a discussion of lawful sexual intercourse when the family is established under the religious law. As clothes protect us from hot and cold weather and give us beauty, male and female play the same role in a marriage protecting each other from deviant sexual intercourse. Based on this understanding, neither the male nor the female is subordinate in a relationship. They each have a

---

[26] Mutahhari (1980), 113.

[27] A. K. Ferdows, "The Status and Rights of Women in Ithna 'Ashari Shi'i Islam" in *Women and the Family in Iran*, ed. A. Fathi (Leiden: E. J. Brill, 1985), 13-36, 18.

[28] Mutahhari (1980), 11.

[29] Ibid., 167.

complementary role to play. The Islamic human-rights system for men and women derives from an Islamic view about the creation of humankind. In rejecting all types of dominant-subordinate relationships between men and women, the Qur'an reveals:

> O People! Be careful of (your duty to) your Lord, Who created you from a single being (Adam) and created its mate of the same (kind) and spread from these two, many men and women. (4:1)

In similar verses, the Qur'an explains that men and women, wives and husbands, are created from the same, unique being.[30] This sameness necessitates the equality of both sexes inasmuch as it maintains their complementary roles. An oversimplified understanding of this view is to replace equality with similarity and sameness in rights and responsibilities. In his book *The System of Women's Rights in Islam*, Mutahhari observes that since men and women are the same in creation they have to be treated equally but not similarly.[31] An insistence on similarity in rights and responsibilities fails to take into account the natural endowments of both sexes. The result of such insistence is the disintegration of their respective roles.

Mutahhari continues by pointing out that, aside from undeniable differences, men and women are similar in many other respects. To support this idea, he quotes a part of the story of Adam and Eve in the Qur'an and concludes that the two were similarly influenced by Satan. Despite many Muslim interpreters who argue that the dismissal of this couple from paradise was the result of Eve's more flexible emotions, Mutahhari maintains that the Qur'an charges the couple with the same responsibility.[32] In the Qur'an it is revealed:

> But the Satan made an evil suggestion to them (both) that he might make manifest to them (both) what had been hidden from them (both) of their evil inclinations, and he said: Your Lord has not forbidden for you (both) this tree except that you may not

---

[30] 16:72; 30:21; 39:6; 42:11.
[31] Mutahhari (1980), 113-15.
[32] Ibid., 116.

(both) become two angels or that you may (not) become of the immortals. And he swore to them (both): Most surely I am a sincere advisor to you. Then he caused them (both) to fall by deceit. (7:20-22)

The repeated use of the specific Arabic pronoun *huma (both)* in the three above-mentioned verses provides a clue. This dual pronoun in Arabic is usually employed in a context where two persons are involved. It indicates that Satan, in his entire approach, including his suggestion, misguidance, and oath-swearing, dealt with the couple simultaneously. This shows that both were equally misguided and equally responsible for their dismissal from paradise. To sum up, we may conclude that men and women, according to the Qur'anic point of view, are endowed with the same type of motivational system. What usually separates men and women can generally be traced back to cultural contexts or varying educational environments.

An important aspect of the equality of men and women in Islam is the equal value of their participation. In our value judgments we always assign a higher value to social activities that are conducted by men. It is, nonetheless, narrated that once, in the time of the Prophet Muhammad, the Muslim women in Medina sent a representative to the Prophet in order to ask him questions as to whether he was only the Prophet of men or of both men and women. They had in mind the fact that the Prophet had mostly handled social and political activities through men. Men participate easily in such matters. The representative of these women talked to the Prophet while he was surrounded by his companions. She reminded him of the significance of their complementary roles in sacred activities, including jihad, which was usually waged by men. The Prophet looked around at his companions and stated that he appreciated her points. Then he replied to the woman, emphasizing the fact that value is never assigned to men because of gender difference or type of activities. The Prophet stressed that value is always assigned where there is full participation, and that women are honoured because of their complementary roles. If women did not cooperate, men would not be able to accomplish their tasks in a jihad.[33]

Tabataba'i observes that this story (and other cases where women are said to have appealed directly to the Prophet) reveals that women deserve the right to have direct contact even with the Islamic leader in order to protect their rights.[34]

Islamic Womanology and the Logic of Nature

To understand the roots of the responsibilities and rights of men and women in Islam, we have to study them in light of the logic of human nature (in Arabic, *fitrah*).[35] Islamic laws, norms, and regulations are compatible with human nature, Misbah argues. Human nature, as revealed in the Qur'an (30:30), is an unchangeable structure which distinguishes humankind from other species. An overview of all species reveals that they are created differently. Human rights and responsibilities find their real meaning within the logic of humankind's specific nature. Humanity, in all its variety, encompasses different aspects and complexities of life. Misbah alludes to other differences between men and women in terms of sex, nervous system, emotions, anatomical structure, and brain function.[36] He attributes these differences to a woman's typical nature. This typical nature determines her abilities to fulfill certain roles and duties on a social level.[37]

Due to these and other differences, some Muslim thinkers argue that women are exempt from certain social responsibilities which require a stronger intellect and less emotion. Dangerous and exhausting

---

[33] M. Mutahhari, *The Islamic Modest Dress*, trans. Laleh Bakhtiar (Albuquerque: ABJAD, 1988), 93-94.

[34] S. M. H. Tabataba'i, *Al-Mizan fi Tafsir al-Quran* [*The Criterion in Qur'anic Exegesis*] (Tehran: Dar al-Kutub al-Islamiyya, 1970), vol. 4:351.

[35] Misbah (1990), 4.

[36] Anatomical differences between the male and female brains in humans have been identified in the area of the hypothalamus, which influences differences in reproductive function. Differences in the cortical region of the brain account for differences in cognition. See Golombok and Fivush, *Gender Development*, 50, who quote from recent research on anatomical gender differences.

[37] Misbah (1990), 5, 8.

positions in the armed forces, legal decision-making and political leadership are just some examples of these excluded responsibilities.[38]

Other Muslim thinkers argue that there is sufficient evidence to prove the legitimacy of women's participation in socio-political activities. The Qur'anic story of Bilqis, the Queen of Sheeba, is considered a good indicator of divine acceptance of women's suitability for political leadership. The Qur'an portrays this queen as a consulting, thoughtful, truth-seeking, and peace-seeking leader.[39] Some also argue that the form and nature of the political system in the present day is completely different from the individual tyrannical dictatorships of the past.[40] Both men and women in present democratic political systems play only the role of consultants. Further evidence of the legitimacy of women's involvement in socio-political affairs is provided by women's *bay'ah* (allegiance) to the Prophet Muhammad[41] and afterwards with Imam 'Ali. The argument finds additional support with reference to: women's *hijrah* (emigration) as a political statement against the oppressive conditions of the time when Islam emerged; their participation in the Prophet's campaigns (as nurses and healthcare workers); and eventually the active participation of the pious and honoured women of Islam, such as Fatimah (the daughter of the Prophet), Umm-i Salamah (one of the Prophet Muhammad's wives),

---

[38] Tabataba'i, vol. 4:343, 347. In his jurisprudential discussion, Ma'rifat provides evidence from the Qur'an, the tradition of the Prophet and Imams, and the consensus of the Shi'i thinkers from Shaykh Tusi (d. 1067/460) up to the recent era. He examines the legal aspects of the capability of women for exercising judgment and political leadership from a Shi'i legal point of view. See M. H. Ma'rifat, "Shayistigi-i Zanan baray-i Qizavat va Manasib-i Rasmi" [Women's Ability for Judgment and Official Positions], *Hukumat-i Islami*, (1997), vol. 4(2), 39-54. Also see M. Mihrizi, "Zan va Siyasat: Girayishha va Nigarishha" [Women and Politics: Approaches and Written References], *Hukumat-i Islami* (1997), vol. 4(2), 166-82.

[39] 27:32-44.

[40] Mihrizi, "San va Siyasat," 171. Mihrizi attributes this argument to Mutahhari to show how he was opposed to interpretation of tradition in such a way as to keep women out of socio-political positions.

[41] 60:12.

and Zaynab (the daughter of Imām 'Ali), in the socio-political events of their times.[42]

In addition to these two opposing views, some Muslim scholars take a middle way and distinguish between women's legitimacy as candidates for political offices such as the presidency and as candidates for other positions. They would deny only the former. This attitude is the accepted policy in the post-revolutionary Iranian constitution (article 115).[43]

In Islamic womanology, views and regulations which are derived from the Qur'an and authentic traditions are claimed to be consistent with the typical nature of women. The reason is that this picture is provided by God, the Creator, who has the most precise and comprehensive knowledge about His creatures. An important parameter in Islamic womanology is the decisive impact of moral values. The Islamic moral system is like an umbrella that encompasses the entire legal system, not only in gender issues but also in all other legal subsystems. It is understandable, therefore, that some attitudes, social roles, and labour divisions, which are considered as the normal or necessary rights of women in other cultures, are challenged in Islam. This is partly due to the contradiction of some gender codes with the Islamic values of motherhood, wifehood, family values, Islamic modesty ('*iffat*), and the Islamic dress code. Islamic methods of gender development, I believe, necessitate a solution which combines womanhood with Islamic values and moral codes.

Closing Remarks

My major concern has been to form a bridge between discussions in Islamic womanology and modern debates over culture, values, development, and the roles women play in these domains. There is a serious need to approach the relation between Islam and women's issues through both theoretical and applied perspectives. In terms of theoretical bases, Islamic references provide a knowledge base that facilitates our discovery of applied solutions. Yet it is vital to take into account other points of reference in our theoretical discussions.

---

[42] Mihrizi (1997), 174.
[43] Mihrizi attributes this idea to the Egyptian Muslim Brotherhood. Ibid.

Characteristics of women's nature are comparable to those of males. I have touched upon the interrelationship between women's rights and their responsibilities; male and female differences in their corporeal and incorporeal aspects, namely physiological and psychological backgrounds; the juxtaposition of the Islamic value system with legal and normative systems; the role of Islamic socialization; and the impact of socio-cultural norms; but there are many more factors that deserve investigation, and those mentioned here could each serve as a topic of much more extended research.

Created as Male and Female: 'Adam, Gender, and the Legacy of Disobedience

W. Derek Suderman

Given its significance in later biblical and theological reflection, it may come as a surprise that no direct quotations or references to Genesis 2-3 appear within the Old Testament itself. Similarly, despite the common description of this passage as the "fall" and the beginning of "original sin" within the Christian tradition, none of the many words for "sin" or "iniquity" appear either.[1] Nonetheless, early Judaism and along with it the New Testament already shows great interest in this passage, and its significance has continued over time.

Indeed, Christian theology often describes the "grand narrative" of the Bible as creation, fall, redemption, and consummation. In this theological shorthand, Genesis 1-3 figures more prominently than any other part of the Old Testament; taken to the extreme, such a perspective leaps from the account of creation and the Garden of Eden past the rest of the Old Testament to the coming of the Messiah in the Gospels. In terms of understanding humanity and its role—biblical anthropology—the "fall" in Genesis identifies the problem which messianic redemption resolves. "Original sin" often proves central in this depiction, and leads some to an extremely negative view of humans as utterly depraved. Further, the "order of creation" has provided a significant basis for depicting men's authority over women as divinely ordained. However, while the Genesis account of creation can be

---

[1] Similarly, despite a later equation of the two, nowhere does the passage itself explicitly identify the serpent as Satan or the devil.

intriguing, complex, and ambiguous, it may in fact challenge both of these common claims.

To consider what the beginning of Genesis contributes to our understanding of biblical anthropology we will concentrate on four key moments: first, the creation of *'adam* as male and female (Gen. 1); second, the portrayal of *'adam* and his wife (Gen. 2); third, the consequences of disobedience for male and female (Gen. 3); and fourth, the depiction of humanity after Eden (Gen. 5:1-3). Finally, we will briefly consider several broader implications of this study for our understanding of the Bible, interpretation, and the role of the believing community.

As we shall see, humanity continues to be formed "in the image of God" after Eden, but challenges remain in dealing with the consequences of disobedience. Rather than seeing men "ruling over women" as divinely ordained or sanctioned, *'adam* as both male and female continues to occupy a unique and exalted status in creation. Thus, a close reading of Genesis 1-5 suggests this tendency to dominate is one that Christians should seek to limit and even overcome.

Creation of *'adam* as Male and Female (Genesis 1)

The Bible begins with the creative act of God: "In the beginning God created the heavens and the earth." In patterned, orderly, poetic language, Genesis 1 describes how God calls the world into being. Time after time, the passage states: "And God said, 'Let there be . . .'" and there was: light and darkness; sea and sky; land and vegetation. Once prepared, each arena is then populated, with the sun and moon in the sky, fish in the sea, birds in the air, and beasts in the field.[2] And all of this is recounted in wonderful rhythm: "and God saw, and it was good. And there was evening and there was morning . . ."

The description builds until, at the end of the sixth day, God says:

> Let us make *'adam* in our image, according to our likeness; and let them have dominion over the fish of the sea, and over the

---

[2] George W. Coats, *Genesis: With an Introduction to Narrative*, The Forms of the Old Testament Literature (Grand Rapids, MI: W. B. Eerdmans, 1983), 1:43–45.

birds of the air, and over the cattle, and over all the wild animals of the earth, and over every creeping thing that creeps upon the earth." (Gen. 1:26-28)[3]

The last element of creation, this new humanity, is both similar to and distinct from other creatures. Like the others, humanity is also created as a living being (*nephesh hayah*) and commanded to "be fruitful and multiply."[4] Unlike its predecessors, the *'adam* is granted both a unique role and attribute: no other creature is given "dominion" over other living things and, most importantly, nothing else is described as being created "in the image and likeness" of God.

For our purposes, verse 27 proves to be of particular interest:

So God created *'adam* in his image, in the image of God he created it (him); *male and female he created them.* (Gen. 1:27, emphasis mine)

The term "create" appears three times in this key verse, and in each case relates to *'adam*. While the first two lines reflect a virtual mirror image of one another, the third expands the singular "it" to the plural "them." In other words, the *'adam* that God creates is none other than the male and female "them."[5]

There are two observations to be made at this point. First, although traditionally translated as "God created man . . ." (KJV), *'adam* here appears in a generic sense that includes both male and female.[6] Second,

---

[3] Unless stated otherwise, biblical quotations will be from the NRSV.

[4] Although complicated because of its frequent translation as "soul" in other contexts, within the Old Testament, *nephesh* does not reflect a body/soul dualism.

[5] Although usually rendered with "his/him," it is worth noting that there are no gender-neutral verb forms or pronouns in biblical Hebrew. Since these pronouns refer to *'adam* which is then clarified as male and female, it may be better to think of this singular pronoun as the neuter "it."

[6] Translations differ at this point, with the traditional "man" (KJV, NKJV, JPS, NIV) being changed to "human beings" (TNIV) and "humankind" (NRSV) in more recent versions. To underscore the generic usage here I have left the term *'adam* untranslated. How this should be understood has been debated within the tradition, from some early proponents who saw *'adam* as an

humanity forms the climax of creation, as both were created in the divine image and given dominion over the other creatures. In addition, in Genesis 1 there is no internal hierarchy between the sexes since, as part of *'adam,* both male and female are created in God's image and *both* are given dominion. Even so, the distinction between creator and creatures remains and is linguistically underscored; while people can form, shape, or make in the Old Testament, only God "creates."[7]

Although beyond the scope of this paper, we increasingly recognize the complicity and negative consequences of an unfettered "domination" view of creation. As Wendell Berry states: "The certified Christian seems just as likely as anyone else to join the military-industrial conspiracy to murder Creation."[8] Thus, in addition to continued discernment regarding the nature of humans as created male and female in God's image, it is imperative to search for alternative ways of interpreting humanity's role both as part of and as uniquely capable of exercising "dominion" over—and in doing so even destroying—creation.

In any case, we have seen that humanity—male and female—is both part of creation and given "dominion" over other creatures. Although similar in the latter respect, we will see that the view of *'adam* shifts as we move into the Garden of Eden.

'adam and his Wife (Genesis 2)

In Genesis 2 the scene shifts to the "genealogy of the heavens and the earth" (Gen. 2:4). Rather than speaking things into being, here the

---

androgynous being that was both male and female to Karl Barth's insistence that the divine image necessarily requires male and female together. The latter view has been particularly significant, since Barth argues from this basis against same-gender organizations; see Karl Barth, "The Doctrine of Creation," in *Church Dogmatics III.* 4, ed. G. W. Bromiley and T. F. Torrance (Peabody, MA: Hendrickson Publishers, 2010), 163–66.

[7] The Qal verb form of the term "create" (*bara'*), used throughout Gen. 1, only appears with God as its subject in the Old Testament. Other forms of the term meaning to "cut," "shape," or even "separate" can be used for people as well.

[8] Wendell Berry, "Christianity and the Survival of Creation," in *Sex, Economy, Freedom & Community: Eight Essays* (New York: Pantheon Books, 1993), 94.

LORD God forms, shapes, plants, and waters.⁹ In contrast to the creation of *'adam* as male and female through the spoken word, here *'adam* is undoubtedly male and formed first among the creatures, while the woman appears at the end of the creation account. As Phyllis Trible states, traditionally interpreters have said this account "proclaims male superiority and female inferiority as the will of God. It portrays woman as 'temptress' and troublemaker who is dependent upon and dominated by her husband."¹⁰ With this issue in the background, we will concentrate on two pertinent aspects of this chapter: the process of naming and the search for a "helper." In doing so we will discover that the narrative proves more ambiguous on this issue than is often recognized, and actually raises serious questions about and even moves against a reading of male priority.

In Genesis 2 the LORD God forms *'adam* from the dust of the ground (*'adamah*) (v. 7), but it is only once God breathes into this "earth creature"¹¹ that he becomes a "living being." Not only the name but also the plight and purpose of the earthling is linked to the ground: "The LORD God took the man and put him in the garden of Eden to till it and keep it" (v. 15).¹² Since the term translated as "till" (*'abod*) also means to "work" or "serve" (even "worship"), one could say that the *'adam*'s purpose is to serve rather than to dominate the land.

God then plants Eden, places the man in it, and commands him not to eat from the "tree of the knowledge of good and evil." Immediately afterwards, the LORD God says: "It is not good that the man should be alone; I will make him a helper as his partner" (v. 19). Using exactly the same language as with the man, God then "forms" animals and birds

---

⁹ Although the divine is referred to as LORD God throughout Genesis 2-3 I will use God and LORD God interchangeably for stylistic reasons.

¹⁰ Trible has provided a classic critique that challenges this view through a close reading of Gen. 2-3. See Phyllis Trible, "A Love Story Gone Awry," in *God and the Rhetoric of Sexuality*, Overtures to Biblical Theology (Philadelphia: Fortress Press, 1978), 72–143. This quotation appears in Trible, "A Love Story Gone Awry," 72–73.

¹¹ A phrase used by Phyllis Trible in "A Love Story Gone Awry."

¹² This verse reconfirms the purpose stated for the man even before he was formed: "there was no one (no *'adam*) to till the ground" (v. 5).

"from the ground" and brings them before the 'adam. Where God breathed into him, here the divine allows the man to name the rest of the creatures, an element that is explicitly underscored twice (v. 19, 20). Where each of these creatures are also recognized as a "living being," the role of 'adam in naming stands in sharp contrast to the depiction of his own creation. While naming also represents a form of authority over other creatures, in contrast to Genesis 1 this role is given to an unambiguously male 'adam in chapter 2. Nonetheless, "there was not found a helper as his partner" (v. 20).

It is at this point that God "constructs" the woman from the 'adam's side and, like the creatures before, brings her to the man.[13] The man's response bears repeating:

> *This* at last is bone of my bones and flesh of my flesh; *this* shall be called woman (*'ishah*), for from man (*'ish*) *this* was taken. (Gen. 2:23, emphasis mine)[14]

Although not readily apparent in translation, the term "this" appears three times without a single use of "she" (or it). The grammar effectively underscores the novelty of this new creature by giving the impression that the man does not know what to make of her. Despite a clear parallel with how the other creatures are brought before the man, here the 'adam does not "name" the woman (the Hebrew term for "name," *shem*, does not appear) but rather states what she "will be

---

[13] The term here is quite different from that used for the man or the other creatures, and is the only occurrence in the creation account in Genesis; whereas "form" is the verb used for a potter, "build" is that employed to construct houses. The term "side" or "rib," when used with reference to construction, can also be translated as "beam" or "plank." Nahum M. Sarna, *Genesis: The Traditional Hebrew Text with the New JPS Translation*, The JPS Torah Commentary (Philadelphia: Jewish Publication Society, 1989), 23.

[14] I have provided a literalistic translation of this verse to emphasize the threefold occurrence of "this." Though awkward to maintain in translation, the term appears as the first and last word of the statement, as well as in the precise middle, at the beginning of the second line.

called." Where "naming" suggests authority over, explicit identification of this element is conspicuously absent here.[15]

In some interpretations, the depiction of the woman as the man's "helper" has been used to support male authority over women. However, while the term "helper" in English suggests a subordinate or secondary role, the term 'ezer in the Old Testament does not.[16] For instance, this term can refer to kings and military allies:

The Egyptians are human, and not God (or gods); their horses are flesh, and not spirit. When the LORD stretches out his hand, the *helper* will stumble, and the one *helped* will fall, and they will all perish together" (Is. 31:3).

In this case it is clear that the "helper" is actually the stronger party (Egypt), to whom the weaker party (Israel) goes for support. Likewise, the term is used frequently to refer to God:

Hear, O LORD, and be gracious to me! O LORD, be my *helper*! (Ps. 30:10).

Thus, the term 'ezer does not imply a subordinate or secondary role but rather quite the opposite. Though sometimes used to support a view of male authority (or even superiority), the term itself does not fit such a portrayal.[17]

As we have seen, the account of creation in Genesis proves more ambiguous regarding the relationship between the sexes than is sometimes assumed. In Genesis 1 God creates humanity together on the

---

[15] Contra Wenham, who sees this as "a typical example of Hebrew naming." Gordon J. Wenham, *Genesis 1–15*, Word Biblical Commentary, vol. 1 (Milton Keynes, UK: Word Publishing, 1991), 70. However, the term "name," explicitly underscored twice with respect to the animals, does not appear here.

[16] Bill T. Arnold, *Genesis*, New Cambridge Bible Commentary (Cambridge, New York: Cambridge University Press, 2009), 60.

[17] "This term cannot be demeaning because Hebrew 'ezer, employed here to describe the intended role of the woman, is often used of God in His relation to man (sic)." Sarna, *Genesis*, 22.

sixth day and gives dominion over the rest of creation to *adam* as both male *and* female. In contrast, in Genesis 2 the LORD God forms the man out of the ground at the outset of creation and gives him (!) the power to name and thus authority over the beasts of the field and birds of the air. While the woman's appearance as the man's "helper" at the end of the account has led some to claim a subordinate role for females based on this "order of creation," the term "helper" does not imply a subordinate in the Old Testament and the man does not name the woman as he does the other creatures.

Finally, the concluding statement of the chapter shows little sign of a hierarchical or uneven partnership: "Therefore a man leaves his father and his mother and clings to his wife, and they become one flesh. And the two of them were naked, the *'adam* and his wife, and they were not ashamed" (vv. 24-25).[18]

Disobedience and its Consequences (Genesis 3)

Few passages have been as influential for Christian theological anthropology (particularly in the West) as Genesis 3, where the account of Adam and Eve eating from the forbidden tree has come to be known as "the fall" and the beginning of "original sin."[19] Along with the order of

---

[18] I have left the term *'adam* untranslated in order to illustrate how it is employed differently here than in Genesis 1. Also, although frequently used in contemporary wedding ceremonies and often taken for granted as an expression of the "nuclear family," the first sentence here is puzzling when considered in ancient Israel. Elsewhere in Genesis (and still today in some cultures) the man does *not* physically leave his parents, but brings his wife into his "father's house" (*beth 'ab*). For the crucial role of women as those with experience in and connections between different households, see Carole R. Fontaine, "The Sage in Family and Tribe," in *The Sage in Israel and the Ancient Near East*, ed. John G. Gammie and Leo G. Perdue (Winona Lake, IN: Eisenbrauns, 1990), 155-64.

[19] While dominant within the Western Christian theological tradition, this view of the "fall" is not universal. As Brueggemann, a prominent Protestant Old Testament scholar, writes: "The text [Gen. 2:4b-3:24] is commonly treated as the account of *'the fall.'* Nothing could be more remote from the narrative itself." Or again, "The text is not interested in theoretical or abstract questions of sin/death/evil/fall. The usual abstract questions of the world (e.g., origin of

creation in chapter 2, the depiction of Eve and the divine punishment for disobedience in Genesis 3 has also long been an important factor in promoting male authority over women within the Christian tradition. Indeed, while Augustine cemented the significance of this passage centuries later, the beginning of Genesis was already linked to debates over the relationship between the genders within the New Testament itself.[20]

Among other things, Eve's response to the serpent has received much attention and contributed to a negative portrayal of Eve within the Christian tradition. Where God previously told the man not to eat from the tree of the knowledge of good and evil (Gen. 2:17),[21] Eve renders these instructions as: "you shall not eat of the fruit of the tree . . . *nor shall you touch it*, or you shall die" (Gen. 3:3, emphasis mine). Some have suggested that this additional phrase represents the real beginning of human disobedience, since humans should not add to the command of the LORD.[22] While there has been much debate over the

---

death and sin, meaning of the "fall") are likely to be false, escapist questions. Such questions are no part of biblical testimony and are of no interest to genuine faith." Walter Brueggemann, *Genesis*, Interpretation: A Bible Commentary for Teaching and Preaching (Atlanta: John Knox Press, 1982), 41, 43.

[20] The New Testament already reflects a diversity of interpretation regarding the implications of this Genesis passage for male/female relations. For instance, I Timothy refers to the "order of creation" as a basis for male authority: ". . . For Adam was formed first, then Eve; and Adam was not deceived, but the woman was deceived and became a transgressor" (1 Tim. 2:11-14). In contrast, 1 Corinthians employs the same passage to emphasize the interdependence and mutuality of men and women: "Be imitators of me, as I am of Christ. . . . Man was not made from woman, but woman from man . . . . Nevertheless, in the Lord woman is not independent of man or man independent of woman. For just as woman came from man, so man comes through woman; but all things come from God" (1 Cor. 11:1, 7-12).

[21] One of the intriguing gaps within the narrative is that God initially warns the man, not the woman, about eating from this tree. Although she clearly hears about this prohibition, the passage does not inform us how this came to be, which has spawned numerous interpretations.

[22] These words have prompted a remarkably different evaluation within some parts of Jewish interpretation, where Eve's response has even provided the basis for her depiction as the first rabbi. Like a good teacher, Eve constructs a "fence around the Torah" by making the requirements more strict than God's

precise nature of this disobedience and the significance of the tree, our primary goal here will be to explore what the beginning of Genesis tells us regarding humans and the appropriate relationship among them in our context *outside* of Eden. To this end we will concentrate on what are sometimes described as the "curses" that the LORD God imposes.

While God curses the serpent (v. 14) and the ground (v. 17) neither the man nor the woman are cursed directly; nonetheless, both continue to bear the effects of what has happened. The woman is told that she will experience great pain in childbirth, and further that: "your desire shall be for your husband (man), and he shall rule over you." The man, on the other hand, now faces the constant struggle to raise food from the cursed ground: "By the sweat of your face you shall eat bread until you return to the ground, for out of it you were taken; you are dust, and to dust you shall return" (v. 19). Though these tasks have become more difficult, in both cases they also relate directly to pre-"fall" purposes: by giving birth the woman fulfills the divine word to "be fruitful and multiply," while through his "toil" the man continues the task of working the ground.[23] However, as these verses make clear, something significant has changed.

The basic difficulty with interpreting God's speech to the woman and man in Genesis 3:16-19 lies in whether these statements should be seen as prescriptive or descriptive. In other words, do they describe or explain the way things are or tend to be, or does this represent the divine will or command going forward? It is at this point, I would suggest, that interpretation has often been inconsistent.

For instance, at its most basic level, should Christians develop and employ means to lessen the amount of effort ("sweat of the brow") required to produce food from the earth? Although often not stated in this way, many Christians would be open to technological advancement if it allows for better food production. Some may even go so far as to

---

initial command and thus safeguarding God's word from being violated. The logic works, since if Eve would have heeded her own statement and not touched the fruit, she would not have eaten it either.

[23] This appears to be a word-play with the previous purpose of the man. Initially, he was meant to till/work/serve (*'abod*) where now he will "toil" (*'abur*).

suggest it is our duty to do so; in a world of hunger we should produce as much food as possible. When applied to Genesis 3, this view sees the curse of the ground as a consequence of the "fall" which we should counteract or struggle against as much as possible.

However, the passage regarding the woman in Genesis 3 has often been seen in precisely the opposite direction:

> To the woman [the LORD God] said, "I will greatly increase your pangs in childbearing; in pain you shall bring forth children, yet your desire shall be for your husband, and *he shall rule over you.*" (v. 16)

For some, the pain of childbirth represents a divinely ordained punishment that needs to be endured and should not be lessened. Indeed, on the basis of this passage women have been prohibited from taking painkillers during childbirth in some settings. Likewise, some have taken this verse as a divine command confirming the order of creation, so that a man's ordained role is to "rule over" his woman/wife. In this view, God's words provide a prescriptive description of how the relationship between the sexes *should* ("shall") function. However, to be consistent this position would also imply that the man's plight is also God-ordained. If women can't take painkillers, men can't use tractors either.

Although less often noted, a direct parallel in the next chapter helps to shed light on this verse. After Cain murders his brother Abel, God says to him: "Why are you angry, and why has your countenance fallen? If you do well, will you not be accepted? And if you do not do well, sin is lurking at the door; its desire is for you, *but you must master it*" (Gen. 4:16-17, emphasis mine). Intriguingly, God's words to the woman and to Cain reflect a parallel structure and identical terminology:[24]

---

[24] Arnold also notes this connection and sees in it a confirmation of a descriptive rather than prescriptive reading of this material. He also notes that the term "desire" (*teshuqah*) is extremely rare, appearing only three times in the Old Testament, which further underscores the connection between these

"... In pain you shall bring forth children, yet your **desire** (*teshuqah*) (shall be) **for your** husband, he **shall rule over** (*mashal b-*) you. (Gen. 3:16) (*we'el-'ishek teshurqathek wehu' yimshol bak*)	"... sin is lurking at the door; its **desire** (*teshuqah*) (is) **for you**, **but** you **must master** (*mashal b-*) it." (Gen. 4:16-17)[25] (*we'eleka teshuqatho w'attah timshol-bo*)

Although the NRSV renders the main verb as "rule over" in one chapter and "master" in the next, the Hebrew wording is identical; the only difference lies in the shift from third person ("*he* shall") to second ("*you* must"), and the change of the final pronoun from "you" to "it" required by the context. Despite virtual unanimity in translating the phrase spoken to the woman as "he shall rule over you," significantly more variety appears in rendering the second: "and thou *shalt rule* over him" (KJV); "but you *should rule* over it" (NKJV); "but you *must rule* over it" (ESV); "but you *must master* it" (NAS, NIV, RSV, NRSV); "you *can still master* him" (NJB); "but thou *mayest rule* over it" (JPS); and "Yet you *can be its master*" (TNK). It must be said that all of these are legitimate translations; one is not more "literal" than another.

The difficulty here lies in the imperfect aspect of the verb, which allows for many possibilities. For instance, an imperfect verb can denote a command ("thou shalt"), a persuasive statement ("you must") or a simple future ("you will"); it can be used as a modal ("you could/should/would"), to express ability ("you can"), or a wish or desire ("may you"); it can even be used to describe continuous or habitual

---

two passages. Its only other occurrence appears in Song of Songs 7:10. Arnold, *Genesis*, 70.

[25] To visually illustrate the similarity between these two verses I have placed the terms that reflect direct correspondence between these two passages in bold type. I have also placed the varying forms of the verb "to be" in parentheses, since these are contextually implied but not explicitly present in either passage.

action ("you constantly," "you tend to"); and more.[26] Given all of these possibilities, and particularly in light of the variety of translations of the imperfect of the identical verb form in Genesis 4, it is striking that God's statement to the woman is repeatedly translated as "he *shall rule over you*." Indeed, out of the ten versions surveyed here, only the NIV and NJB offer an alternative translation, with "he will rule over you" and "he will dominate you" respectively.

Taken on its own it is possible, as some do, to read this passage in a prescriptive sense where God's words to the woman mandate how things *should* be: "he shall rule over you." However, I find it problematic to do so and then treat the statement to the man as merely descriptive, so that the toil involved in producing food is a difficulty that one should attempt to limit. If, on the other hand, the difficulty of working the ground is understood as a difficulty we should attempt to overcome, then the same should be said of the depiction of gender imbalance. Thus, one could just as accurately read the phrase: "(unfortunately) he will tend to rule over you."[27] In other words, this statement neither reflects the original plan of God nor a divinely mandated "Plan B" after the "fall," but reflects a tendency arising from human disobedience that all too often plays itself out.[28] Thus, a

---

[26] Verbs in Biblical or Classical Hebrew do not have "tenses" but rather are conjugated (or "built," to use the Hebrew idiom) based on aspect. As a result the division between past, present, and future commonly assumed in other languages proves more complex and ambiguous. Thus, while an imperfect commonly refers to a future or potential action, it can also be used to describe ongoing action in the present or even habitual action in the past. For instance, "I will go to the store," "I go to the store every week," and "Last year I went to the store every week" all reflect an imperfect aspect, even though they reflect future, present, and past tenses respectively.

[27] Arnold discusses the issue of descriptive vs. prescriptive readings and concludes: "Whatever the nuanced meanings of the archaic poetry and terminology, now partly lost to us, the rulership of the man is no more prescriptive than pain in childbirth." Suggesting that the phrase may reflect an "attempt or endeavor rather than fact" he proposes the translation: "he will attempt to rule over you." Arnold, *Genesis*, 70, 71.

[28] Many scholars take this view. The following quotations come from a Jewish and Catholic Christian scholar respectively: "It is quite clear from the description of woman in 2:18, 23 that the ideal situation, which hitherto

descriptive view seems to make better sense of the surrounding narrative context than one that sees this phrase as prescriptive in nature.

Finally, it is noteworthy that the man only explicitly "names" the woman Eve *after* the "fall" and the description of its consequences (Gen. 3:20). If one sees God's statement to the woman as a normative command then this confirms the man's authority over the woman. If, however, one sees masculine dominance as an unfortunate consequence of the fall, the man's action may immediately illustrate this tendency. In any case, 'adam gives the woman a proper name here, which is different than "naming" a species of creature as he does with the animals. It is also striking that the passage explains the name "Eve" as the mother of "*all* living" (not just humanity), which puts her on fairly even footing with the 'adam. Might this suggest a joint priority over creation in this chapter similar to the "dominion" granted to 'adam (both male and female) in Genesis 1?

As we have seen, although Genesis 2-3 has often been read as confirming men's priority over women as instituted by God and reflected in the "order of creation," this view does not account well for all of the material within this narrative. Despite its connotations in English, the term "helper" does not reflect a secondary or subordinate role in the Old Testament, but is often used of the stronger, more authoritative or even dominant party. While the overwhelming tendency to translate God's speech to the woman as "he *shall* rule over you" suggests that this is a prescriptive statement or even command, the

---

existed, was the absolute equality of the sexes. The new state of male dominance is regarded as an aspect of the deterioration in the human condition that resulted from defiance of divine will." Sarna, *Genesis*, 28. As with many others, David W. Cotter sees vv. 14-21 as "etiological" and describes these verses as follows: "It should be noted that these, especially male dominance, are the undesired realities of a sinfully disordered world. Our author is attempting to explain the mysterious realities of the world in which he (or she) lived." David W. Cotter, *Genesis*, Berit Olam (Collegeville, MI: Liturgical Press, 2003), 35. In contrast, Wenham argues that the man has authority over the woman, since she is formed from man and "twice named by man (2:23; 3:20)." As a result, "It is therefore usually argued that 'rule' here represents harsh exploitive subjugation." Wenham, *Genesis 1-15*, 81.

breadth of possible translations is less often recognized. Further, when considered in light of the consequences for the man and a parallel verse in the next chapter, this statement seems to be descriptive rather than prescriptive. In other words, the tendency for men to "rule over" women appears as yet another unfortunate consequence of the "fall," which humans should struggle to overcome.

Still "In the Image" (Gen. 5:1-3)

Though the beginning of Adam's genealogy attracts much less attention than the preceding chapters, Gen. 5:1-3 proves significant for our topic:

> This is the list of the descendants of Adam ('*adam*). When God created humankind ('*adam*), he made them (it) in the likeness of God. Male and female he created them, and he blessed them and named them "Humankind" ('*adam*) when they were created. When Adam ('*adam*) had lived one hundred thirty years, he became the father of a son in his likeness, according to his image, and named him Seth ... (Gen. 5:1-3)

This passage brings together the perspectives of Genesis 1 and Genesis 2-3 in a very striking way. While we would expect '*adam* to appear as a proper name at the beginning of a genealogy (and the term clearly continues as such in verse 3),[29] this list of descendants is immediately interrupted by a rehearsal of Genesis 1:26-27. Precisely where the human genealogy begins we are taken back to the initial creation of '*adam*, where the term appears not as male over against female or as a proper name, but as male *and* female. Although hidden in translation, these verses combine two very different uses of the term '*adam*; the contrast could not be more stark or the difference more

---

[29] Though its significance lies beyond the scope of this paper, the phrase "the generations of ..." appears over ten times within Genesis and functions as an organizational or structural element within the book. Except for Genesis 2:4 ("these are the generations of the heavens and the earth"), each genealogy begins with the name of a character in the account: Adam (5:1); Noah (6:9); the sons of Noah (10:1); Shem (11:10); Terah (11: 27); Ishmael (25:12); Isaac (25:19); Esau (36:1, 9); and Jacob (37:2).

jarring.[30] For our purposes, I would like to mention three implications of this brief passage.

First, this passage appears *after the expulsion from Eden*. Despite their disobedience in the Garden and its negative consequences, humanity—both male and female— still reflects the "likeness of God." Although some Christian groups and theologians have insisted on "human depravity," the "fall" does not alter humanity's status or erase the divine likeness instilled in them as 'adam at creation. At the same time, the statement that "he (Adam) died" (Gen. 5:5) serves as an important reminder that humanity is *not* divine, but a creature.

Second, although the "likeness of God" continues to be passed on, the means by which this occurs has fundamentally changed to that of procreation. Where 'adam as male and female was created directly by God, Adam in turn fathers Seth "in his likeness, according to his image." Further, since Seth is in the likeness of Adam who is in the likeness of God, this passage also suggests that the divine "image and likeness" resides in each and every human being.

Third, while the divine image is passed on, the child appears in the likeness of Adam and not immediately of God.[31] While a link to Eden

---

[30] One of the intriguing and puzzling characteristics of biblical material lies in its frequently unharmonized nature. Biblical scholars have long argued, on the basis of such shifts, that Genesis reflects different traditions or written "sources" that were collected and put together at some point. In doing so, some treat the beginning of Genesis as containing two different creation accounts that have little to do with one another; for a classic example of this approach see: E. A. Speiser, *Genesis*, introduction translation, in The Anchor Bible (Garden City, NY: Doubleday, 1964), 3-28. While there may have been previous "versions" of such material, the passage in Genesis 5:1-3 reflects the intentional intermingling of perspectives or even "sources" to create a new whole. Whatever its prehistory, the canonical text(s) of the Bible provide the basis for ongoing Christian interpretation.

[31] As Brueggemann states: "The text may realistically recognize that Seth and his heirs are a strange, unresolved mixture of the *regal* image of God and the *threatened* image of Adam. Such a double statement recognizes the ambivalence of humankind, even as Paul later experienced it (cf. Rom. 7:15-23)." Walter Brueggemann, *Genesis: A Bible Commentary for Teaching and Preaching*, Interpretation (Atlanta: John Knox Press, 1982), 68.

remains, this also points to a new stage in which the difficulties and problems begun in the Garden continue to have ongoing effects.

Although it often does not receive much attention, Genesis 5:1-3 provides an important corrective or even a textual antidote for an overly bleak view of humanity espoused in some western Christian theology. Instead of, or at least alongside, a thoroughgoing "original sin" endemic to all humanity, this brief passage confirms that people, men and women, continue to bear the "likeness of God" even after their expulsion from Eden. Thus, it refuses to allow a negative view of biblical anthropology to effectively erase the divine image and likeness granted at creation.

Where some cite the "order of creation" to uphold views regarding the priority or authority of men over women, the "order of *Scripture*" suggests otherwise. Having narrated the "fall," Genesis returns to reaffirm the creation of *'adam* as both male and female, and thus implicitly the dominion of *both* over creation as described in Genesis 1. In doing so, it bounds the account of Adam and Eve in the Garden before and after with an affirmation that questions an imbalance in authority or status between men and women, and so cautions us against such a conclusion. Indeed, given the patriarchal culture and perspective from which biblical material emerges, I am actually amazed at how much fodder the account provides to critique and challenge such a perspective.

Implications

In this paper we have looked at the beginning of Genesis to consider its implications for biblical anthropology. In doing so we have also encountered broader issues worth highlighting regarding the nature of the Bible, the significance of interpretation, and the role of the community of faith.

First, we have seen that, as is often the case with the Bible more generally, these chapters are remarkably unharmonized. Genesis 5:1-3 provides a microcosm of this issue by using *'adam* in two very different ways within the same sentence: first as a proper name, then as a generic term that includes male and female, and finally as a proper name again. Far from being hidden, the passage highlights these shifts in such a way as to make them unmistakable. While we may be tempted to either smooth over such differences or to heighten them to the point where we see no connection between two different "creation accounts," these verses provide an example where divergent views have been incorporated into a meaningful whole. Rather than a problem to be solved, recognizing such differences can prove fruitful for interpreting the document we have before us.

Second, we have seen both the significance and inevitability of interpretation. The ambiguity of the language and gaps within the story inevitably draw readers into the process of interpretation. As our discussion of the term "helper" and the phrase "he shall rule over you" demonstrate, translation adds yet another level of complexity to the interpretive enterprise. The latter case also illustrates that it is impossible to avoid interpretation and "just read" a biblical document even when working in the original language; differences in translation often make explicit the ambiguity that lies implicit within the original grammar itself. Similarly, the traditional view that Genesis 3 describes "the fall" and the beginning of "original sin" necessarily goes beyond the words on the page.[32] This does not mean that such a perspective should be necessarily deemed mistaken or inaccurate, but simply that it needs to be recognized as an interpretation within the ongoing tradition.

Third, given the unharmonized nature, gaps, and ambiguities reflected in biblical material, the role of the community as both the site and embodiment of interpretation proves essential. The relationship between genders provides an excellent example where life affects interpretation and interpretation informs life. This example also illustrates how proposing a different interpretation opens the possibility and challenge of embodying an alternate understanding of the tradition; and it is the community of faith where such interpretations take place and are tested in practice. After all, the ultimate goal of Christian biblical interpretation, whether of the Old Testament or the New, is to reveal and embody the gospel of Jesus Christ under the guidance of the Holy Spirit.[33]

---

[32] Brueggemann, *Genesis*, 41-44.

[33] This is not simply a linear process or one in which a New Testament view necessarily trumps the Old. It may well be, for instance, that a rereading of the

In light of the three elements just described, it is also important to state that our interpretation is always provisional. Conclusions are not settled for all time but represent our best contextual attempt to understand and embody the gospel in our time and place, building on and being faithful to the tradition that has been passed down to us. And once again, it is hard to overemphasize the role of the community in this process. Although a Scripture may theoretically exist on its own, it cannot *function* as such without a community committed to engage it and live in accordance with it. At the same time, Christian Scripture does not contain or monopolize God. Within the Christian tradition the Bible is not the revelation in and of itself, but rather functions as a pointer witnessing to the divine that lies beyond it. Since the Gospel lies before us as well as behind us, our preceding tradition—as essential as it is—does not hold a monopoly on appropriate interpretation but prompts us to return again and again to rediscover, recommit to, and continue to embody the gospel it reveals.

Conclusion

In this paper we have reconsidered some of the most influential biblical material for understanding the role and nature of humanity within the Western Christian tradition. Indeed, it would be difficult to overstate the influence the "order of creation," the "fall," and "original sin" have had within this tradition.

Nonetheless, we have also seen that interpretations linked to these concepts do not account for all of the material present in the first chapters of Genesis. Perhaps most significantly I have argued that Eve's role as Adam's "helper" as well as God's speech to the woman should not be understood to support male dominance as divinely mandated Rather, the common tendency for men to "rule over" women reflects a consequence of the "fall" that we are called to limit and overcome as much as possible. In a similar vein, if one jumps from the "fall" to "redemption" in the Gospels it becomes possible to miss or downplay the insistence in Genesis 5 that humanity continues to be formed in the divine likeness, even on this side of Eden. Thus, I have argued against a

---

beginning of Genesis and other New Testament material may well lead us to re-evaluate Timothy in light of the gospel as much as the inverse.

view of humanity as thoroughly "depraved," although the ongoing repercussions of human disobedience were—and remain—all too real.

Finally, while it has attracted much attention, in my view one of the most striking aspects of the account of the Garden in Genesis lies in its brevity. Humanity quickly emerges out of an earthly paradise, so that the vast majority of the Bible proves concerned with life on this side of Eden rather than an extended pining for how things "used to be." However, since creation remains good but things are not right in their current arrangement, it is the task of the church to embody and thus be a witness to how things should be rather than accepting them as they are. I believe the human tendency to "rule over" or dominate, whether men over women, one people over another, or humanity over the rest of creation, remains a major issue that the church is called to address. Doing so is not primarily a philosophical problem, but rather a challenge of imagining and incarnating a different reality.

PART VI:

THE SELF

In the Name of Allah, the Beneficent, the Merciful

THE ROLE OF TURNING TO THE SELF: INTROSPECTION IN QUR'ANIC DISCOURSE

MOHAMMAD MOTAHARI FARIMANI

Every book brings some questions to our attention for which it tries to provide us with some answers. If we face some questions in a book to which no responses are put forth, that is usually either due to the fact that the author is not sufficiently prepared to present the answers, or that he does not deem it opportune to do so and intends to broach them at a later time.

In the Qur'an we encounter a number of verses that raise questions but are seemingly left unanswered. Here are some examples:

Is there any reward for goodness—other than goodness? (55:60)

Is one who worships devoutly during the hour of the night prostrating himself or standing (in adoration), who takes heed of the hereafter, and who places his hope in the mercy of his lord (like one who does not)? Say: "Are those equal, those who know and those who do not know?" It is those who are endued with understanding that receive admonition. (39:9)

Of course, we never justify these types of questions in the Qur'an by saying that God did not have a response handy, or that He wants to respond to it in some other book. For, according to Muslims, the Qur'an is the last and ultimate scripture sent down to humans. So, what is the reason behind this silence?

A little deliberation leads us to an answer. Namely, that these questions belong to a special category, as they have not been put forward by a human for other humans, but rather, they have been tabled by the Creator of all human beings. And He knows us much better than we humans know ourselves. Hence, He knows that we know the answers—the answers being providentially provided and innate to all human beings.

Leaving the questions unanswered is a divine contrivance whereby all are encouraged to introspect and refer to our selves. It is worthy to note that no one needs to do any research to get the answers to these types of questions. In fact, as soon as one "turns to himself" or "to his self," he has the answer.

In this paper, I intend to explain a notion used in the Qur'an, that is, turning to oneself. After explaining the notion, I will refer to its situation and import in Islamic teaching. This will be followed by some practical suggestions that might be helpful for our spirituality. Finally, I will explain how this discussion can provide us with responses to some frequently asked questions concerning both God and religion.

Certain scientific points in the Qur'an—which are astonishingly compatible with some new scientific discoveries—have received a lot of attention by some people, such as the compatibility between the Big Bang theory and continuous expansion of the universe on the one hand and the following verse on the other:

We built the heaven with might, and we are expanding it. (51:47)

Nevertheless, it seems that what the Qur'an says with regards to the human soul or self and its relation to God is much more fascinating and profound. Furthermore, things like the Big Bang are nothing more than theories, and as such it is not reasonable to give them too much attention.

At any rate, the notion of turning to the self has been mentioned in the Qur'an directly and indirectly. One of its direct and clear usages occurs in the midst of relating a story regarding Abraham. There is no mention of such a story in the Bible, but a somewhat similar story, with no mention of "turning to the self," has been mentioned in what is called the Oral Torah in Midrash Bereishit 38:13.

The story goes: Once when the people were in the midst of celebrating a festival, prophet Abraham made his way to the temple where the idols were kept. Going inside, Abraham took out an axe and broke all the idols, except for the biggest one of them, which he purposefully spared. When he had done his deed, he left the axe hanging around the shoulder of the biggest idol. When the people came to the temple to worship their idols, they were astonished to see the sad state of their gods.

> They said, "Who has done this to our gods? He must indeed be some evil-doer!" A group responded, "We have heard a youth make mention of him: he is called Abraham." They said, "Then bring him before the eyes of the people, that they may bear witness." When he was brought, they charged, "Are you the one who did this to our gods, O Abraham?" He said, "Nay, he did it– this is their biggest one! Ask him, if he can speak!" (21:60-64)

It is here that the Qur'an uses the phrase: "so the idolaters turned to themselves:"

> So they turned to themselves and said, "Surely you are the ones in the wrong!" (21:65)

It can be understood from this verse that what led the idolaters to the truth was turning to the self.

A question might arise here: Is it not the case that almost everyone in some way or another has some sort of "turn to the self"? If so, why does this referring to the self not show them the true way?

What makes the question more serious is that, as the Qur'an indicates, the "turning to the self" of the idolaters did not last long since after a short time they called the people to gather and decided to burn Abraham alive in order to defend their gods. A big fire was set up and, as punishment for breaking the idols, Abraham was thrown into it. But the fire miraculously failed to burn him and turned to flowers. Allah protected him and the people were amazed to see it—they could not believe their eyes! But it was so; Abraham was happy and his persecutors felt sad and helpless.

An example can help us to answer this question as to why referring to the self does not lead to truth. Every day, we witness that many quarrels and disputes take place between governments, politicians, believers, nonbelievers, family members, etc. We also see that there are a number of people who are able to prevent such quarrels from happening in their personal lives. But these altercations are not as important as another type of quarrel that occurs inside each and every person—there being no person who does not experience such internal disputes. For instance, one side of a person asks him to stop eating, while the other motivates him to go on. An internal voice invites him to avoid sin, while another voice incites him to be careless. When he gets angry, there are two voices that speak to him from inside his self: one says, "Take a hold of yourself;" while the other says, "Go on, vent your feelings!"

In other words, the dispute here is between two selves, or two "Is" and egos acting in opposite directions. It is "me" who has the temptation to eat more, and it is "me" who warns myself about that. Obviously, this does not mean that everyone is indeed composed of two distinct persons—in which case there would be two levels of the same entity trying to take control. But to follow up on this point would make the discussion more philosophical than Qur'anic, and this is not what we intend.

An important point with regards to the above example comes from incisively noting the kind of feelings we have after each dispute is finished. If the winning side or action is in accordance and in harmony with the good and the moral, we feel happy and victorious. Conversely, when we do evil or do something wrong, after the dust settles, we feel disappointed and ashamed. But if it is really true that in both cases it was "me" who did the deed, then why do I feel defeated and dejected in one case, and the opposite in the other? In short, who has defeated whom?

Scrutinizing when we feel victorious and when we feel defeated helps us to recognize the real self. To explain, when we resist evil desires, a sense of victory comes to the fore and we recognize the "I" that stands on the winners' podium to be the real self. The significant conclusion here is that the self who orders the good is our real self, and the other self is the imaginary or false self; or, one may call it the "non-self."

On this account, the Qur'anic phrase "they turned to themselves," can be explained in this way: At the moment when Abraham requested them to ask the biggest idol, they suddenly noticed what their real selves were saying, and had no choice other than to concur with Abraham at the moment. But why did they then go on to punish Abraham? Because their imaginary selves or non-selves took control of them again. Since their real selves were defeated after a short time, they returned again to their previous position.

The question still remains as to why the idolaters were unable to continue partaking of their real selves. In other words, why did their imaginary selves re-emerge and become dominant again so quickly?

The answer can be derived from the Qur'an. The Qur'an greatly emphasizes the fact that the only way for one to identify with the real self and have it be his active self—thereby preventing the imaginary self from taking control of his soul—is the remembrance of and invocation to God.

A fascinating and thought-provoking verse of the Qur'an takes us to the heart of the issue. In verse 19 of the Surah Hashr, God talks about the punishment of those who, despite frequent divine reminders to not forget God, still forget Him:

> And do not be like those who forget Allah, so He makes them forget their own selves. It is they who are the transgressors. (59:20)

As we see, the punishment is that God makes them forget their selves. At first sight, it seems strange that someone forgets himself. The first priority for everyone, believer or nonbeliever, good or wicked, is to do something for himself and improve his personal life—no one takes any step against himself. All humans do what they think is to their advantage, whether that advantage be spiritual or material. The substantial point here is that forgetting God makes one forget one's real self; hence, one begins to work in the context of an imaginary self, thinking all the while that one is working for oneself. He is not aware that by committing a sin he is actually going against his own self, as in fact the Qur'an sees committing a sin as an act of "oppression (*zulm*) to oneself." So what we can conclude is that, according to the Qur'an, there is a mutual relation between remembering God and remembering our souls and selves.

Here, a point of clarification is indispensable. Worldly desires are integral to human nature, and Islam by no means asks us to extinguish those desires. Rather, what is asked for in Islam is to direct them and manage them in such a way that they do not hinder the relation between the real self and God. What's more, Islam stipulates that satisfying the instincts and human desires in a religiously permissible way actually helps in the restoration of the real self.

Here, one of the reasons behind the religious injunctions to remember God in each and every moment of our lives comes to light. In Islam, just as in Christianity, there are stipulated prayers for many occasions. But in the case of Islam, it seems that such occasions are more numerous and wider in scope. The Muslim is encouraged to pronounce certain prayers, or at least the general invocation of the *basmalah* (i.e., In the Name of God, the Beneficent, the Merciful), prior to and during even the most mundane of activities. Hence, there are prescribed invocations for eating, sleeping, leaving the home, marital relations, childbirth, forbearing an illness, accompanying a funeral procession, and visiting a graveyard.

By the same token, a Muslim is strongly encouraged to turn all of his activities into a sort of worship by making his intention for that act to coincide with the pleasure and will of God. Hence, it does not matter whether one walks to the university or to see a friend, or whether one writes a paper or gives a lecture—all of these can become a sort of worship if they are done for the sake of God, although they can never replace the compulsory daily worship which is equivalent in weight to canonical liturgy. Therefore, invocation to God and the remembrance of Him is not just a part of a daily routine, but rather it ideally permeates life and inspires each and every moment.

Not only is there a mutual relation between remembrance of God and remembrance of self, but also the knowing of self has been put forth as a way of knowing God. I do not have the opportunity to delve into this issue here. Suffice it to mention the well-known saying of the Prophet when he said: "He who knows his self knows his Lord." There are some mystical and philosophical interpretations and explanations for this saying which should be explained on another occasion.

Let me summarize what has been put forward so far. Having started with the story of Abraham, we saw that God admired turning to the self as a means of reaching the truth. But which self can play such a role? There are two selves that can act and take control of us, but only one of them is the real human self. The duty asked of us by God is to prevent the imaginary self—who is in fact alien to the real self—from misleading us. God has shown us the unique way of turning to the self. The real and innate self cannot act and become activated without first being in an intimate connection with its Creator—such as would lead it to be in perpetual invocation to God and to be in continuous remembrance of Him. Knowing this self is tantamount to a continuous knowledge and remembrance of God. In a nutshell, remembrance of God leads us to His obedience, and this forms the unique way to restore the real self.

From here an essential distinction between the Qur'anic view on the turning to the self and the perspective of many philosophers, mystics, theologians, and others who have raised the issue of turning to the self comes to the fore.

As the Canadian philosopher Charles Taylor indicates in his famous book *Sources of the Self*, "Some sort of 'turning to the self' was relatively common topic among ancient moralists".[1] He adds that "Foucault has mentioned the importance of the 'care of oneself.'"[2] Likewise, in Hinduism, "turning to the self" is a commonly employed term. However, none of these approaches looks at the issue of the real self as the Qur'an looks at it. They commonly try to solve the issue by mere introspection and mental effort and there is neither mention of the remembering of God as the unique way of becoming free of the imaginary self, nor is the real self considered as a gateway towards knowing God. Nietzsche is mistaken to say that our souls are too small, for the human soul can continue to magnify and expand as long as it is connected with God. But if by "soul" Nietzsche means "the imaginary self," then that statement is in order.

---

[1] Charles Taylor, *Sources of the Self* (Cambridge: Harvard University Press, 1989), 130.
[2] Ibid.

Based on what has been presented here, the importance of turning to the self is such that it can hardly be exaggerated. This is evidenced by the fact that when it comes to this subject, everyone feels a sense of innate apprehensiveness or perilousness. This is because the all-present danger is that we dwell in the imaginary self instead of the real self. In so doing, we lose the wholeness of our identity and consequently fail to be servants of God. And we can do all this without even noticing!

In order to shed further light on this, Mawlana Rumi, the great Muslim poet, employs a parable. He recounts the story of a person who happily spares much time, effort, and money to construct a big building for himself. The day he wants to move in he notices that he inadvertently erected the building on someone else's property and is now empty-handed. This is the story of many of us humans on the Day of Judgment, when we will be made to see that what we have done has been in part, mostly, or even totally for an alien being—our false and imaginary self. The Qur'an succinctly summarizes this existential hazard by saying:

Truly, those in loss are those who lose themselves. (39:15)

What the prophet Muhammad says in this regard is illuminating: "The most terrible enemy to you is the self within you." How should we not be worried when our enemy is not merely close to us, but rather lives within us!

By the same token, when the Prophet was asked what is the most reassuring verse and also the most disappointing verse of the Qur'an, he mentioned a verse which is closely connected with the false self:

Shall we inform of those who are the greatest losers in respect of their life? Those whose striving is lost in this world's life and yet they reckon that what they are doing are good deeds. (18:103-104)

As we see here, since they have lost their real selves, they think that their efforts are for themselves, whereas in truth, they have mistaken their imaginary selves for their real ones.

Now, given that this spiritual disease approaches us so clandestinely, is there any way for us to recognize whether we seriously suffer from this disease? In other words, are there some signs that can help us come to know whether our imaginary selves are sometimes acting in us?

I think there are, and I confine myself to one instance. As we know, two very important elements that influence the quality of prayer are the intensity of concentration and the complete attention of the worshiper during that prayer. At first glance, the fact that a believer is ready to spend some of his time for enacting a religious precept and to actually pray should be given the higher value. However, why is there such a great difference between a prayer done with concentration and one done without—at least as far as Islam is concerned? To underline this difference, some Muslim mystics have made the remark that we need to repent for many absentminded prayers.

In light of what was noted with regards to the difference between the real self and the imaginary self, it would seem that the main point of praying is to connect with God; and if attention were to be lacking, this connection would not be between the real self and God. To put it differently, when someone is absentminded, with his attention wavering in and out during the prayer, it is his imaginary self that has taken control of him while the real self has failed to become sufficiently connected with God. The purpose of praying is not to stop from doing other jobs and do something as a ritual or as a formal liturgy. Rather, the main purpose is the invocation of the real self to God, and, so to speak, to connect the real self with God in the way designated by God. On this account, a criterion by which we can evaluate and compare the powers of the real self and the imaginary self in each one of us can be set. If one sees that despite his efforts he is still unable to pay full attention during prayers, it could be a sign that his real self is not the full governor of his self.

Turning to the last section of the paper, I believe the distinction between the real self and the imaginary self can be used as a key to provide good and even new answers to some frequently asked questions of which I will briefly mention three.

One of the criticisms frequently directed to believers is that obeying God is against human freedom and in some way or another suppresses it. The proponents of this objection think that by ignoring religion and

God they experience complete freedom. You might have heard someone say: "I do not practice any religion because I want to be the master of myself!"

The answer is clear. Everyone is either the servant of the real self, which is the same as being the servant of God, or the servant of his imaginary self—and there is no third option that can be derived from the Qur'an. Therefore, disobeying God is a clear example of slavery because such a person follows the dictates of his carnal desire, selfishness, vanity, and lust. But being in communion with the real self, as acting self, is tantamount to emancipation from the desires of the carnal soul. The one who obeys God connects himself with the infinite ocean of knowledge, love, and goodness. Such a connection existentially fulfills him and suffices him such that he becomes free from the need to follow his worldly desires.

The second question that can be answered in a similar manner is: Why does God invite us to worship Him? Does He need our worship?

The answer is that it is us who are in dire need of emancipation from the imaginary self, and this emancipation is entailed in the worship of God. Therefore, the need is on our side not God's.

Another question that can find a proper response in light of the above has to do with identifying the main reason that the secular worldview—and the solutions it offers to human issues—is not acceptable from the Islamic point of view. The answer is that the bulk of its "solutions" are premised on the imaginary self and are oblivious to the real self. In the atmosphere in which there is no room for any understanding of the real self, that is, for the secular mentality, there can be no reason to see profanity and blasphemy towards the sacred as being problematic. Such a mentality cannot understand why the limits of freedom should be assigned by God, why provocative pictures are not art, why mutual consent is not enough to condone any and all financial activity, and many other whys.

I will end by reciting the following two verses:

On the earth are signs for those of assured faith, as also in your own selves: will ye not then see? (41:53)

And keep thy soul content with those who call on their lord morning and evening, seeking his face; and let not thine eyes pass beyond them, seeking the pomp and glitter of this life; not obey any whose heart we have permitted to neglect the remembrance of us, one who follows his own desires, whose case has gone beyond all bounds. (18:28)

Conscience, Dissent, and Church: Theological Anthropology in Mennonite Perspective

Jeremy M. Bergen

At the second Mulsim-Mennonite Dialogue (Qom 2004), our friend and colleague A. James Reimer presented a paper on revelation, law, and conscience. Reimer explained how early Anabaptists understood the church as a "free church" that was "defined no longer by automatic [infant] baptism but by voluntary membership based on individual conscience and free choice, signified outwardly by adult baptism. Although entrance into the community was based on such free, non-coerced adult decision, once the choice had been made, a strong communal ethic set in."[1]

The role of individual conscience in the Christian tradition embodies several tensions which Reimer touches on in this brief quotation. First, the Anabaptist movement itself was a movement of conscience, especially of those moved to dissent from the broad consensus of Christendom Christianity (for example, regarding infant baptism), even at the risk of persecution. Secondly, as highly committed persons moved by conscience formed early Anabaptist communities, the "strong community ethic" that emerged could, in turn, create the conditions for internal dissent by members of these communities with somewhat different visions of the Christian life. These tensions lead to a third, which is a theological debate about the very category of

---

[1] A. James Reimer, "Revelation, Law, and Individual Conscience," *Conrad Grebel Review* 24, no. 1 (Winter 2006): 13. The title of the Festschrift presented to Jim Reimer on the occasion of his retirement, *Creed and Conscience* (Kitchener, ON: Pandora Press, 2007), indicates the significance these themes played in his life's theological work.

conscience, especially as this category has been shaped by Western modernity. In his paper at Qom, Reimer argued for a strong link between individual conscience and divine law precisely because in Western thought these connections are no longer assumed. In the West, the conscience is often taken to be the seat of the autonomous individual, a right of "free choice" perhaps compatible with dissent, but not with the recognition of the authority of God nor the community of faith.

In this paper, I will situate the role the conscience plays in Anabaptist-Mennonite theology and practice within the wider Christian tradition. Drawing from both Roman Catholicism and Anabaptism, I will address the second tension about the relation of the individual and the church; drawing from both Protestantism and Anabaptism, I will address the third tension by developing the Christological and pneumatological grounding of conscience. The first tension, Anabaptism's position of conscientious dissent from dominant forms of Christianity, lurks within any attempt to think both from a Mennonite perspective and within the wider Christian tradition, a theme that characterized Reimer's entire theological project. I will comment on this dimension briefly. Finally, because what Anabaptist-Mennonites believe is often implicit in practices, I will conclude by examining two historical episodes in which conscience played a key role.

Theological Developments: Conscience and Modernity

In Western thought the concept of conscience has not been static and therefore resists simple definition. First, a biblical account links it with the person as a whole. Though the Old Testament does not employ a term equivalent to our conception of conscience, the heart is often described as the centre from which thoughts, emotions, actions, and moral judgments issue, and is the key point of contact with God. God's Word dwells in the heart (Deut. 30:14), and God's law will be written on the hearts of God's people (Jer. 31:33). In turn, God may look upon the heart (Ps. 44:21) and test it (Ps. 17:3).

Secondly, the Latin *conscientia* and the Greek *syneidesis* both imply a "knowing with." The apostle Paul addressed the church at Corinth with a slightly different though related sense of the significance of conscience. Some Corinthian Christians had no objection to eating meat that had been sacrificed to idols; since idols are unreal, the meat is the same as any other. Other Christians did not eat this meat, perhaps because they lacked full knowledge that idols had no power.[2] How were persons with different consciences to coexist in one church? Paul does not give a "modern" response; he does not say that each should eat or abstain according to her conscience. He counsels that those whose consciences are strong should not exercise their freedom to eat meat, but should rather abstain in certain circumstances for the sake of those of weak conscience for whom this would be scandalous (1 Cor. 8:1-13). Thus, there is not a simple correlation between individual conscience and action; conscience is exercised, even moderated, in the context of community.

Thirdly, conscience in the Christian tradition has been identified with the "voice of God, present in the heart of every person," as one Catholic-Protestant dialogue has put it.[3] Yet, since the Montanist heresy of the second century, in which so-called prophets claimed to receive new revelations from the Holy Spirit, the church has guarded against claims that the content of individual conscience is simply and automatically identical with revelation. The tradition has affirmed that the Spirit indeed speaks in conscience, though not in isolation. Because the same Spirit constitutes the church and preserves it in truth, the Spirit that speaks in conscience cannot *ultimately* be incompatible with the church, though our limited human knowing may not always discern the *form* of that compatibility.

Fourthly, the ethical dimension of conscience, especially in the Catholic tradition, is embodied in a key statement from Vatican II: "In the depths of his conscience, man detects a law which he does not impose upon himself, but which holds him to obedience . . . . For man has in his heart a law written by God; to obey it is the very dignity of

---

[2] Wendell Lee Willis, *Idol Meat in Corinth: The Pauline Argument in 1 Corinthians 8 and 10* (Chico, CA: Scholars Press, 1983), 94. There is, however, an extensive debate about the identity and character of those "weak" in conscience.

[3] Disciples of Christ-Roman Catholic International Commission for Dialogue, "Conscience and Community: Formation and Practice [Agreed Account]," *Mid-Stream* 40, no. 6 (2001).

man; according to it he will be judged. Conscience is the most secret core and sanctuary of a man. There he is alone with God, Whose voice echoes in his depths."[4]

Fifthly, contemporary notions of interiority, a theme traced by genealogists of Western modernity,[5] highlight the reflexivity in self-consciousness. Conscience exists as the self relates to the self, especially in the detection of disharmony in that relation. The inner dialogue of conscience may provide a guide for future action or a framework for reflecting on the morality of past action, but even more so is the key to an "integrated" and "authentic" life.

Sixthly, the "turn to the subject" ingredient in the Enlightenment's suspicion of external authorities and tradition invested individual conscience with a new status as a self-contained authority. For Immanuel Kant, conscience is "the subjective reflective principle of directing or orienting oneself to an ideal interpreter."[6] This ideal interpreter is the supremely rational one; in this sense conscience is practical reason judging itself according to reason, the truth of which is manifest in universality. For Kant, the existence of God is postulated as the basis for the *authority* of conscience, though special revelation is no longer the material basis for its content. Modern thought soon came to recognize that if God is merely a formal guarantor of conscience, then God is an unnecessary hypothesis. With this move, conscience emerged as a supremely human source of appeal and judgment.

Roman Catholicism: Church and Conscience

The focus on the "depth" of conscience in the Vatican II statement need not imply individualism, but rather Catholicism's high estimation of the human being created in the image of God. It is also coupled with a strong role for the church in the formation of conscience. The church has an obligation to form consciences, and persons have an obligation to let their consciences be thus formed. Accordingly, instruction in the

---

[4] Second Vatican Council, *Gaudium et Spes: Pastoral Constitution on the Church in the Modern World*, no. 16 (1965).

[5] See Charles Taylor, *Sources of the Self: The Making of Modern Identity* (Cambridge, MA: Harvard University Press, 1989).

[6] G. Felicitas Munzel, *Kant's Conception of Moral Character* (Chicago: University of Chicago Press, 1999), 218.

Word of God, the authorized teaching of the church, participation in the sacraments of Eucharist and Reconciliation (Penance), works of mercy, and prayer all give proper shape to conscience.

However, conscience also gives shape to the church, even the consciences of those who dissent. Though Catholic theologians deny that dissent is ever acceptable, what they usually mean is that falsehood cannot be endorsed. But dissent grounded in conscience is not the same as falsehood. The church must hear the echo of its formation of consciences in the dissent of its members, and thus presume to defer definitive judgment. Dissent takes issue with the operative assumptions of the day, and it may prove to be prophetic, to reflect an acceptable diversity, or to be partially, or fully, in error.

The 1997 confession of the French Catholic Bishops of what the church did and did not do during the Holocaust may be understood as a recognition that the dissenting minority during the war, the small number of cleric and lay Catholics who took risks to protect Jews and enjoined the church hierarchy to do the same, had in fact been right. They acknowledged that "the Church of France failed in her mission as teacher of consciences and that therefore she carries along with the Christian people the responsibility for failing to lend their aid, from the very first moments, when protest and protection were still possible as well as necessary."[7] They judged the source of the church's collective failures to be rooted in patterns of excessive institutional self-preservation, and in anti-Jewish beliefs and practices. In particular, "an anti-Jewish tradition stamped its mark in differing ways on Christian doctrine and teaching, in theology, apologetics, preaching and in the liturgy."[8]

The bishops did not pass judgment on the consciences of persons at the time. (An inculpably erroneous conscience is one which is malformed through no fault of the subject's, a plausible possibility for some given the church's acknowledgement of failure. Consequent acts are not morally good, but the will is not evil and the subject is not guilty. Others may have avoided proper formation through self-deception or willful ignorance and are therefore culpable.) However, in

---

[7] French Catholic Bishops, "Declaration of Repentance [Drancy Declaration]," *Origins* 27, no. 18 (16 October 1997): 305.
[8] Ibid., 304.

light of the recognition of the particular shape of this past wrong, the church's obligation to form proper consciences in the future is served by an examination of the past.

The church in France ought to have heeded dissent in its midst, and eventually did. Recognition of the horrors that Christians have visited upon Jews has led to the explicit rejection of supersessionism[9]—the idea that God's covenant with the Jews has been rescinded—a functionally operative teaching in Christian thought for centuries.

The churchly dimension of conscience goes both from the community to the individual (the failure of which during the Holocaust the bishops acknowledged was a principle fault of the church, and which they sought to correct in part by a public act of repentance), and from the individual to the community, even in the form of dissent. Crucially, the formation of conscience takes a tremendous amount of time, not just the lifetime of an individual, but years and centuries as the church continues to be challenged to greater faithfulness by dissonant voices in its midst. Of course, dissent *may* be the espousal of falsehood, but it cannot be assumed that it is nor that it is always a simple matter to determine. Furthermore, as a *minority* Christian movement, Anabaptist-Mennonites believe that dissenters may in fact bear a truthful witness to the entire church, even if this takes years or centuries to recognize.

Protestant developments: Christ and Conscience

The reformer Martin Luther famously wrestled with a guilty conscience. Young Luther doubted that any of his efforts to live a righteous life could merit God's favour. His great insight was that while he was still a sinner, God *declared* him righteous. For Luther, God's law did not exist as an achievable pattern of life, but rather as the occasion by which he came to realize, in his conscience, the bondage of his will to sin and thus the need for God's grace. A "happy conscience" was the result of faith, not works. While Luther (and Calvin) intended their reforms to turn the attention of Christians away from themselves and their actions and towards God's grace in Christ, some who followed in their traditions sought greater *human* assurance. For example, some

---

[9] Second Vatican Council, *Nostra Aetate: Declaration on the Relation of the Church to Non-Christian Religions*, no. 4 (1965).

Pietists and Puritans wondered whether the conscience itself might be examined for evidence of one's relationship with God. Individuals examined their consciences, conversion experiences, and prayer practices for signs, even assurance, that salvation was being extended to them.[10]

Twentieth-century Lutheran theologian Dietrich Bonhoeffer's account of conscience differs from Luther's because Bonhoeffer starts from a different theological anthropology, one which takes into account some of the dangers represented or even introduced by Luther. For Bonhoeffer, Christian salvation solves not the problem of a guilty conscience (as for Luther), but the problem of the individuated self which seeks to dominate others. The attempt of the atomized self to ground its own unity in itself—in conscience—reflects not the voice of God but flight from God. Bonhoeffer describes Adam's hiding from God (Genesis 3:8-10) as the origin of human conscience. Adam flees from God's judgment to his own, and by his own deluded standards, and self-serving accusation of Eve, attempts to justify himself before God. In his conscience, Adam projects a god of his own making.[11]

Thus, Bonhoeffer indicts a modern notion of conscience in favour of a distinctly Christian one. "When conscience is said to be an immediate relation to God, Christ and the church are excluded, because God's having bound the divine self to the mediating word is circumvented." Thus, "[o]nly when Christ has broken through the solitude of human beings will they know themselves placed into truth."[12] This truth is not a set of affirmations or principles; in fact these are typically the refuge of the conscience that flees God. Rather, the truth is a person—Jesus Christ. And because of the person Jesus Christ is, humans who are "in Christ" are set in a web of true relationships with themselves, with others, and with God.

---

[10] William C. Placher, *The Domestication of Transcendence: How Modern Thinking About God Went Wrong* (Louisville: Westminster John Knox Press, 1996), chap. 6.

[11] Dietrich Bonhoeffer, *Creation and Fall*, trans. John C. Fletcher (London: SCM Press, 1959), 82–84.

[12] Dietrich Bonhoeffer, *Act and Being: Transcendental Philosophy and Ontology in Systematic Theology*, trans. H. Martin Rumscheidt (Minneapolis: Fortress Press, 1996), 141.

Jesus Christ determines and reveals the true sociality of human beings, and consequently the true nature and content of conscience. For Bonhoeffer, Jesus Christ is the man for others, not only in his earthly ministry but also in his role as the representative of all of humanity to God, and all of humanity to each person. To be "in Christ" is to surrender oneself to God—and because Jesus Christ is both God and man—to others as well. The consequently liberated conscience ultimately seeks unity not with itself but unity with Christ, which transforms both being and action.

The liberated conscience is not restricted merely to adherence to the law, or to established morality (which for Bonhoeffer are efforts by which we justify ourselves), but is rather free to respond to the concrete distress of the neighbour—the "being for others" reflecting our true humanity—even to assume guilt in the process.[13] That for Bonhoeffer this meant involvement in a plot to assassinate Hitler may give pause to the pacifist, but it also serves as a reminder that pacifism ought not to be its own principle, but rather a serviceable description for a set of practices that follow from consistent adherence to Jesus.

Anabaptist-Mennonites may partially disagree with Bonhoeffer about the concrete ethical implications of a Christ-centred conscience, and worry that "being for others" can become an abstract principle contrary to Bonhoeffer's intentions. Whereas Mennonites have sought to follow the example of Jesus as revealed in the New Testament, Bonhoeffer places emphasis on how God continues to confront and to call the human person in Jesus Christ. Given that Mennonites have interpreted the radical obedience of Jesus to God as a paradigm of human obedience, these approaches are not as different as they may appear.

In Christ, God has acted to reorder human life. We are judged and we are acquitted. We are reborn by Christ's Spirit. Contemporary Protestant theologian John Webster describes the conscience as an aspect of the human person which comes to recognize its being placed in the truth. Evoking a traditional understanding of the Holy Spirit as

---

[13] Dietrich Bonhoeffer, *Ethics*, trans. Neville Horton Smith (New York: Macmillan, 1955), 244–45. See also Christine Schliesser, *Everyone Who Acts Responsibly Becomes Guilty: Bonhoeffer's Concept of Accepting Guilt* (Louisville, KY: Westminster John Knox, 2008).

applying the benefits of Christ to each person, he explains: "Spirit and conscience are related in such a way that, through the Holy Spirit, Christ appropriates me to himself, displacing my self-will and desire for mastery of good and evil through reflection .... I come to judge not on my own authority but only in the repetition of the authoritative judgment of God."[14] The formation of conscience is, first of all, discernment about what is most true about me, a "me" understood not in terms of modern autonomy, but in terms of truth given in Christ by the Spirit, and subsequently of discernment (together with the church) about what it might mean to act within such a "moral field."[15]

Early Anabaptism: Conscience and New Life

Early Anabaptist writers did not produce treatises on the conscience, even though their break with Roman Catholicism and with other Reformers grew out of convictions of conscience. An Anabaptist account of conscience shares with Catholicism a strong role for the church and with Protestantism a decisive role for God's action in Christ and the Spirit. The interconnection of these elements may be seen in the way Anabaptists understood the transformation of new life in Christ, and baptism.

South German Anabaptist Leonhard Schiemer is reasonably representative in his description of the process by which God brings about this new life through divine-human cooperation in three stages or "graces." The three graces are the inner light, outward righteousness, and finally, comfort and joy. First, God gives each person the light of understanding which enables the discernment of God's power as well as God's law. Schiemer explicitly identifies this light with the conscience, and the capacity to reject all that is "shameful" and "unjust," such as "whoring, anger, greediness, evil ... hatred, murder, quarreling."[16] This light (conscience) is not simply a given aspect of human nature but the light which the Gospel of John (1:5) identifies with the Word—Jesus

---

[14] John Webster, "God and Conscience," *Calvin Theological Journal* 33 (1998): 118.

[15] Ibid., 123.

[16] Leonhard Schiemer, "Three Kinds of Grace Found in the Scriptures, the Old and New Testaments [1527]," in *Early Anabaptist Spirituality: Selected Writings*, ed. Daniel Liechty (New York: Paulist Press, 1994), 88.

Christ—and must be activated and drawn into the second and third graces in order to effect salvation. Schiemer explains that while the light is given to all, not all respond. Some will snuff it out, others will respond half-heartedly but ultimately fall away at a time of trial. However, "with all diligence [some] set themselves against sin; they pray and listen to much preaching. They read much and ask many questions, all with a true heart."[17] Thus, the will is not in total bondage (as per Luther) but has the freedom (and burden) to respond to an initial gift. According to Anabaptist Balthasar Hubmaier, the power to will what is right and good "is not in us as if it were from us, for it is originally from God and his image . . . . Nevertheless, it is not possible to extinguish entirely this breath of God in us."[18]

Schiemer's second grace, outward righteousness, entailed concrete behaviour as well as baptism and membership in the church. The Anabaptist practice of baptism exhibited the relationship of the individual to the community, as well as the "inner" to the "outer." They dissented from the nearly universal (in the sixteenth century) practice of infant baptism because it was contrary to the biblical order of teach, then baptize (Matthew 28:19-20), and thus failed to hold together the inner work of the Spirit with outward expression in discipleship. The outer sign of water baptism was not saving per se, but neither was it dispensable. It was a public commitment to express the inner transformation by concretely following the example and teaching of Christ, to manifest the fruits of the Spirit, and to be held to these outward expressions by a community of persons likewise transformed. For some, including Schiemer, all who were "of Christ" must hold in common "all the gifts which God has given them, whether gifts of teaching and understanding or of goods and wealth or anything else."[19]

The ban refers to the practice of binding and loosing, chiefly discussed in Matthew 18:15-18. Jesus taught that "if another member of the church sins against you," you ought to point out this sin in private. If this admonition is not received, bring others when you speak to the

---

[17] Ibid., 89.

[18] Balthasar Hubmaier, "Freedom of the Will, I [1527]," in *Balthasar Hubmaier: Theologian of Anabaptism*, ed. H. Wayne Pipkin and John H. Yoder (Scottdale, PA: Herald Press, 1989), 437–38.

[19] Schiemer, "Three Kinds of Grace," 92.

offender. If the offender still does not listen, "let such a one be to you as a Gentile or a tax collector," that is, outside the community though continually invited to join the community through repentance. Anabaptists understood the ban as a practice given by Jesus Christ through which the church is enabled to visibly manifest obedience to Jesus. It is a means by which Christians hold each other in the truth and light by which they have already been transformed and to which they have publicly committed.

Yet, it is not simply that transformed individuals come together to constitute the church; such would be a merely human institution. While the church is a consequence of the Spirit's work in individuals, the Spirit also constitutes the community that in turn helps bring individuals to the recognition of God's light within them. The church is a community constituted by the Spirit; the Spirit makes it the Body of Christ. Moreover, to the extent that the Anabaptist dissent with respect to wider Christianity was/is a faithful one, it must be understood theologically not as a human work, but as Christ reforming his church through the consciences of a minority.

For Pilgram Marpeck, an Anabaptist writing in the 1540s, the cross is both the event through which Jesus Christ willingly makes his Spirit available to others and which gives concrete shape to the church. Christ's victory over sin and death is through suffering; in like manner Christ's Spirit in the church is effective not through coercion but patience.[20] Thus, Marpeck counsels patience in matters of church discipline, an approach at odds with many in the movement. On the one hand, the giving and receiving of counsel within the church is the basis for the discernment of the Holy Spirit. On the other hand, Christ's humble suffering has crushed "our presumption and attempt to do everything by our own wisdom, law, commandment and prohibition."[21] Those in Christ are freed from these human bondages, which the church ought not to reproduce. "For true love in Christ—indeed, the Spirit and God himself—is a free and willing fulfillment of all that is

---

[20] Stephen B. Boyd, *Pilgram Marpeck: His Life and Social Theology* (Durham, NC: Duke University Press, 1992), 73.

[21] Pilgram Marpeck, "Concerning Hasty Judgments and Verdicts [1542/43]," in *Jörg Maler's Kunstbuch: Writings of the Pilgram Marpeck Circle*, ed. John D. Rempel (Kitchener, ON: Pandora Press, 2010), 146.

good."[22] Thus, while members of the church warn and admonish one another, they ought to do so not in self-certainty but in Christian humility that recognizes that the Spirit may be at work in the seemingly errant sister or brother, and that God is the final judge.[23] The authority of the church to use the ban, which was to be exercised in love in order to draw a wayward sinner back to the commitment made in baptism, was premised on confession that the *same* Spirit was at work both in regenerating and restoring each person and in the decision of the community.

Anabaptists held that church unity, and in this sense social order, was achieved not by the physical coercion employed by state churches, but by the appeal to conscience presupposed by *voluntary* church membership. Neither true faith nor true community could be coerced. Coercion in belief would ultimately result in an insecure conscience, since human effort not the Spirit would be the source of such unity.

Nevertheless, the church in its humanity has been called and empowered to actually manifest obedience to Christ and the fruits of the Spirit. The promise of a church "without spot or wrinkle" (Ephesians 5:27) undoubtedly led to the abuse of the ban. The ban could become punitive rather than restorative in purpose, authoritarian rather than communal in expression, legalistic rather than Spirit-driven in application, dangers Marpeck termed "running ahead of Christ."[24] The ban silenced dissent, even when this dissent might have pointed to the correction of some abuse, or prophetically to a deeper understanding and practice of Christian faith. While there is a great deal of discomfort with the idea of discipline in contemporary Mennonite churches,[25] its pivotal place in Anabaptist understandings of conscience, community, and the Christian life calls for its reformation and renewal, though not outright rejection.[26]

---

[22] Ibid., 156.

[23] Ibid., 154.

[24] Ibid.

[25] Often expressed in works of literature, most notably Patrick Friesen, *The Shunning* (Winnipeg: Turnstone Press, 1980).

[26] See Harry J. Huebner, "Church Discipline: Is It Still Possible?" in *Echoes of the Word: Theological Ethics as Rhetorical Practice* (Kitchener, ON: Pandora Press, 2005), 107-114.

Schiemer's third grace is the consolation, comfort, and inexpressible joy the Spirit bestows on Christians, a grace especially welcome to those early Anabaptists who could expect persecution and suffering. While this third grace may be interpreted as the future, even eschatological, vindication of the Anabaptist minority position, Schiemer's text also reminds readers that the Holy Spirit is not under human command and control: "No one can be comforted or strengthened by the Holy Spirit until he has forsaken and relinquished all human comfort and strength."[27] Though the Spirit does indeed work through the consciences of individuals, as well as dissenting minorities, one cannot therefore assume that the conviction of conscience or minority position is therefore endorsed by the Spirit. In humility, any Christian community must recognize that the Spirit may be working through it in ways that cannot be clearly discerned, and thus cannot with certainty point to the form and content of the Spirit's consolation. This ought to temper any present assessment of just what the Anabaptist contribution has been to the recovery or reform of true Christianity. Needless to say, faithfulness (and sinfulness) on the part of the Anabaptist movement must be viewed in light of the integrity and faithfulness of Christianity as a whole and the call of the church to unity, rather than the preservation or vindication of any particular group that might be called Anabaptist or Mennonite.[28]

---

[27] Schiemer, "Three Kinds of Grace," 94.

[28] For an extensive and complex reflection on these themes, see Ephraim Radner, *The End of the Church: A Pneumatology of Christian Division in the West* (Grand Rapids: Eerdmans, 1998). Radner's indictment of church schism and division may be understood as a plea for Christians to radical patience in the face of claims by various Christian groups to know where the Spirit is and what the Spirit is doing. He provocatively suggests that the Spirit may be seeking the unity of Christ's church by temporarily withdrawing itself from the divided churches. He calls attention to the exemplary witness of the Jansenists in the seventeenth and eighteenth centuries, who sought significant reform in the Catholic Church but refused to leave that church. Because of this refusal, there was no distinct community to preserve their sufferings as a distinct witness, or to point to any "Jansenist church" as the true remnant. Thus, they experienced a profound "death for the faith" in the "hiddenness of 'ignored sufferings'" (130). However the Spirit might console such witnesses, the question is whether anyone will recognize that consolation.

The War of the Lambs: Confessions vs. Conscience among Dutch Mennonites

Tensions between individuals and community have surfaced at many points in Mennonite history. One instructive case is that of Dutch Anabaptism in the late-sixteenth and seventeenth centuries. Dutch Mennonite churches came to be characterized by a rigorous use of the ban, disagreements about discipline, and a strong congregationalism which together resulted in numerous schisms. Key Mennonite leaders attempted to bring together the divided church by drafting and proposing written confessions of faith. The status of these confessions became, ironically, a new source of conflict.

The details of the various splits need not confuse us at this point. I will leap ahead to the middle of the seventeenth century in which a controversy developed between the "Zonist" Mennonite congregations and the "Lamist" ones. The Zonists had high regard for confessional documents which, though developed for the sake of church mergers, they regarded as authoritative statements by which individuals may be assured of true doctrine and consequently right action. By contrast, the Lamists denied that an individual's conscience could be bound by church authority. They did not deny that confessional statements had some value, but assigned to them a strictly representational authority. While they were helpful to the extent that they represented biblical truth, the Lamists argued that to make them tests for membership was to place human standards above those of the Bible and the Spirit.

Both groups may be understood to espouse both optimistic and pessimistic anthropologies. The Zonists were more pessimistic about one's capacity to follow Christ as an individual and thus emphasized the role of the church in maintaining discipline. At the same time, their high view of the church's capacity to actually bear witness to the truth, through doctrinal statements, church discipline, and the formation of individual consciences, was rooted in a particular (and controversial) "celestial flesh" Christology. According to this view, Jesus' flesh came from heaven not Mary. The Zonists drew a particular ecclesiological conclusion: the church was called to be, and enabled to be, visibly holy in its outer forms, to be "without spot or wrinkle."[29] The Lamist

---

[29] Karl Koop, *Anabaptist-Mennonite Confessions of Faith: The Development*

optimism lay in the potential for each person, equipped by the Spirit, to choose the good and to manifest holiness in their lives. According to Karl Koop, their "locus of renewal and obedience . . . was centred on those who, through the new birth, have inwardly become a part of the body of Christ."[30] Their more orthodox Christology, in which Christ's flesh was more fully human flesh, may have resulted in an ecclesiology more amenable to a mixture of sinners and saints.[31]

The Zonists' confessional approach resulted in clearly defined communal boundaries which, in the context of the Dutch Republic, allowed them to maintain a social position as an officially tolerated minority. Within this social context members achieved significant material success, in part because confessionalization prevented the idiosyncratic views of individuals (moved by conscience) from being ascribed to the group as a whole, an ongoing danger for the Lamists. From a sociological perspective then, the Zonists limited internal dissent in order to maintain their status as a community of dissent from society as a whole (or as a community whose dissent was known, stable, and acceptable).[32] While this analysis might appear to suggest the Zonists aspired to accommodate, Zonists could charge the same of Lamists, whose "laxity" in church discipline more readily accepted the actions of individuals going outside traditional moral boundaries.

Conscientious Objection to War: Canadian Mennonites and World War II

In the 1930s and 40s, Canadian Mennonites faced the challenge of responding to World War II. The historic position of nonresistance was traditionally expressed in the refusal to join the armed forces and fight in war. The Canadian government recognized conscientious objection to military service on the basis of religious beliefs.[33] Of the

---

of a Tradition (Kitchener, ON: Pandora Press, 2004), 94–95, 116–17.

[30] Ibid., 117. Koop here refers to the Waterlander Mennonites who were closely aligned with the Lamist group.

[31] Ibid., 116–17.

[32] Michael D. Driedger, *Obedient Heretics: Mennonite Identities in Lutheran Hamburg and Altona During the Confessional Age* (Aldershot, UK: Ashgate, 2002), 50–51.

[33] Exemptions were not granted for political or "secular" reasons. See David Fransen, "Canadian Mennonites and Conscientious Objection in World War

approximately 17,000 Canadian Mennonite men between fifteen and thirty-five in 1941, 7,500 did alternative service, and 4,500 enlisted in the armed forces.[34] Mennonite leaders did not generally propose a structural critique of Canadian participation in war,[35] but focused rather on the exemption of individuals from participation, and more generally on how young men might serve the public good at a time of crisis in ways that would not violate their consciences and/or church teachings.

During World War II, jurisdictions such as Ontario granted conscientious-objector status and exemption to young men on the basis of lists submitted to the government by the church. This assumed that individual members personally espoused the official teachings of the churches, even though in reality not all individuals did so.[36]

By contrast, young men in Manitoba were required to appear before the Chair of the Mobilization Board, Judge J. E. Adamson, to explain the bases, coherence, and sincerity of their beliefs. Some young men found it difficult to articulate their objections to military service (especially to outsiders, with whom many Mennonites had little contact) beyond the fact that it was a church teaching. Others were more successful. Nevertheless, Adamson believed that Mennonite bishops and preachers unduly influenced their young members. Addressing Mennonite leaders, he said: "[D]o not attempt to influence these young men. Leave them free. Remember it is their conscience, not yours."[37] He believed that the consciences of young men would naturally be inclined to military service for the sake of their country were it not for their "indoctrination" by authoritarian Mennonite leaders. Though Adamson may have believed there was a "natural"

II," MA thesis (University of Waterloo, 1977), 147, 193.

[34] T. D. Regehr, *Mennonites in Canada, 1939-1970: A People Transformed* (Toronto: University of Toronto Press, 1996), 35.

[35] Critique of structural violence and injustice would develop later. See Leo Driedger and Donald B. Kraybill, *Mennonite Peacemaking: From Quietism to Activism* (Scottdale, PA: Herald Press, 1994), and Ervin R. Stutzman, *From Nonresistance to Justice: The Transformation of Mennonite Church Peace Rhetoric, 1908-2008* (Scottdale, PA: Herald Press, 2011).

[36] Fransen, "Canadian Mennonites and Conscientious Objection in World War II," 137.

[37] Ibid., 141.

content to conscience, the shaping power of Christ and church on conscience that I have highlighted points to the role of community in the formation of conscience, whatever that community may be.

At the same time, the inability of many Mennonites to articulate their faith served to remind the church that faith is not only communal, but must be embodied in each person, and in each conscience. As a result, Canadian Mennonites in the postwar period developed educational institutions and increased sophistication about theology as well as nonviolence, peace, and justice. Heightened global awareness including dialogue and encounter with various "others" has in turn shaped the contours of communal commitments and individual consciences.[38]

Some Mennonites dissented from church teaching and enlisted in active military service. One young man explained that "Canada gave our parents a new life and an opportunity to live in peace and harmony and raise a family in the best country in the world, and [is] therefore worth fighting for."[39] Many Mennonite ministers responded harshly to soldiers who returned to their congregations. Most were not welcome and effectively banned without attempts to understand how these men understood their military service in light of their faith. Many were lost to the Mennonite church (and to the church in general), leaving "scars that healed slowly" and "Mennonite communities diminished and impoverished."[40] Is this an example of faithfulness to biblical pacifism, or running ahead of Christ? Perhaps this history instructs Mennonites more about the importance of patience in judgment than about pacifism and war.

Laureen Harder has documented the more nuanced approach of Stirling Avenue Mennonite Church, in Kitchener, Ontario. That church called on its young men to be conscientious objectors, but emphasized the importance of each person following his conscience "based on Christian principles as found in Scripture," and maintained ties with

---

[38] See David Schroeder, "Theological Reflections of a CO: Changing Peace Theology Since World War II," *Journal of Mennonite Studies* 25 (2007): 183–93.

[39] Regehr, *Mennonites in Canada, 1939–1970*, 36.

[40] T. D. Regehr, "Lost Sons: The Canadian Mennonite Soldiers of World War II," *Mennonite Quarterly Review* 66 (1992): 478.

those who joined the army.[41] Pastor Andrew Shelly preached at the memorial service of an adherent killed in combat in which he did not explicitly advocate the nonresistance he forcefully articulated in other contexts. To this day the church organ bears a plaque with the name of that young man: Frederick Shantz. While this might be interpreted as capitulation to the "world," Harder proposes that by remaining in fellowship with those who disagreed with the church's stance, "the congregation modeled Christian love in the face of disagreement," which may have even strengthened the congregation's capacity to work concretely with a variety of others for justice and peace down to the present day.[42]

Conclusion

In the theological anthropology to which Anabaptist-Mennonites subscribe, the conscience is not simply a given part of human nature, but always understood Christologically, pneumatologically, and ecclesiologically. As a result, the tension between the individual and the community is both necessary and necessarily unsettled. In contemporary Mennonite churches, there is dissent from the "teaching position"[43] on a number of convictions, including human sexuality, the exclusivity of Jesus Christ for salvation, and whether non-baptized persons may participate in the Lord's Supper. To some, dissent on these and other issues compromises the church's public witness and the formation of members. On one level, such ambiguity will be frustrating. However, I believe Mennonites are bound to take seriously both the light of conscience in each person as possibly the light of Jesus Christ reforming his church, as well as the communal context of the Body of Christ, whose ongoing deliberation in these matters is crucial for the formation, even correction, of consciences. Humanly speaking, the church always seeks to grow in understanding and faithfulness, guided

---

[41] Laureen Harder, "One Photograph, Many Stories: A Mennonite Congregation's Diverse Response to War," *Journal of Mennonite Studies* 25 (2007): 139. I am a member of Stirling Avenue Mennonite Church.

[42] Ibid., 142.

[43] The phrase sometimes used to describe the status and purpose of the *Confession of Faith in Mennonite Perspective* (1995).

by the Holy Spirit; this implies a long and patient view of theological and moral discernment.

Epilogue

In the discussion immediately following the presentation of my paper, our Shi'i dialogue partners probed whether my account of conscience can serve as a practical guide for Christians in daily life. I readily admitted that my approach was not immediately applicable, especially as I problematized the conscience as a potential hiding place from God. Mohammed Motahari Farimani's paper, "The Role of Turning to the Self': Introspection in the Qur'anic Discourse," which was presented in the same session as mine, made the helpful distinction between the real self and the false self. I believe he and I would agree that our respective traditions affirm that the conscience of the real self, which is the self properly oriented to God, is a guide to true faith and life. The emphasis in Shi'i Islam on the mutual relation between remembering God and remembering our true selves resonates deeply in the Christian tradition, most notably in Augustine's *Confessions*. The Muslim practice of invoking God before daily activities is an instructive one for Christians[44] and also highlights the positive role in the formation of conscience for the community and the family that teach such practices.

While affirming the distinction of real self and false self, I would be reticent to claim that a Christian can be clear or ought to be clear, even to herself, about when she is acting on the basis of the one rather than the other. Western Christianity's ambivalent relationship with the legacy of the Enlightenment and Modernity, which Islam has experienced differently, as was explored in the First Dialogue,[45] contributes to this. I worry that appeals to conscience may too easily reflect individualism, the quest for human certainty, or the inability to distinguish the voice of the Holy Spirit from other spirits. Thus, my task as a theologian is to draw to my community's attention the dangers of the conscience of the "false self."

---

[44] It echoes 1 Thessalonians 5:16-18: "Rejoice always, pray without ceasing, give thanks in all circumstances; for this is the will of God in Christ Jesus for you."

[45] Papers published in *The Conrad Grebel Review* 21, no. 3 (Fall 2003).

If I have this reticence at the individual level, am I warranted in my more positive assessment of the capacity of conscience to effect the kind of dissent in the religious community that may lead to positive reforms and greater faithfulness? In response, I reiterate my emphasis on the "long view," and thus resist any formulaic relationship between dissent and faithfulness. Prophetic truth is typically recognized long after the prophet has spoken. I believe that Mennonites have much to learn from the Muslim discipline of prayer, for example, as a way of remembering our true selves in God, and to see the reform of the community, whether occasioned by dissent or not, through that lens. The dynamics by which Mennonites understand their own status as a dissenting minority within Christianity might be illuminated, even challenged, by hearing from our Shi'i dialogue partners about their own communal identity within the wider Islamic community, especially as it may be conceived in terms of conscience. Moreover, what is their experience of whether and how dissenting individuals or groups within their own tradition may come to be recognized in retrospect as genuinely prophetic? Probing such questions together will reveal deep assumptions as well as new understandings of theological anthropology, the nature of the religious community, and ways by which the voice of God continually guides both persons and communities.

Contributors

Jeremy M. Bergen received his PhD from the University of St. Michael's College (2008). He is Assistant Professor of Religious Studies and theology at Conrad Grebel University College, University of Waterloo, Canada. He is the author of *Ecclesial Repentance: The Churches Confront Their Sinful Pasts* (2011) and co-editor of two books. He also serves as editor of *The Conrad Grebel Review*. He has published articles and chapters on Mennonite theology, ecclesiology, ecumenism, collective apologies, pneumatology and martyrdom.

Jo-Ann Brant has taught at Goshen College in the Bible, Religion and Philosophy department since 1993. She completed her doctoral work at McMaster University in Hamilton, Ontario in 1991. From 1991-1993, she taught at Canadian Mennonite Bible College (now Canadian Mennonite University) in Winnipeg, Manitoba. Her major publications include *Dialogue and Drama: Elements of Greek Tragedy in the Fourth Gospel* (2004) and *John: Paideia Commentaries on the New Testament* (2011), a commentary that situates the Gospel of John within the rhetorical and narrative conventions of Greco-Roman literature.

Peter Dula is Associate Professor of Religion and Culture and chair of the Department of Bible and Religion at Eastern Mennonite University. He received a PhD from Duke University in theology and ethics in 2004. He is the author of *Cavell, Companionship, and Christian Theology* (Oxford, 2011). Before teaching at EMU (began 2006) he was the Mennonite Central Committee Iraq Program Coordinator. He has taught at Lancaster Mennonite High School and at the Meserete Kristos College in Addis Ababa, Ethiopia where he was a Fulbright scholar in 2001-2.

Mohammad Fanaei Eshkevari is Associate Professor of Philosophy and Mysticism at the Imam Khomeini Education and Research Institute in Qom. He studied in the Islamic seminaries in Qom before earning his doctorate in the philosophy of religion from McGill University. His published works include Persian introductions to Western and to Islamic philosophy and numerous articles on Islamic philosophy and mysticism. His most recent book is *An Introduction to Contemporary Islamic Philosophy* (London: 2012).

Mohammad Motahari Farimani is Assistant Professor of Religious Studies at the Imam Khomeini Education and Research Institute in Qom. After studying in the seminaries in Qom, he earned his PhD in Religious Studies from the Toronto School of Theology. He has published numerous articles in Iran on religious and social issues.

Gerald Gerbrandt is President Emeritus and Professor Emeritus of Bible at Canadian Mennonite University in Winnipeg, Manitoba. He completed a PhD at Union Theological Seminary in Richmond, Virginia in 1980, with a dissertation on *Kingship in the Deuteronomistic History*, published by Scholars Press. He is currently completing a commentary on the book of Deuteronomy for the Believers Church Bible Commentary series.

Aboulhassan Haghani is Associate Professor of Psychology at the Imam Khomeini Education and Research Institute in Qom. After his seminary studies in Qom, and graduate work in Canada, he earned his PhD in psychology from the Imam Khomeini Education and Research Institute in Qom. In addition to teaching and counseling, he has translated English works on the psychology of religion in Persian, and is currently writing on Islamic psychology.

Harry J. Huebner is Professor Emeritus of Theology and Philosophy at Canadian Mennonite University in Winnipeg, Canada. He is a graduate of St. Michael's College in Toronto with a PhD in theology. He is co-author of *The Church as Parable: Whatever Happened to Ethics?* (1993), author of *Echoes of the Word: Theological Ethics in Rhetorical Practice* (2005), and *An Introduction to Christian Ethics: History, Movements,*

People (2012). He has edited several books and contributed several articles in books and journals.

Muhammad Legenhausen is Professor of Western Philosophy at the Imam Khomeini Education and Research Institute in Qom. He completed his PhD at Rice University in Houston, Texas, with a dissertation in metaphysics. He has published in English and Persian on the philosophy of religion, including a book, *Islam and Religious Pluralism* (London: 1999), and a number of articles in which he advocates non-reductive religious pluralism. He has translated Ayatullah Misbah Yazdi's *Philosophical Instructions* (1999) and Muntazir Qa'im's *Jesus (peace be with him) through the Qur'an and Shi'ite Narrations* (New York: 2005).

Ali Misbah is Associate Professor of Philosophy at the Imam Khomeini Education and Research Institute in Qom. He earned his PhD in the philosophy of religion from McGill University. In addition to numerous publications on the philosophy of religion, he has recently edited *The Relation between Science and Religion* (in Persian) by Ayatullah Muhammad Taqi Misbah Yazdi (Qom: 2013). He is the editor of the journal *Ma'rifat-e Falsafeh*.

Abolfazl Sajedi is Associate Professor of Philosophy at the Imam Khomeini Education and Research Institute in Qom. He earned his PhD in the philosophy of religion from Concord University after seminary studies in Qom. His publications include *Religious Language and the Qur'an* (in Persian), and he is editor of the *International Journal of Hekmat*.

Abbas Ali Shameli completed his PhD in education at McGill University after seminary studies in Qom. He is currently teaching at *Jam'at al-Mustafa* in Qom. He has written on Islamic education, psychology, and philosophy, including work on the soul-body relation in the philosophical psychology of Avicenna and Mulla Sadra.

David W. Shenk is an internationalist with particular interest in the role of religions in modern societies. That interest has taken him to some 100 countries; he has lived in East Africa, the United States, and in Lithuania in the former Soviet Union. He has become engaged in Christian-Muslim Dialogue especially in regard to peacemaking. He has authored or co-authored some fifteen books including *A Muslim and A Christian in Dialogue,* in which he and a Muslim friend, Badru D. Kateregga, share their faith with one another. He has a PhD in Religious Studies Education from New York University.

Mohammad Ali Shomali studied in the Islamic seminaries of Qom, and earned his doctorate in philosophy (ethics) from Manchester University. He is currently the director of the International Institute of Islamic Studies in Qom. His publications include *Self-Knowledge* (2nd ed., 2006), *Ethical Relativism* (2001), *Discovering Shi'a Islam* (2003), *Shi'a Islam: Origins, Faiths and Practices* (2003), and *Principles of Jurisprudence: An Introduction to the Methodology of Fiqh* (2006). He has also co-edited several collections of papers resulting from Shi'a-Catholic dialogue, and is the editor of the *Islamic Reference Series* (six volumes). He is the editor-in-chief of the journal *Spiritual Quest.*

W. Derek Suderman is Associate Professor of Religious and Theological Studies at Conrad Grebel University College, University of Waterloo. He received a PhD. in Biblical Studies (Old Testament) from the University of St. Michael's College in Toronto, Ontario (2007), a Masters in Theological Studies from Conrad Grebel (2000). He has published articles, chapters, and reviews on the Psalms, Wisdom literature, Hermeneutics, and violence in the Bible, as well as biblical study guides for a general audience. He has been a member of the Editorial Council of the Believers Church Bible Commentary series since 2004 and is currently completing the "Psalms" article for the upcoming *Fortress Commentary on the Old Testament.*

Gordon Zerbe is Professor of New Testament at Canadian Mennonite University, Winnipeg, Manitoba. He received his PhD in New Testament from Princeton Theological Seminary and is the author of *Non-Retaliation in Early Jewish and New Testament Texts: Ethical Themes in Social Contexts* (1993) and *Citizenship: Paul on Peace and Politics* (2012). His published articles include two essays in the recent volume *The Colonized Paul: Paul through Postcolonial Eyes* (ed. C. Stanley, 2011).

. . .